VOLUME ONE: GENESIS–KINGS

THE WORD MADE FRESH

compiled by
ANDREW EDINGTON

with foreword by
James A. Wharton

JOHN KNOX PRESS
ATLANTA

Library of Congress Cataloging in Publication Data

Edington, Andrew.
   The word made fresh.

   CONTENTS: v. 1.   Genesis-Kings.—2.   Chronicles-Malachi.
   1. Bible   O.T.—Paraphrases, English.   I. Title.
BS895.E33   221.5'2   75-13457
ISBN 0-8042-0075-0 (v. 1)

The text is reproduced from type set by
the Herring Printing Company, Kerrville, Texas

© copyright 1975 John Knox Press
Atlanta, Georgia
Printed in the United States of America

FOREWORD

More than two centuries have elapsed since old Johannes Bengel gave this advice to people who would study his edition of the New Testament in Greek: "Apply your whole self to the text; the whole matter apply to yourself." *The Word Made Fresh* gives the reader a delightful opportunity to enjoy the fireworks that crackle and flash when Andrew Edington applies his whole self to the Bible and the whole Bible to himself.

No one knows better than Andy Edington that the Word of God is never stale, as if it were our job to make it fresh. But he knows better than most of us how stale we can make the Bible seem when we read it with dull and unimaginative hearts. He knows especially well how a wrong sense of the holiness of Holy Scripture can keep us from seeing how deeply it plunges into the ordinary fabric of human life, where the Holy Lord is always challenging us, loving us, and calling us to be his kind of people. And he knows that God is always ready to make His Word fresh to us when we give our whole selves to the reading of Scripture and apply the whole matter to ourselves.

The Word Made Fresh is neither a commentary nor a new translation. It is not, above all, a substitute for reading the Bible in one of the excellent modern translations that tries to give us the most accurate possible rendering of the best Hebrew and Aramaic and Greek manuscripts of the Biblical text (such as the *RSV, The New English Bible, The Jerusalem Bible).* What Andrew Edington has done in *The Word Made Fresh* is to give us his own paraphrase of Scripture as it impacts on his own life and changes the way he looks at himself, at us, and at our contemporary world. It is not the work of a professionally trained Biblical scholar, even though countless hours of devoted study and rich experience have gone into its preparation. It is instead a layman's challenge, full of genuine humor and much wisdom, to come always fresh to the reading of the Bible. As such it is a hymn of praise to the Lord who makes all things fresh.

James A. Wharton
Austin Presbyterian Theological Seminary

CONTENTS

GENESIS

In the beginning God created everything from nothing, for there was no earth or heaven and darkness was total and only the spirit of God moved.

And God said, "Let there be light", and there was light. God checked it and found it to be good. God designated the presence of light as "day" and the presence of darkness as "night". This was the first phase of creation.

Next God said let there be a firmament dividing all the various waters in their varied forms. God divided the waters underneath from those that were above and he called the upper part Heaven. This was the second phase.

Then God ordered the waters under the heavens to be gathered together and dry land appeared. This dry land was called 'Earth' and the waters which were gathered together were called 'Seas'. God said, "Let the grass now grow, and the plants, and the fruit trees, each after it's kind," and God checked all this and saw that it was good, and this was the third phase of creation.

God then decided there should be specific lights in the heavens, working orderly, to control the seasons and the times. The two principal lights God made were one greater for the day and a lesser one for the night. God also made the stars and set them in the firmament. After all this was done God checked it and found it to be a good system. This was the fourth phase of creation.

Then God's planned creation began developing in living creatures of the sea, even such as whales, and also the winged fowl of the air and God encouraged their productivity and he saw the way it was working and thought it was good. This was the fifth phase of creation.

God then saw to it that the earth began to bring forth living creatures, each of its own kind and he made the cattle, and the creeping things, each different. God saw that this was good and so He decided to make man; to make him different from all the other creatures, to model man after the image of God, and to empower man to look out for all other living things, to have dominion over the fowl of the air and the fish of the sea, and over all the creeping things. God made man male and female, and he blessed them, and he instructed them to multiply. God also told them to exercise proper care of the earth, to replenish and conserve.

God told man that all things were given to him for his benefit and to properly use God's creation. God observed all that He had done and He considered it a good plan.

Now the seventh phase of God's creation was for rest and growth. God blessed the seventh phase particularly. God watched the clouds form, and rain come, and plants grow and the earth and all His creation becoming active. It was during this phase that God breathed into man a living soul, and man's difference became permanently established.

The first area to develop as a garden was called Eden. There were four rivers having their source here and God watched as man developed this area and lived in it.

God ordered man, however, not to eat of the tree of knowledge, for knowledge of life would bring into man's experience knowledge of death. God let man name all of the plants and animals and God provided woman for man. God called the helpmate woman for she was made from man and was of the same flesh. It is proper, therefore, that a man cleave to a woman and that they become one for this is the beginning of family, the basic unit of God's plan for man.

Sometime after this, Curiosity, the name of the first serpent, began working on a woman named Eve. The serpent said that God was running a bluff, and that all knowledge would mean would be equality with God. The fruit of the tree looked good and the reasoning seemed adequate; so Eve disobeyed God and then induced Adam rather easily to join her in disobedience. The knowledge which the two acquired for all mankind was knowledge of their nakedness, knowledge of the existence of good and evil, and knowledge of death.

And God said to the woman, "What is this that you have done?"

She replied, "Curiosity got the best of me."

And God said to the serpent Curiosity, "From henceforth you are to be cursed and despised over all cattle and all beasts, and you shall crawl on your belly in the dust the remainder of your existence. I will also create enmity between you and woman, and you shall bite at the legs of her and her offspring, and they shall strike at your head."

To the woman God said, "Your punishment shall be labor in childbirth and you shall be subject to man."

God spoke to Adam and said, "Because you joined Eve in this folly, you will have to work. You will plant, and fight weeds, and you shall live and prosper by the sweat of your brow."

God, however, still caring for His special creation, provided skins for clothes for Adam and Eve.

God then noted that man would have to be expelled from the presence of the place of God; and this place known as Eden was closed to man. Enclosed in God's place is the tree of eternal life and this was no longer available simply for man's easy taking.

It was not long after this that Eve became pregnant and her first son was named Cain. Later there came another son and his name was Abel. In due time Cain was assigned the job of looking out for the farm and Abel was the rancher. Each brought appropriate offerings to God, but Cain had a poor attitude. The Lord was therefore pleased with Able's gift and not with Cain's. This disturbed Cain and he vented his anger on Able, and killed him. God punished Cain by relating a vagabond and lost feeling to sin, and Cain groaned under the penatly. God also placed a mark on Cain that would encourage others to let him live and prolong him in his misery.

Cain departed from the area with his wife and started a new life. Down through the years there were many descendants of Cain, and there began to develop through the years skills in music, and art, and the working of metals. Eve had still another son, Seth, and he was a fine boy and he began another line and gradually man began to work at the job of subduing the earth, and about this time man became sensitive to his need for God.

Chap.
5

Now there were multiple descendants of Adam and finally there came one named Enoch. Enoch was the first great seeker of God, and Enoch walked with God. In his later years, one day Enoch walked off with God and did not return.

Chap.
6

Many generations later, as time had passed and man was expanding in numbers and in wickedness, there was born a man named Noah, and he worshipped God. It was now that the Lord began to restrict the longevity of man. God said that He would not always be at odds with man, but since man was of flesh his time should be limited.

There were big men on the earth in these days and they chased the girls, taking many wives. Wickedness increased and God wondered if He had been wise in turning man loose on the earth. Now Noah was a good man, and God rejoiced in him. The earth was full of violence and evil and God revealed to Noah that He planned to clean up the place.

God told Noah to build an ark, large enough to hold all of Noah's family and representatives from all the animals. Noah gathered stores of food as instructed, and he built an ark, and he ignored all the smart remarks made by local yokels.

Chap.
7

God gave Noah seven days to load the ark after it was finished and then He caused the rains to descend for forty days and forty nights and the earth was flooded. As the waters increased the ark was lifted and the ark floated, to the great joy of Noah. All living substance that was not in the ark was destroyed, all men, and cattle, and the creeping things.

Chap.
8

God did not forget Noah, but He sent a wind to begin to blow upon the waters and the rain was stopped. There was no way for

Noah to tell if the waters were receding and so he sent forth a raven who never returned. After waiting a long time, Noah sent forth a dove and the dove returned weary from flying. After another period of waiting, Noah sent the dove a second time, and this time the dove returned with a green twig, an olive leaf. Finally mountain tops became visible in the distance.

At long last the Ark rested on dry ground and God spoke to Noah and told him it was time to lower the gangway and start life going again on the earth.

Noah was the first down the ramp and onto the dry ground, and he immediately built an altar and thanked God. This pleased God mightily and God smelled a sweet savor, and so God said in His heart that He would not again curse the ground because of man and again smite every living thing at once. God further promised not to tamper with the seasons, but that without interruption there would be seedtime and harvest, cold and heat, summer and winter, day and night, without ceasing.

God blessed Noah and He renewed His instructions to man through Noah to be fruitful and multiply, to keep the earth in good shape, to practice conservation, and to avoid the shedding of the blood of his fellowman.

God made a covenant with Noah and with mankind that He would not again destroy as He had with the flood and that the sign of the covenant would be the rainbow, and the rainbow would be a reminder to God of His agreement.

Now Noah had three sons and he named them Tom[1], Dick[2], and Harry[3] and they scattered and through them came into being all the races of the world.

Noah was at a loss for something to do and so he planted a vineyard. After this he gathered the grapes, made wine, and got drunk. Harry saw the old man naked and drunk and left in disgust, but the two older boys took pity on Noah and covered him with a garment. When Noah learned of this, he chewed out his younger son and praised the other two, telling the younger that he would never amount to anything but that the older boys would prosper.

And at the proper time Noah died.

Noah's sons had children, and their children had children, and so went the development and spread of mankind. Among one of the generations there developed a young man named Nimrod and he was the first of the great hunters.

As man progressed, he also began to develop arrogance and one group decided that they were now smart enough to look God in the eye. All men spoke one language and as the making of bricks was

[1]Shem   [2]Ham   [3]Japheth

4

devised, the men began to build a tower which was to reach to Heaven.

The Lord brought this project to a screeching halt by confounding their language; so that the confusion prevented communication. Then God called the name of this place Babel. The men ceased then in their efforts and scattered themselves abroad, as the Lord had planned for them to do.

Time went by, and many, many generations came into being, and man spread himself across the face of the earth.

There was born eventually a man named Joe[1] and he had a son named Abe[2]. Now God inspired Joe to take his family to the land of Canaan and establish there a new nation, but Joe stopped on the way at a place called Palm Springs[3], and he liked it there and there he stayed.

In time God spoke unto Abe and challenged him saying, "Get yourself out of this country, get away from your kinfolks and from the protection of your father, and I will show you a new land and give you a chance to found a great nation. I will give every reasonable help, and if you take advantage of the opportunity, yours shall become a great name, and the families of the earth shall be blessed because of you."

Abe took Sara, his wife, and a nephew named Lot along with a few herdsmen and departed on the great trip of his life. The group journeyed to the land of Caanan, and the Lord assured Abe that this was the promised land. In recognition of this occasion Abe built an altar and thanked God.

In due time a famine arose in the land because of the drought, and so Abe gathered his possessions and headed for Egypt.

Abe had inquired a bit about Egypt and its customs and so he spoke to Sara, his wife, as they neared the land of Egypt and said, "Sara, you are a very beautiful girl. The Egyptions will notice this and they will decide to kill me in order to possess you; so I want you to pose as my sister, then I can bargain with them for you."

Sure enough, the Egyption girl watchers noticed Sara, and word was passed to the palace crowd and then to Pharoah, and Sara was taken into the girls' dormitory of Pharoah's palace in exchange for numerous sheep, oxen, men servants, maid servants, camels, and similar booty.

The Lord began to create problems in Pharoah's house because Sara was actually Abe's wife.

Pharoah soon learned that Sara was Abe's wife, and that this was the source of his difficulties and so he sent for Abe and told him to take Sara, take his possessions, and get out of Egypt. Abe left, of course, and he was now a pretty rich man.

[1]Terah   [2]Abram   [3]Haran

Abe and Lot returned to the homesite in Canaan, and both men were wealthy from their trip to Egypt. In fact, both became so affluent that there was not room enough in one area for the two of them. Soon strife arose between the herdsmen of Lot and those of Abe.

Abe one day suggested to Lot that in the interest of peace that they separate. Abe said that he would move with his possessions in the opposite direction from Lot and that Lot should choose first.

Lot agreed and immediately began to figure on the best direction. It did not take him long to decide to go east to the fertile plains of Jordan, toward the cities of Sodom and Gomar[1]; so Abe dwelled in Canaan and Lot in the city of Sodom. Now the men of Sodom were wicked and sinful and Lot lived in the midst of them.

Then the Lord told Abe to travel the length and breadth of the land and to become acquainted with it, for the Lord planned that Abe and his offspring should rule it. Abe did as he was told, and at some places, such as St. Louis[2], he built an altar to God.

And it came to pass that the various kings began to do battle with one another, and there was strife and rebellion in the land. The kings of Sodom and Gomar banded together and in an encounter on the plains they were defeated, and they lost their possessions and also many of their people were taken captive, including Lot.

A messenger came and reported this to Abe and he decided to rescue Lot. Abe assembled a group of about 318 roughriders and he went in pursuit of the victorious kings. By using the strategy of dividing his men and attacking at night, Abe rescued Lot and recovered the people and the lost possessions. Needless to say, Abe was given a triumphant and hearty reception when he returned the people to Sodom. The king of Sodom offered to give Abe all the booty, but Abe said, "Let me keep some of the people and you can have the goods." Abe said that he served the one true God, and that he would not take so much as a shoe lace that did not belong to him. Among other things, Abe said he did not want the king of Sodom to be able to say that he had made Abe rich.

Abe did allow the three platoon leaders who were with him to take their share of the booty, but for himself Abe kept nothing.

Sometime after this Abe sensed the presence of God in a vision and God reminded Abe of His support and the promise of reward.

"How can this promise be fulfilled if I remain childless?" asked Abe. The nearest thing to an heir, Abe pointed out, was some kid who happened to be born in Abe's house.

Again the word of the Lord came to Abe saying that the child in the house would not be the heir, but the promise was renewed of an offspring of his own flesh and blood. Abe believed this, and was

[1]Gomorrah   [2]Mamre

comforted. God promised Abe that as he viewed the heavens and saw the many stars so ultimately would be the number of his descendants.

Abe thought often of these things and asked God for a sign of encouragement. As a result, Abe initiated a little ceremony, with burnt offerings, and after the long and intense ceremony, a deep sleep fell upon Abe and a nightmare of darkness.

While in his sleep the Lord came to Abe saying that his descendants would have difficulties and would spend 400 years as captives, but that God would punish the captors. Abe, however, was assured that he would die in peace, and that ultimately the land of Canaan would belong to the seed of Abe.

Chap. 16

Sara still was not pregnant and she was worried about the descendant problem. Sara had a house maid that was a nice girl named Lilly[1] and Sara reasoned that if Abe would marry her and have two wives in one tent that this would double the chances of offspring. The arrangement was agreeable to Abe and as a result Lilly became pregnant.

The new arrangement did not work smoothly, however, as Lilly elevated herself to number one wife and Sara began to fret. When Sara complained to Abe he told Sara that Lilly was her problem and to do with her as she pleased. Sara immediately began to make life so miserable for Lilly that Lilly headed for the hills.

Now when Lilly found herself weary and in poor circumstances in the wilderness by an oasis, she prayed and an angel of the Lord appeared to her and advised her to return and submit herself to Sara's rule and that as a result God would see to it that her child would be born, that the child would be a boy, and that she should name him Mike[2]. The angel promised that God would make Mike the father of a great race of wild and vigorous people.

Lilly was grateful to God and she named the place of her prayer Holy Water[3]. Lilly returned as instructed and had her son and she named him Mike.

Chap. 17

Time rolled along and still there was no sign of pregnancy with Sara and Abe was beginning to think that maybe he and Sara were too old to have a child; so God renewed his covenant with Abe. Because of Abe's great faithfulness, God changed his name to Abraham, and again God renewed His promise to eventually give unto the seed of Abraham the land of Canaan.

As a sign of recognition of this covenant, Abraham agreed to see that every male child would be circumcised and that this would be a physical symbol of a spiritual agreement.

God said that since to Sara there was to come God's extra blessing that a superlative was to be added also to her name, and she

---

[1]Hagar   [2]Ishmael   [3]Beerlahairoi

would be called Sarah.

God said that Sarah would be pregnant soon and that the son was to be Isaac. God reminded Abraham again that God was a keeper of the promises and that both Mike and Isaac would become established heads of future great races. Then God ceased talking to Abraham.

Abraham immediately began the process of circumcising all the males attached to his household or under his command.

One day Abraham was sitting in front of his tent in meditation in the presence of God, and he saw three men approaching. Abraham rightly assumed that these three had been sent by God and he welcomed them profusely, offering coffee, water, bread, and instant cookies.

Abraham then went and selected a fine calf and had one of the servants prepare it and before long there was a wonderful steak dinner with all the trimmings prepared for the visitors.

One of the men said, "Where is Sarah, your wife?"

"She's in the tent," replied Abraham.

"I will return unto thee, in accordance with Sarah's time of life, and see that Sarah has a son."

Now Sarah overheard this and she laughed in derision.

Abraham said to the men, "But Sarah has passed the menopause."

The Lord said then to Abraham that Sarah should not have laughed for nothing is impossible with God. The representatives of God again affirmed that Sarah would have a son.

Sarah then denied that she had laughed but she knew she was wrong, and she was afraid.

God spoke through one of the visitors and said, "Because the howling of Sodom and Gomar is great and their sin even greater, we are going to check on them and if it is as it appears, we will destroy the cities."

As soon as the visitors departed, Abraham appeared before God and prayed saying, "Will you destroy the righteous with the wicked? If there are 50 good people in the city, will you save it?"

"Yes," replied God, "if there are 50 good people in Sodom I'll save it."

"Perhaps there are only 45. Would you save the city for 45?"

"Yes," replied God. "I'll save it for 45."

"What about 40?" said Abraham.

"I'll save it for 40," replied God.

"How do you feel about 30?" asked Abraham.

"I'll save it for 30," said God.

"Ten less would be 20," asserted Abraham.

"I'll save it for 20," said God.

"This is the last time I'll speak, but God, will you save it for 10?"

"Yes," said God, and at that God ceased communicating with Abraham.

Shortly after this two men, representatives of God, came to Sodom and Lot invited them to spend the night at his house. They finally accepted his invitation and that evening enjoyed a fine dinner at Lot's home.

Some of the wild and unruly men of Sodom, however, learned that there were strangers at Lot's house and they came to make sport of them and harass them. Lot pleaded with the people, but to no avail. In fact, Lot said that he had two daughters that he would release to the pleasure of the crowd, but that the two men were his guests and shouldn't be violated.

This was not well received and the unruly mob began to threaten Lot so that the two guests finally pulled Lot into the house for his own safety. The representatives or angels of God then detonated a tear bomb on the front porch and men "wearied themselves trying to find the door."

The angels then turned to Lot and said, "Get your family together. The Lord has sent us to destroy Sodom and we want to get you and your family to a safe place first."

Now Lot had a couple of married daughters, but Lot's sons-in-law laughed at his warning and would not leave; so he took his wife and two daughters and left the city.

One of the angels told them to flee to the mountains and that they were not to look back on the city. Lot bucked at this injunction, however, as he claimed he was no rancher or mountain man and that he needed to live in the city. Lot said that a little city would do, but that it had to be a city.

The angels agreed and headed Lot to Zoar. Brimstone and fire then rained down upon Sodom and Gomar, and Lot's wife couldn't resist looking back on the disaster and she was burned to where only salt was left.

Abraham saw the smoke rise from the destruction of Sodom and Gomar and trusted that God had delivered Lot as promised.

Lot, however, became unhappy in Zoar as the people were not friendly to him, a refugee from hated Sodom; so finally Lot left Zoar with his two daughters and began to dwell in a lonely mountain region.

The oldest of Lot's daughters decided that the two girls would be left forever in the mountains and would never have any children; so she proposed a plan whereby they would get their father drunk and then lie with him when he was too stoned to know what was happening. The eldest daughter was the first to pull the trick and then she talked the youngest into doing the same thing. As a result both girls became pregnant by their father, without his knowledge, for he was apparently real drunk on both occasions.[1]

The Lord provided, however, that the sons of Lot's daughters would be the source from which came the people of Mississippi[2] and the Moscow Muggers[3].

Again Abraham decided to journey to the south and to visit in the land of Winston,[4] king of Filter[5]. As he had done once in Egypt, Abraham explained that Sarah was his sister. Because of this, Winston asked Sarah to be one of his wives and she was placed in the girls' dormitory.

God revealed to Winston, however, the fraud, and Winston was afraid, for he believed it to be a great wrong to take another man's wife. As a result, Winston gave Abraham a big fee to take his wife back and Winston explained that he had not had an occasion to go to bed with Sarah; so there was no harm done.

When Winston complained to Abraham about the deceit, however, Abraham said that actually Sarah was his half-sister anyway, and so his lie was not as bad as Winston thought. Abraham also said that he had mentioned the sister deal for fear of the ungodly attitude of Winston's people.

For the second time in his life, Abraham returned to his homeland with significant riches. Winston could not resist criticising Sarah and he told her that she didn't need to wear a veil any more with a husband that did such a deceiving job for her.[6]

Because of the generous fee, Abraham asked God to bless Winston and to let pregnancy again abound in his household, and God relieved the tension in the palace and children were again in process.

God fulfilled also his promise to Sarah, and she conceived and gave birth to a son, who was named Isaac. Sarah and Abraham were both middle aged and they were elated over the baby. Sarah said that the Lord had finally made her happy and she wanted everyone to be joyful. Abraham gave a big barbecue in celebration.

Now Lilly's son began to tease Sarah about her baby and so Sarah asked Abraham to send Lilly and Mike away. Abraham did not want to do this, as he was fond of both of them.

God told Abraham not to worry, however, as it would be good for Lilly to leave and take Mike to another area and begin another nation. When Lilly left, Abraham gave her provisions.

Lilly was never much of an outdoor person and soon she was lost in the wilderness and the water was all gone as well as the food. Lilly put the child Mike in the shade and then she went apart as she

[1] I personally never cared for Lot, anyway
[2] Moab
[3] Ammon
[4] Abimelech
[5] Gerar
[6] "You don't need a veil" is no longer an insult

said she could not stand to see him die.

The little boy then prayed to God for help and God heard him so that when Lilly opened her eyes she found water and gave it to the boy. As a result, the two lived and the boy became very proficient with the bow and arrow and when he was old enough, Lilly selected a wife for him among the Egyptians.

Winston and Abraham met some time later and Winston urged that the two of them agree to arbitrate any difficulties that might arise and discuss things together so there would be no war.

A chance to practice this came pretty soon as some of Winston's men captured one of Abraham's wells. Winston assured Abraham that he had known nothing of it and so the error was corrected and Abraham offered public sacrifice so all would know that things were well between Abraham and Winston. Abraham gave Winston seven ewe lambs so that Winston would remember that the well was dug and owned by Abraham. Abraham used this occasion to praise God, and to establish a place of worship.

Chap. 22

A few years later when Isaac was still a small boy, God spoke to Abraham and told him to take his only son Isaac, whom he dearly loved, and to go to a holy mountain and to sacrifice him. Abraham obeyed, and he took Isaac, two servents, and wood for the altar of sacrifice. En route to the mountain Isaac said to his father, "We have the wood, but where is the sacrifice?"

Abraham replied, "The Lord will provide."

Upon arriving near the site, Abraham left the servants behind and took only the wood and Isaac up the mountain. Once there Abraham built an altar and then tied Isaac to the altar. As Abraham raised very slowly the sacrificial knife, the voice of the Lord came to him saying that he should stop and look behind him. When Abraham turned around there was a ram caught in the bushes and God told Abraham to sacrifice the ram instead of Isaac.

God told Abraham that because of his extreme willingness to obey God to such a degree that God would see that ultimately all the nations on the earth would be blessed through the descendants of Abraham.

Upon returning home, Abraham was told of the various additions to the family through his brother Nat[1], who had now totalled 8 children by one of his wives, a girl named Mildred.[2]

Chap. 23

Sarah died on a trip and Abraham wanted to bury her on the spot so he could see that it was properly done. Abraham found a cave in a field and he sought to purchase this from the owner, a young man called Ronnie.[3] The purchase was agreed upon and Abraham bought the field and the cave, and Abraham mourned for Sarah, his true wife.

[1]Nahor
[2]Milcah
[3]Ephon the Hittite

11

As Abraham became very old he worried about getting a wife for Isaac and he called his trusted ranch foreman and made him promise to find a wife for Isaac in the next county and not to let him marry a local girl who might simply be after his money.

Abraham told the foreman to go seeking a wife in the area of Palm Springs[1], but not to take Isaac on the trip.

The foreman said, "How do I select a wife?"

Abraham replied, "I will ask God to have an angel help. If the chosen girl won't return with you, you are released from this vow."

The foreman took ten camels and many provisions, plus jewelry and gifts and went into the next county, stopping at a prominent water well. At this point the foreman prayed saying, "O Lord, help me. Send the right girl today so that I will make a wise choice. As a test, I will ask each girl that comes for water for a drink, and if she says she will give me to drink from the pitcher and then offers to water the camels, I will know that this is God's choice."

Sure enough, a beautiful girl, Becky,[2] a granddaughter of Mildred, came to the well and responded favorably to the foreman and she also offered to water the camels.

The foreman thanked Becky and gave her beautiful rings as well as some hard cash and gold earrings. Then the foreman asked for her name and if it was possible for him to spend the night and meet the family. Becky invited the foreman to the house. The foreman thanked God for his help.

Of course, Becky ran home and told everybody what had happened and she impressed her brother Laban very much with the jewelry and the money. Laban then ran to meet the foreman and offered him the full hospitality of his house.

After washing his feet, the foreman came to dinner, but said that he could not eat until he had explained his errand.

"First, let me admit that the Lord has made my boss, Abraham, very rich and very powerful. Now Abraham has an only son who will inherit everything and I've come to secure a wife for the son," said the foreman.

The foreman then went on to explain how he had prayed and he had selected Becky.

Becky's father was dead and the eldest brother, Laban, ruled the ranch, and so he spoke, "This is apparently a matter of God's doing. You may take Becky and let her become your master's son's wife."

At this point the foreman thanked God again, and then broke out the jewelry, money, and gifts for the family. A feast ensued and an all night celebration took place.

The next day the foreman was ready to take Becky back, but the brother and sister asked to keep Becky a few days so she wouldn't have to pack in a hurry.

[1] Haran   [2] Rebecca

The foreman urged them and they decided to let Becky decide for herself.

Becky said, "Saddle up, I'm ready."

The home folks waved good-bye to Becky, saying such encouraging things as "Be the mother of thousands!"

As Becky, her two servants, and the foreman neared the ranch headquarters back home, Isaac was sitting on a rock meditating and he arose to meet the group approaching.

"Who is that?" asked Becky.

"That's Isaac," said the foreman.

Whereupon Becky coyly covered her features with her veil.

Shortly thereafter, however, the young couple were married and Isaac who had been grieving over his mother's death was comforted in Becky, and he fell in love with her.

Abraham soon made a gift to Isaac of all his major possessions, but he gave many gifts and what he considered a fair amount to the sons of his other wives as well as to his illegitimate children and asked them all to leave the area so that Isaac might begin his own operations as head of his own family.

Shortly after this Abraham died, and he was buried in the cave with Sarah his wife.

Mike[1], Abraham's son by Lilly[2], died after a fruitful life and after properly establishing a new nation.

Isaac prayed to God that Becky would become pregnant and she wondered during her pregnancy about all the discomfort. God told her, in response to her prayer, that she would be the mother of two nations, and they would often struggle, with the younger being stronger than the elder.

Becky in time gave birth to twins and the first, a hairy boy, was named Esau and the second was named Jacob.

The boys grew and Esau became a cunning hunter and Jacob was a mother's boy, and stayed close to the house. Now Isaac was particularly fond of Esau because he enjoyed the venison he brought him, but Becky was partial to Jacob.

One day Esau came in famished and pooped out from deer hunting.

"How about some food?" he asked.

"I'll sell you some," said Jacob.

"If I don't eat I'll die; so what's the price?" asked Esau.

"Your right to the ranch," said Jacob.

Whereupon Esau sold his rights to the ranch for a square meal. Esau obviously placed very little value on inheriting the ranch.

A periodic drought came to the land and Isaac did as his father had done and went south in the land of Winston[3], king of Filter[4].

[1]Ishmael   [3]Abimelech
[2]Hagar   [4]Gerar

Isaac also remembered about his father's fear of being killed because of having a beautiful wife and so he told the people that Becky was his sister, for she, as Sarah had been, was beautiful.

Isaac prospered in the land and his possessions grew. One day, however, Winston was looking out the window and he saw Isaac loving Becky; so he sent for him. Winston told Isaac that he knew that Becky must be his wife and he lectured Isaac, saying that some of the Fascists could have gone to bed with Becky and defiled themselves; so he asked Isaac to leave the country.

Winston told Isaac that he could not order him out as Isaac had more men than Winston had, but Issac agreed to leave in the interests of harmony and peace. Isaac had, however, become rich in the process.

Isaac took his people to a portion of the country where his father had dug wells, but the wells had been plugged by the Fascists.

The servants of Isaac went to work and dug again one of the wells of Abraham in a valley, and herdsmen from Filter came and claimed the well. Isaac then dug another of the wells, and then another, surrendering each when claimed by Fascist herdsmen. Winston had observed the continued prosperity of Isaac and thought that God was providing continuous water for Isaac; so he journeyed to Isaac and made a covenant of peace with him.

After this Isaac dug another well and no one contested it. Isaac was pleased with this, but he and Becky were both displeased to learn that the eldest son Esau had married two Hippie[1] girls.

In time Isaac became old and almost blind and one day he sent for Esau and asked him to go kill a deer and bring him some fresh venison for he loved deer meat very much. Becky heard this and she told Jacob to kill two kid goats and bring them and she would cook them like venison and let Jacob present them to Isaac and receive Isaac's blessing.

"But, Mother," said Jacob, "Daddy will know it is me by feeling my smooth hands, for Esau is hairy."

"Don't be so stupid. Just do as I say," replied Becky.

So Becky fixed the meat and made it savory, and then she dressed Jacob in Esau's clothes and put on his hands the gloves she had made from the young goats' hides. Jacob then took the meat to his father.

"Hello, Father," said Jacob.

"Which one are you, son?" asked Isaac.

"I am Esau. I have done as you asked. Bless me and enjoy the meat."

"How did you get the deer so quickly?" asked Isaac.

"The Lord, thy God, helped me," said Jacob.

[1] Hittite

14

"Come near," said Isaac, "that I may feel thee, and know you are Esau."

Jacob came near and Isaac felt his hands and said, "The voice is the voice of Jacob, but the hands are the hands of Esau."

Again Isaac said, "Art thou Esau?"

Again Jacob replied, "I am."

So Isaac bestowed his blessing on Jacob and thereby his possessions. Isaac smelled the garments of Esau which Jacob wore and he said, "These are of the field which God has blessed and may the Lord give thee the dew of heaven, the abundance of the earth, and plenty of corn and wine, and let everyone that despises you be despised and everyone that blesses you, let him be blessed."

Shortly after this Esau returned with the venison and brought it to Jacob, saying "I am Esau, thy son, and I seek thy blessing."

Isaac trembled with anger and told Esau that Jacob had used subtility to secure the blessing, but there was only one blessing that he could give and it was given.

Esau wept in his anguish and vowed that after his father's death he would kill Jacob.

The words of Esau about killing Jacob were reported to Becky and so she sent for Jacob and said, "Esau plans to kill you. Flee to Palm Springs and visit my brother Laban until Esau has had time to cool it. I will send for you when all is well." Becky then came to Isaac and said that she was afraid Jacob would marry locally and that was a sickening thought.

Chap.
28

As a result, Isaac sent for Jacob and ordered him not to marry locally but to find a girl from his mother's country, and he then dismissed Jacob with his blessing.

When Esau learned that Isaac had blessed Jacob again and had sent him to Palm Springs to find a wife because the girls of Canaan did not please him, then he took additonal wives of Mike's descendants for himself, in hopes of pleasing Isaac.

As Jacob proceeded toward Palm Springs he tarried to rest on the way and used a stone for a pillow. While he was asleep he dreamed that he saw a ladder reach from the earth to heaven and the angels of God going up and down the ladder. In his dream he heard the voice of God from the top of the ladder saying that for Abraham's sake he would bless Jacob and his offspring. Jacob awoke and was afraid for he reasoned that surely the Lord was in this place. As a result, Jacob took the stone he had used as a pillow, poured oil on it, and made it an altar, vowing that if God would bring him home safely that he would worship God and believe in him completely. In his enthusiasm, Jacob also promised to tithe.

Chap.
29

As Jacob traveled east he found a well and there were three flocks there being watered. Jacob asked the herdsmen if they knew a rancher named Laban and they said they did.

"Is he alive and well?" asked Jacob.

"Yes," replied one of the herdsmen, "In fact, there comes one of his daughters, Rachel, bringing the sheep to water now."

As Rachel approached, Jacob rolled away the stone which closed the well, told Rachel that they were kissing kin, and kissed her. Rachel ran to tell her father about the new cousin she had found and Laban came forth to meet Jacob.

Jacob stayed on the ranch working for Laban for about a month, and Laban said one day that he thought he should start paying Jacob.

Now Laban had two daughters, the eldest was Leah, a plain but wholesome girl, and Rachel, who was very beautiful.

Jacob fell in love with Rachel and he told Laban that he would work for seven years and his wages would be the hand of Rachel in marriage. The seven years seemed but as a few days to Jacob because of his love for Rachel.

At the end of the seven years, Laban ordered a marriage feast and Jacob was married to the heavily veiled girl that Laban brought to the church. The next morning, when the sun made bright the honeymoon tent, Jacob had his suspicion confirmed that he had married the wrong girl, for it was obviously Leah at his side.

Jacob at once complained bitterly to Laban about the trick played on him.

Laban explained that it was an old family custom that the eldest daughter had to be wed first.

"Next week," said Laban, "we will have another wedding and you can marry Rachel and work another seven years."

Jacob married Rachel the next week, and he loved Rachel more than Leah.

Because Jacob showed favoritism to Rachel, the Lord blessed Leah with children and caused Rachel to be barren. Leah had four straight sons, Reuben, Butch[1], Max[2], and Judah, and each time she had a son she expected to impress Jacob.

Rachel envied Leah and complained to Jacob about not having children. Jacob said, "It is God's doing. Don't blame me."

Rachel then asked Jacob to have intercourse with her maid Babe[3] so that Rachel could count a child to her tent's credit. As a result Babe produced two sons, then Leah became jealous and threw her handmaid into the contest. When Leah's handmaid Zelda became pregnant, she was so large that Leah said she looked as if she was going to give birth to an army and she named the large son that was born Troop[4].

During all of this Jacob had quit going to bed with Leah. One day, however, Rachel asked Leah for some material and Leah said

[1]Simeon   [2]Levi   [3]Bilhah
[4]Hebrew word is Gad

she would sell it for one night again with Jacob. When Jacob came in that evening, Leah told Jacob that he was purchased for her tent that evening and so he lay with Leah and from this she had her fifth son by Jacob. Leah then had a sixth son by Jacob and a daughter that she named Dinah[1].

The Lord now remembered Rachel and she finally had a son who was named Joseph.

Jacob decided that it was time to return to his homeland and he also asked permission from Laban to leave, but Laban said, " You can deal with me for a raise in pay, but you can't leave." The ranch had been prospering and Jacob had been doing most of the work.

Jacob pointed out to Laban how everything had increased under Jacob's supervision, and he agreed to remain and to care for all the ranch and cattle, but he said, "I will go through the ranch and select all the spotted cattle for myself and leave all the blemish-free for you. From now on, Laban, all the speckled are mine and all the solids are yours."

Jacob then moved his tents about ten miles away on another part of the ranch, but he continued to feed and water all the stock of the ranch.

Now Jacob devised a way of doctoring the feed of the cattle so that all of the offspring began to be produced with specks, and in a very few years, practically all of the cattle everywhere were flecked. Jacob omitted this treatment only in the case of weak or sick cattle. Jacob flourished and became rich while Laban sat on the porch and rocked, not knowing that his cattle were gradually all being marked for Jacob.

Chap.
31

Some of the sons of Laban, however, began to wise up a bit and Jacob decided that he had better make his move. The Lord favored Jacob's plan to move back to Canaan.

Jacob called Leah and Rachel to him and told them how Laban had always cheated on his wages and that God had been on the side of Jacob and had caused the speckled rams to leap upon the pure cattle and that God was helping Jacob. At least Jacob said that's what he dreamed.

Rachel and Leah said Laban had never given them anything and they were ready to take all they could get and leave; so Jacob rose up and departed with his wives, and sons, and all his goods. While Laban was away shearing sheep, Rachel had slipped into the house and taken the jewelry.

Three days later, Laban was told of the departure of Jacob; so he pursued him and in seven days he caught up and God warned Laban in a dream to be careful of what he said to Jacob.

When Laban came to talk with Jacob, he accused him of

[1]She had 10 brothers; so nobody was in the kitchen but Dinah

stealing away with his daughters and grandchildren. Laban even suggested that he might have given Jacob a farewell party.

Laban went on to say that except for the warning of God he might get physical with Jacob for stealing all his goods.

Jacob insisted that nothing had been stolen and told Laban he could search, for Jacob did not know that Rachel had stolen the jewelry.

Laban immediatley went into Jacob's tent, then to Leah's tent, and then to Rachel's. Rachel had taken the jewelry and was sitting on it when Laban entered. Laban searched the tent and did not find the jewelry. Rachel told Laban not to be displeased that she did not rise when her father entered but that she was in her menstrual period.

When Laban failed to find anything he could claim, Jacob became angry and yelled, "What's eating you? What do you think I've done? Why do you pursue and harass me? I worked hard for 20 years and this is all the thanks I get. I've been out in the cold, looked out for your ranch, and you've cheated me ten times on my wages. In fact, if it weren't for God I'd be broke.[1] Furthermore, the daughters are mine, the sons are mine, the cattle are mine. Now put up or shut up, though I'll offer an agreement for the sake of the children."

So a place was marked with stones and Laban said let this place be a witness between us and "the Lord watch between me and thee when we are absent one from the other." And Laban added that neither would ever cross the pile of stones seeking to harm the other.

Jacob then offered a sacrifice and early in the morning Laban arose, kissed his daughters and grandchildren good-bye, and returned home.

Jacob proceeded toward Canaan and the angels of the Lord met him, and Jacob named the place God's Country[2].

Jacob dispatched messengers to Esau to tell him of his return and inquire into the state of affairs. The messengers returned and said that Esau was coming to meet Jacob with 400 men and the news terrified Jacob; so he instructed his followers to divide into two groups and he told them that when Esau attacked one group, the other was to flee to safety.

At this point Jacob prayed saying that he was completely unworthy of God's mercies, but that he was afraid of Esau and that he needed to be delivered. Jacob also mentioned that Esau would probably kill mothers and their children.

Jacob then assembled an abundance of gifts for Esau, separated widely one group of gift bearers from the other and Jacob told the first of the servants to tell Esau that all the possessions were Jacob's and that they were gifts for Esau. He commanded the same for the second, third, and all the gift bearers. Jacob also told the servants to tell Esau that Jacob was coming last, and Jacob hoped that by the time Esau got to Jacob the gifts would have soothed him.

[1] I doubt if anyone present believed this.   [2] Mahanaim

After the gift bearers had crossed the boundary stream and it was night, Jacob sent his two wives, the two handmaidens, and his eleven sons[1] and they forded the brook. Jacob remained on the safe side.

During the night a man appeared and he wrestled with Jacob. Jacob would not release the man, although the man threw Jacob's hip out of joint. Jacob was certain that the man was an angel of God and Jacob promised to release him in exchange for a blessing. The man blessed Jacob and told him that henceforth his name would be Israel for he had overcome his difficulties and he had shown strength in dealing with man and God.

From this time forth the children of Israel no longer ate meat from the hollow of thighs in remembrance of this occasion.

The next morning Esau arrived with 400 men. Jacob sent the handmaidens with their children first, then Leah and her children, then Rachel and Joseph last.[2] Jacob then went forward himself, bowing seven times en route and when he came near Esau embraced him and welcomed him with forgiving love.

"Who are all these people?" asked Esau.

"My family," replied Jacob.

"What was all that convoy I met?"

"They were my servants with gifts for you," replied Jacob, "as I wanted to please you."

"Keep your stuff, brother, I have plenty."

Jacob, however, insisted, saying that God had prospered him and that he was making the gifts as a blessing and so Esau accepted the presents.

"Let's go," said Esau.

"My people are not in shape, Esau, and the feet of my stock are tender; so let us go slowly and we will see you later at the ranch."

"All right," said Esau, "but at least let me leave a few servants to help you as I am interested in being helpful to you."

Jacob proceeded to Kansas City[3] and there built a house and stockyards. Jacob also began to buy land in the surrounding area.

Dinah, the daughter of Jacob, went roaming around looking at the new land and one of the native sons saw her. He grabbed her and lay with her, and ended her virginity. The young man, whose name was Sandy[4], actually fell in love with Dinah and began to speak sweetly to her. Sandy then asked his father to make a deal with Jacob so that Sandy could marry Dinah.

In the meantime, Jacob had heard that Dinah had been raped, but he took no action, waiting until all his sons were home. Soon Harvard[5], the father of Sandy, came to Jacob and said that Sandy

---

[1] Dinah no doubt also, but girls were rarely counted in this era   [2] Obvious partiality   [3] Succoth   [4] Shechem   [5] Hamor

19

wanted to marry Dinah and that he thought it would be good to have some of the new people to intermarry with the natives.

Harvard was very gracious and expressed a willingness to pay any reasonable dowry and to encourage friendliness in the land.

The sons of Jacob were very angry so they decided to deceive the Harvard people. The spokesman for the group told Harvard that their sister would not marry into an uncircumcised family, but that if every male would consent to be circumcised that the marriage would be approved.

As a result, Sandy and Harvard returned to their neighborhood and persuaded all the men to consent to being circumcised, telling them of the benefits of accommodating the tourists. Consequently, every male was circumcised.

On the third day following this, when the wounds of circumcision were the very sorest, Butch[1] and Max[2], the blood brothers of Dinah, took their swords and attacked the helpless men, killing Harvard and Sandy, taking Dinah forcibly home, while the other brothers made spoil of the neighborhood, taking all the sheep, oxen, jewelry, wives and children, and vandalizing the whole community.

Jacob rebuked his sons claiming that they had ruined his reputation and that the other inhabitants would rise up against them. All the sons said was that they weren't going to let anybody take advantage of their sister.[3]

Jacob then declared a household reform and told all his family to put on clean clothes, to destroy all false gods and images, and Jacob collected all the jewelry representative of pagan concepts and then he led the whole crowd on the journey to Bethel.

God appeared to Jacob and renewed his blessing and told Jacob that because of his recent faith and trust, that God was changing his name to Israel, and that he would receive the promise given to Abraham and Isaac; so Jacob built a small memorial church on the spot.

As they journeyed from this place Rachel came into labor and died giving birth to a son named Benjamin.

Israel, formerly named Jacob, continued to have some family problems. It was noted, for instance, that his eldest son Reuben had been trifling with Israel's mistress.

At last Jacob (Israel) journeyed to see his father Isaac who was very old. Not long after this Isaac died and Esau and Jacob attended the funeral.

[1] Simeon   [2] Levi

[3] How much advantage is questionable

Esau, in the meantime, had prospered so greatly that he felt the land was too small for all that he and Jacob both owned, so Esau gethered all his people and all his possessions and departed from Canaan.

Joseph remained in Canaan and helped his older brothers feeding the cattle, but he also reported critically on them to his father. Now Jacob loved Joseph more than his other sons and they all knew it; so they hated Joseph.

Joseph did not help matters by telling his older brothers that he dreamed that all the family were binding sheaves in the field and that Joseph's sheaf stood upright while all the others bowed to him.

"Does this mean that you will rule over us?" asked the superstitious brothers.

Joseph poured it on with another dream that showed the sun, and the moon, and eleven stars bowing to him and they hated Joseph all the more.

Not many months later Jacob sent Joseph to find his brothers and get a report on where they were and how well they were doing with the cattle.

Joseph, who had received a spectacular sport coat of many colors from his father, set forth on the trip. The brothers, who were by now jealous of Joseph and the coat, saw him in the distance and they plotted to kill him.

Reuben, however, argued against killing Joseph and suggested that he be thrown into a nearby pit. Reuben secretly planned to save Joseph from the pit.

Consequently, when Joseph arrived his brothers took his coat and then threw him in a deep, dry pit.

Later, while they were eating, a group of slavetraders came along and one of the brothers suggested that they sell Joseph and split the money. This sounded like a good idea. Unknown to the brothers, however, some gypsies found Joseph, took him from the pit, sold him to the slave traders, and the slave traders took Joseph to Egypt.

Reuben discovered the empty pit and was extremely upset. The other brothers, however, decided to take the coat of Joseph, dip it in goat's blood, and tell their father that Joseph was killed by a lion.

On returning home, this was the story they told and Jacob believed it, and Jacob went into deep and sorrowful mourning for his favorite son. No one could comfort him and Jacob said he would grieve all his life for his dead son.

The slave traders sold Joseph to a man named Pat[1], a big shot friend of Pharoah, ruler of Egypt.

[1]Potiphar

One day Judah, a grown son of Jacob, went to visit his friend Tommy[1] in the next county and during the visit he fell for a girl named Sheila[2]. The marriage to Sheila resulted in Sheila having three sons by Judah, the eldest being named Al[3]. When Al became of age Judah arranged for him to marry a girl named Dolly[4]. Al, however, was a bad boy and the Lord deprived him of his life before he could become a father.

Judah was worried about the widow Dolly having no children so he instructed the second son, Olaf[5], to have intercourse with Dolly and produce a son. Olaf did not want to have a son through his brother's wife and so he spilled his sperm on the ground when he was in the tent with Dolly. The Lord then caused Olaf to lose his life.

Then Judah told his daughter-in-law Dolly to return to her father's house until the third son Sam[6] was old enough to marry.

Shortly after this Sheila died and Judah sought comfort in travel, visiting again his friend Tommy. Dolly learned of this and she was unhappy that Judah had not provided marriage and a son for her, as Sam was grown and no arrangement had been made with Dolly.

Dolly was a desirable woman and so she shed her widow's garb and dressed herself fetchingly, covering her face with a veil, and she placed herself in a prominent place knowing that Judah, her father-in-law, would see her. Judah saw Dolly and thought that she was a whore; so he propositioned her.

"What will you pay?" asked Dolly.

"A kid from the flock," replied Judah, "and I will leave you a pledge until the kid arrives."

"I'll take your ring, a bracelet, and your staff," said Dolly.

Judah gave it to her and then he lay with her, not knowing it was Dolly. After this episode Dolly returned to her father's house and put her widow's clothes on again.

Judah later asked his friend Tommy to take a kid to the harlot and retrieve his ring, bracelet and staff. Tommy sent word to Judah that no one knew of a harlot answering Judah's description in the little town of Camelot[7] where this incident occurred.

About three months later word came to Judah that his daughter-in-law Dolly was pregnant, and that the child would be illegitimate.

"Bring her here and we'll burn her to death," said Judah.

Dolly appeared before Judah.

"Hello, Dolly," said Judah, "you have played the part of a harlot."

[1] Hirah   [4] Tamar
[2] Shuah   [5] Onan
[3] Er   [6] Shelah

[7] Timnath

"Yes," said Dolly, "and the man left me a pledge," and so saying she showed Judah the ring, bracelet and staff.

"You have been more right than I have been," confessed Judah, "for I failed to remember my promise about Sam. You are forgiven." Judah had no further dealings with Dolly, who later had twins.

In the meantime, Joseph, who was sold in Egypt to Pat, was progressing nicely. Joseph was a good boy and smart and the Lord blessed the work that he did for Pat so that Joseph had finally been promoted to General Manager and handled all of Pat's affairs.

Trouble started, however, when Pat's wife asked Joseph to go to bed with her.

Joseph said, "I just can't do it. Your husband has trusted me with all his affairs, and it would be not only a sin against God, but a dirty trick to play on Pat. I'm real sorry, but I can't go to bed with you."

The wife disregarded this negative reply and began to speak daily to Joseph, suggesting that they at least do a little necking, but Joseph continued to refuse.

One day the wife caught Joseph alone in the house and grabbed him by the shirt saying, "Love me!"

Joseph ran, but in leaving a part of his shirt was left torn in the lady's hand. This really tore it for the wife and she called to the servants and made a little speech saying, "Pat brought this Hebrew Joseph in to mock us and rule our lives. He actually tried to attack me and so I yelled, and in running away he tore his shirt and here is the piece of it."

When Pat returned he heard his wife's story and had Joseph thrown into prison. The Lord, however, was with Joseph even in prison and soon Joseph became a trusty and was really running the prison.

Sometime later Pharaoh's butler and baker were sent to prison and came under Joseph's jurisdiction.

One morning the butler and the baker appeared especially sad and they explained to Joseph that each had dreamed the night before and neither one could interpret their dream.

Joseph asked them to relate their dreams. The butler said that he dreamed he saw a vine and there were three branches and the buds came forth and grapes grew and he gathered them, squeezed them into a cup and gave them to Pharoah.

Joseph said that this simply meant that in three days the butler would be restored in favor and get his old job back with Pharaoh.

"Now when this occurs," Joseph said, "remember me, and ask Pharaoh to get me out of this dungeon."

The chief baker said that he had dreamed of three white baskets on his head and that the birds began eating the goodies out of the top basket.

Joseph said this dream meant that in three days Pharaoh would cut off his head and hang his body out to be pecked by the birds.

Three days later Pharaoh had a birthday and to celebrate he restored the butler to his former position and he had the baker hanged.

Unfortunately, the butler forgot all about Joseph.

Chap. 41

Two years later Pharaoh dreamed that seven fat cows came out of the river and began grazing and along came seven skinny cows and they ate the fat ones. Pharaoh also dreamed that seven good, full grained ears of corn were consumed by seven poor ears. Pharaoh was glad to wake up and realize it was a dream, but he wanted an interpretation.

Pharaoh sent for the educators, the astrologists, and the consultants, but none could interpret the dream.

The chief butler spoke up, however, saying, "A couple of years ago when I was in prison along with the baker, we had dreams and a trusty there named Joseph interpreted our dreams and did so correctly."

Joseph, after shaving and dressing properly, appeared before Pharaoh, as requested.

Pharaoh told Joseph of his problem and Joseph said that God alone could interpret dreams, but that God sometimes worked through Joseph. Pharaoh then repeated the dreams to Joseph.

Joseph said, "God has decided to show Pharaoh what God is planning to do. The seven good cows and the seven good ears represent seven years of plenty and the seven skinny cows and poor ears are seven years of famine. This is the cycle that is forthcoming, for there shall be seven years of gracious plenty in Egypt and then seven years of grievous famine and hardship."

"Ugh," said Pharaoh.

"My suggestion," said Joseph, "is for you to appoint one man to take charge. Select a wise person who knows what this is all about, and let him gradually corner the grain market in Egypt, and store grain in the good years to provide for the lean years. When the lean years come, Pharaoh's warehouses will have all the grain that is available. It will be a financial bonanza."

"How can I find anyone who is better qualified than you? God has shown you these things and so I hereby make you General Manager of Egypt."

Whereupon Pharaoh put a special ring on Joseph's finger, bought him some fancy clothes, and arranged for him to ride in the second chariot during Mardi Gras parades. Pharaoh publicly declared Joseph the chief ruler saying, "Let no man lift a hand or a foot without permission from Joseph."

Pharaoh then said that Joseph's new name was to be Bing[1] and Pharaoh also gave him a wife, Arlene[2], a high class local favorite.

Joseph was a young man at this time and with great energy and enthusiasm he went forth and during the seven good years he accumulated corn as sand of the sea until it was too much to be numbered.

Joseph had two sons during this period, the eldest, who made him forget how tired he was, he called Zip[3], and the second son he named Carl[4], who reminded him of God's blessings.

The seven years of plenty ended and throughout the whole Middle East there came a time of great need, and there was food only in Egypt, in the warehouses under Joseph's control. Soon the people began to cry unto Pharaoh and he sent them to Joseph, and Joseph sold the grain to the Egyptians and to the people from the far countries who came to buy.

Meanwhile, back at the ranch in Canaan, Jacob said to his sons, "Why do you sit around staring at each other? There is corn in Egypt, and we've got to have corn; so go down and buy some, else we die."

The ten older brothers set out for Egypt, leaving the youngest, Ben, at home, for he was still a bit young for such a hazardous trip.

The brothers arrived in Egypt and as was the case with all foreign buyers, they had to present themselves before Joseph to make a plea for corn. Now Joseph recognized his brothers, but he was careful to see that he was disguised enough so that they would not know him.

Joseph spoke harshly to them saying, "From where did you birds come?"

"We are from the land of Canaan and we come to buy food."

"You are spies. You have come to see how bare our land is."

"No, sir. We are one man's sons, we are sincere people, and we are not spies."

"You look like spies to me."

"We are twelve all told. The youngest we left at home and one brother is no longer alive."

"You are spies! In fact, I'll test you. You stay in Egypt until the youngest comes here. I will let one go back to Canaan for the youngest and I'll keep the others here in jail until the two return."

Whereupon he put them all in custody for three days. At the end of this period, Joseph told them that since he was a God-fearing man, he would give them a chance to live and told them to leave one brother bound in prison, take the corn that was needed, and then return later with the youngest.

[1]Zaphenathphaneah   [3]Manassahs,
[2]Asenath   [4]Ephraim

Joseph was speaking to them through an interpreter and they did not know that he knew their language, but Joseph understood perfectly the conversation they had following his final pronouncement.

"We are guilty concerning our lost brother," said one, "therefore this trouble has come upon us."

Reuben said, "I told you meatheads not to sin against the child and you would not listen."

The brothers agreed to the arrangement and they left Butch[1] bound. Joseph then ordered their sacks to be filled with corn and secretly he had their money placed back in the sacks, also provisions. The sacks were placed on the donkeys and they departed. The first night on the road one of the brothers opened one of the sacks to feed his donkey and saw the money in the mouth of the sack.

"My money is restored," he told his brothers.

This scared all of them and they said that it must be part of God's punishment.

Upon arriving at home, they told the whole story to Jacob.

Jacob immediately complained, "You are gradually getting rid of all my children. Joseph is long gone, Butch is lost in prison, and you want to take Ben away. You're doing all these things to spite me."

"I'll be responsible for Ben. Let me have him and I'll bring him back. If I fail you can kill my two sons, your grandsons," said Reuben.

"You're nuts. Ben shall not go to Egypt. Joseph's dead and Ben is the only son of Rachel left, and it would be too much if anything happened to him."

Chap. 43

Famine, however, grew worse in the land and the corn from Egypt was gone.

Jacob said, "All right, boys, go again to Egypt."

Judah spoke, "The man made it clear. No Ben, no corn. We will

go if Ben goes."

"Why did you big mouth goofs tell the man that there was another son in the first place?" asked Jacob.

"He asked us," they replied. "How were we to know that he'd want to see the youngest one?"

"Send the lad with me," said Judah, "so that we can all live. If I don't bring Ben back I'll take the full blame."

"All right," said Jacob, "if you must go, take plenty of gifts, take exotic aftershave lotion, some honey, salted pecans, and take double the money, both the money you brought back and the new amount needed. Maybe the money left in the sacks was an oversight.

[1]Simeon

26

Take your brother Ben, and God Almighty give you mercy before the ruler of Egypt that he may release Butch and let you bring Ben home. If I lose my children I lose everything."

The brothers came again and appeared before Joseph and this time Ben was with them. When Joseph saw Ben he told his aides to invite the brothers to lunch. The brothers were terrified to learn that they were invited to the ruler's house, and they feared that they would be attacked and made slaves.

The minute the brothers hit the door of Joseph's house they began explaining about the money to the business manager.

"Peace be with you, and fear not," said the business manager, "your God and the God of your father hath put the money in the sacks." Then he presented Butch to them.

The business manager saw that the brothers had a chance to wash and prepare for lunch.

When Joseph arrived the brothers gave him the presents and bowed themselves to the earth.

"Is your father well?" asked Joseph.

"Yes," they said.

Joseph then looked upon Ben and asked if this was the youngest son and they told him that it was. Joseph blessed him then. In fact, Joseph was so happy to see Ben and the other brothers that he had to leave to get hold of himself before the time for eating.

There were separate tables for lunch for Joseph, a Hebrew, could not eat with the Egyptians present, the Egyptians could not eat with the foreigners from Canaan, and the foreigners did not know that Joseph was a Hebrew.

Joseph, however, sent the food from his own table to the brothers' table but he put the choice cuts on Ben's plate. They all ate, drank, and were merry.

Chap.
44

After the meal, Joseph privately told the business manager to fill the sacks again with corn, to again replace the money, and this time to conceal a silver cup in Ben's sack. Needless to say, the business manager did it.

The next morning the brothers departed for Canaan.

Joseph instructed his business manager to let them get a couple of miles out of town and then they were to be stopped and searched by the customs people. The customs people were to say such things as "Why do you repay a kind host in such a manner?"

This was done and the brothers replied, "Why do you accuse us? We would not do anything wrong. Did we not bring the money back that was left in our sacks before? If there is anything stolen, search us and the culprit will surely die, and we will voluntarily be slaves."

The customs officers said, "That is not necessary. I will merely take as my slave anyone who is trying to steal or smuggle."

So beginning at the eldest, each was searched and the silver cup was found in Ben's sack.

The brothers tore their clothes and gnashed their teeth, and returned together to face the ruler again. Upon arriving, they fell on their faces again before Joseph.

"What deed have you done? Do you think I'm so stupid as to let you get away with this theft?"

Judah spoke then, "What can we say? How can we clear ourselves? We are even now your slaves, all of us."

"Sorry about that," said Joseph, "but I must keep the guilty on as my slave and the rest of you can return to the ranch."

Judah stepped forth then and said, "Don't get mad, but please listen. We know you are as powerful as Pharaoh, but listen. Do you remember asking if we had a father or a brother? Well, we said we had a father, an old man now, and a younger brother, a son of his old age, a little one, and his blood brother is dead, and only the little one is left of the mother, and the father loves him dearly. Then you said, 'Bring him down.' We said the old man would die if anything happened to the boy. Now father reminded us that his great love, Rachel, had only two sons, and one was torn to pieces, and if he loses this last one, he will perish. As a result, I declared myself surety for Ben. Let me therefore be your slave instead of Ben, for I cannot return to my father without Ben for I could not stand to see him suffer so much."

Chap. 45

After this speech, Joseph could not contain himself and he ordered everyone from the room except the brothers and then he declared himself unto them. In fact, Joseph carried on so everyone in the house could hear him.

The brothers couldn't believe it. It was too startling to comprehend.

Joseph then approached to them and said, "I am Joseph, your brother, whom you sold into Egypt. Do not be grieved or angry with yourselves that you treated me as you did, for God did send me before you to preserve life. For two years now there has been famine and there are five more years to come. God has really sent me before you to preserve a posterity for you in the earth, and to save your lives by a great deliverance; so really, it was not you, but God who did this thing, for God has made me as a father to Pharaoh, and a ruler throughout all Egypt.

"Make haste. Go to my father and say to him, 'Thus saith thy son Joseph. God hath made me ruler of Egypt, come to see me, and make haste.

I will give you land in Texas[1], where there is room for all of you, and your children, and your flocks, and all you have, and I will

[1]Goshen

28

feed you during the remaining years of famine. Look, you can see now that I am Joseph, and so can Ben. Don't forget to tell father of all my glory in Egypt, and hurry, and bring my father to me."

Joseph then embraced his brother Ben and then all the brothers got into the act.

The word of this soon leaked out and Pharaoh heard of the coming of Joseph's father and he was glad. Pharaoh ordered wagons to be acquired and given to the brothers to help with the move and Pharaoh said that what they didn't bring, Pharaoh would supply. So the brothers departed, with many gifts and many provisions.

Finally they arrived in Canaan and told Jacob that Joseph was alive and governor over the whole land of Egypt, and then Jacob fainted. As soon as he could listen they told Jacob all the things that Joseph said, and they showed him the wagons, and Jacob began to recover.

Jacob then said, "It is enough. Joseph my son is alive. I will go and see him before I die."

Chap.
46

As soon as everyone was packed Jacob and all his sons, and grandsons, the wives, the servants, and with all the possessions, they departed in one group. At a place where they stopped, the Lord spoke to Jacob and said, "I am God. Be not afraid to go to Egypt. I will be with thee. I will make of you a great nation and will in time deliver your descendants from Egypt. You will also see Joseph."

Judah went ahead to confer with Joseph and to locate Texas. Joseph then went in a chariot to meet his father and embrace him.

Joseph told his father and his brethren that although they had been raising sheep and goats that they were to tell Pharaoh and all the Egyptians that they were cattlemen and not to mention being shepherds, as a shepherd was an abomination in Egypt.

Chap.
47

Upon arriving in the presence of Pharaoh, however, the five selected brothers were asked by Pharaoh, "What is your occupation?"

"We are shepherds," they replied. "We have no pasture in our land and we would like to dwell in Texas, which we understand is not widely settled and there is much space there."

"Fine with me," said Pharaoh, "and if any of you have any experience in the cattle business I will be glad to employ you to help on my ranch."

Joseph brought Jacob to meet Pharaoh and Jacob blessed Pharaoh.

"How old are you?" asked Pharaoh.

"Older than seems possible, yet younger and more evil than my fathers," said Jacob, and then he departed.

Joseph saw to it that his father and his brethren were all nourished and well settled in Texas.

Joseph began gathering together all the money that was owed for all the corn that had been sold and he brought the money to Pharoah for safekeeping.

Now as the famine increased the people came to Joseph for corn, but they had no money. Joseph said that he would accept cattle in place of money so the people brought their cattle in exchange for food for a year.

The next year the people came for food and Joseph said that in exchange for food he would take land and the people then transferred all their deeds to Joseph for a year's supply of food.

Finally, Joseph told the people that they would now work the fields, all of which were now owned by the government, and they would be given food for their labor. And so it was made a law that the people would work and 20% of all that they made was given to Pharoah. The only land exempt was church property.

Jacob was getting old to the point of thinking of death and he sent for Joseph and made him promise to bury him back home. Joseph promised.

Word came to Joseph some months later that his father was dying; so Joseph took his two sons Zip and Carl and went to his father's bedside. At the approach of Joseph, the old man revived a bit and began to talk. Jacob said that he would like to bless the two sons of Joseph and they drew near, Jacob placed his right hand on the head of Carl, the younger, and the left on Zip.

Jacob prayed, saying, "God, before whom my father and grandfather walked, God who fed me all the days of my life, and the spirit which redeemed me from evil, bless these boys, let my name be their name, and let them grow into a multitude in the midst of the earth."

When Joseph saw that the right hand of Jacob was on Carl's head he told his father that the hands should be changed, but Jacob said he knew what he was doing, for great as the older boy would be, the younger would be greater.

"Joseph, I die," said Israel[1], "and I am leaving you an extra portion of my property, being some land I took away from a Frenchman[2]."

Then Jacob called the whole family together and pronounced a prophecy on each tribe.

"Reuben, your tribe represents power and strength, but it is not stable, and shall not excel, because of that incident with my mistress."

"Butch[3] and Max[4] are cruel. They are cursed for their violence

[1]Same as Jacob
[2]An Amorite
[3]Simeon
[4]Levi

30

and their wrath. I will divide them and scatter them."

"Judah shall be praised. The rule shall not depart from Judah and his tribe shall be neat and well kept."

"Jack Tar[1] shall be the seafaring ones, and in charge of the ports."

"Jeeves[2] is a worker and he shall be the servant tribe."

"Dan shall be a judge, and full of tricks."

"Troop[3] shall have trouble with troops, but will finally be victorious."

"Duncan Hines[4] shall be the eater and and furnish the gourmet cooks."

"Hubert[5] is a great talker with a mouth full of goodly words."

"Joseph is a fruitful bough growing by a well. The archers shoot at him and worry him, but he is made strong by the mighty God of Jacob. The blessings of my father shall be on the head of Joseph."

"Ben shall be like a wolf prowling in the morning and then counting his money at night."

Then Jacob blessed them all and charged them to see that he was buried in the same cemetery with Sarah, Abraham, Isaac, Becky and Leah.

Jacob, who sat for the blessing period, then climbed into bed and died immediately.

Joseph mourned the passing of his father. Having had his father embalmed, he then at the end of the mourning period went to Pharaoh for a visa to leave the country to go and bury his father as requested.

There went with Joseph a great company of chariots and horsemen and the sons of Jacob buried him as he asked.

The brothers of Joseph then began to worry that Joseph might seek some revenge on them since their father was no longer alive to be a peacemaker, and so they went to Joseph and asked for forgiveness for their cruel behavior to him when he was a boy.

"Be not afraid," said Joseph, "I am not God. Granted that you planned evil against me, but God meant it for good, to bring to pass, as illustrated now, to save many people. Fear not, for I will continue to nourish you and your little ones." Thus he comforted them and spoke kindly to them.

Joseph lived to see his grandchildren grow and then as his own death approached he said unto his people, "I am going to die. God will visit you though and finally bring you out of this land, as he promsied Abraham, Isaac, and Jacob."

Joseph died and was embalmed and buried in a tomb in Egypt.

[1]Zebulon   [3]Gad
[2]Issachar   [4]Asher
[5]Naphtali

EXODUS

The twelve sons of Jacob prospered and multiplied and their descendants became strong and plentiful in the land. Many years later, long after Joseph was dead, a new Pharaoh came into power who had never heard of Joseph or all that he had done for Egypt.

The new Pharaoh, however, was increasingly alarmed over the growing power of the Hebrews and he reasoned that if an enemy attacked the land the Hebrews might join them and Egypt would be doomed. As a result, he began to take various steps to prevent this.

One thing he ordered was work. Pharaoh made the Egyptian overseers or taskmasters compell the Hebrews to make brick and do the laboring and servant chores of the land.

In view of the population explosion problem among the Hebrews, Pharaoh ordered all the midwives to kill any male Hebrew as soon as he was delivered. Because of the fear of God and the madness of this order, the midwives refused to obey. When challenged by Pharaoh, they denied their disobedience, telling Pharaoh that Hebrew women were more lively than Egyptian women and that the sons were being born before the midwives arrived. Pharaoh said, "A likely story."

God blessed the midwives for their attitude.

Pharaoh finally ordered the death of every male Hebrew child.

There was born one day to a Hebrew family a boy and the couple managed to hide the baby for over three months. Then the mother fixed a small boat out of reeds and during the day the teen-age sister would baby sit while the infant floated in the boat, hidden in the marsh grass.

One day some young ladies came down to the creek to frolic and swim. One of them was Pharaoh's daughter and she saw the baby and immediately went soft-hearted and said, "This is a Hebrew baby, but I want to keep it."

At this point the quick-thinking baby sitter arrived and said, "Do you want me to go and employ a nurse for you to use for the baby?"

"You bet I do," said Pharaoh's daughter.

Whereupon the sister went and brought the baby's mother.

"Take the baby and nurse it and I'll pay you wages," said Pharaoh's daughter.

The child grew, and the mother brought the baby, now named Moses[1], to Pharaoh's daughter regularly and Moses lived and grew up in a palace.

When Moses became grown he moved about the city observing all the work being done, and one day he saw an Egyptian striking a Hebrew slave. Moses carefully looked in every direction and decided

[1]Means one drawn from the water

32

that he was not observed, so he attacked and killed the Egyptian.

The next day Moses saw two Hebrews fighting and he attempted to be a peace maker, but he was rebuked by one of the Hebrews who mentioned that he knew Moses had killed a man and probably considered himself above the law.

Word of this shortly reached Pharaoh and he put out an APB on Moses, who had already fled to the wilderness in the land of Midian.

Moses visited an oasis as this was the place to see about getting a job. One of the county commissioners in this area who was also a prominent rancher had seven daughters but no sons; so the daughters brought the flocks to the oasis for water. Here the herdsmen from the other ranches made them wait until last to water. Moses, who was a trained Egyptian warrior, told them this was not fair, and began to beat the herdsmen with his war stick. In a few minutes the herdsmen decided Moses was right, and they let the seven girls water their stock first.

Upon returning home early for the first time, their father, Mr. Cartwright[1], wondered how they got to water early.

The girls said, "An Egyptian, Hoss Moses, delivered us and also drew the water."

"Where is this fellow?" asked the old man. "Invite him to dinner."

Hoss Moses found a happy home on the range. Soon he was given his choice of daughters to marry and he chose Zsa Zsa[2] and Moses began a period of great joy and contentment. He had it made.

In the meantime, however, back in Egypt, Pharaoh had died, and the bondage of the Hebrew people was increased and they began to cry mightily to the Lord for deliverance. God heard their moans and groans and He was not unmindful of His promise to Abraham and Isaac, and He looked upon the children of Israel and decided to help them.

Chap.
3

One day when Moses had the duty on a faraway part of the ranch, an angel of the Lord appeared in the middle of a bush which though it burned, it did not seem to be consumed.

Moses said to himself, "I think I'll ease over and see more closely this strange sight."

As Moses approached, God called to him saying, "Moses."

"Here I am," said Moses.

"Put off your shoes, this is a holy place, and holy ground, for I am here," said the Lord. "I am the God of your father, and the God of Abraham, Isaac, and Jacob."

Moses was afraid and hid his face.

"I have seen the affliction of my people," the Lord continued, "at the hands of the Egyptians and I know their sorrows, and so I am

[1]Reuel (Jethro)   [2]Zipporah

33

here to initiate their deliverance, for I want them to leave Egypt and go to a good land, flowing with milk and honey, a place now inhabited by Canaanites, Hippies[1], Indians[2], Anglo-Saxons[3], Canadians[4], and Germans.[5] I have heard the prayers of my people of Israel and I am depending on you to return to Egypt and to lead in their liberation."

"Who am I, Lord?" asked Moses. "I am a nobody to Pharaoh."

"I will be with you," said God, "and I promise that after the deliverance of the people you will return here and serve God at this very place."

"When I come to the children of Israel and tell them that the God of their fathers has sent me, they shall surely say 'what is His name?'"

"Tell them that I Am That I Am," said God. "Tell them I am the God of Abraham, Isaac, and Jacob. Tell them to gather their leaders together and tell them of my promise, and they shall finally listen to you. It will not be easy, Moses, for the king of Egypt will work against you, but in the long run the Israelites will follow you, and they will receive gifts from the Egyptians to help them with their journey."

Chap. 4

"But, God, these people won't believe me," insisted Moses.

"All right, Moses. Take the rod that is in your hand and throw it on the ground."

Upon doing this, Moses saw the rod turn into a serpent and he jumped at least 12 feet.

"Now pick it up, Moses," said God. When Moses grasped the tail of the snake it turned again into a rod.

"Feel better, now?" asked God. "Then put your hand in your shirt."

Moses put his hand in his shirt and when he withdrew it, he was a leper.

"Now put it back in your shirt." Moses placed his trembling hand in his shirt and when he withdrew it he was whole again.

"Believe me, Moses," said God, "I will work as many signs as are necessary to get my people free from Egypt."

"All this sounds fine, O Lord," replied Moses, "but I am not a public speaker. When I get up before a crowd my tongue sticks to the roof of my mouth."

"Who do you think made you? Who made the dumb or the deaf or the seeing or the blind? Have I not made them all, and they are mine. Now get up and go and let me worry about your mouth."

"But, God, why not send someone who is already prepared?"

[1]Hittites   [2]Amorites   [3]Perizzites
[4]Hivites   [5]Jebusites

And God became miffed with Moses and said reluctantly, "All right. I will have Aaron meet you and Aaron is a great speaker, though he can do nothing else. You can put words in Aaron's mouth after I have placed them in yours. Now take the rod which I have blessed and for the last time 'get gone!'"

Moses returned to the ranch house and told his father-in-law of his encounter with the Lord and the father-in-law blessed him and sent Moses away in peace.

The Lord then comforted Moses by telling him that his picture was no longer in the Post Office in Egypt and that the group who had sworn to kill him were all dead.

Moses then put his wife[1] and sons on a donkey and departed for Egypt. En route Moses had a fight at a motel which apparently Moses interpreted as objection from God that the eldest son was not circumcised. As a consequence, Zsa Zsa[2] took a sharp stone and circumcised the son, which was a bloody operation, and then she threw the foreskin at Moses[3], calling him a bloody brawler.

After this incident, the mother and boy returned to the ranch.[4]

As promised by God, Aaron met Moses in the wilderness and there Moses told Aaron all the words of the Lord and told him of all the signs which were at Moses' disposal.

Upon arriving in Egypt Moses and Aaron gathered together all the leaders of the children of Israel and Aaron spoke to them, telling them all the words of the Lord, and the people bowed their heads and worshipped God.

Shortly thereafter Moses and Aaron visited Pharaoh and told him that God had a message for Pharaoh and it was "let my people go".

"Who is the Lord that I should obey him? I don't know him and I won't let Israel go," replied Pharaoh.

"We believe in God and He has met with us and ordered us to take the people into the wilderness for a feast. How about letting them off for three days, just a long weekend?"

"You're trying to get the people out of work. Nuts to you both!"

As a result of this confrontation, Pharaoh ordered the workload to be increased on the Hebrews, including requiring them to secure their own straw for the bricks. All this was done and the punishment was severe.

The local leaders of the Hebrew people then came to Pharaoh and asked, "What brought all this trouble on us?"

"You are idle," said Pharaoh, "and want to spend time in the wilderness at a feast. Your workload will stay as I ordered."

---

[1]Some scholars question her enthusiam for the trip
[2]Zipporah   [3]Some scholars were right
[4]Indications are that wife and sons all returned.

After leaving the palace the leaders encountered Moses and Aaron and denounced them saying, "The Lord should judge you all and punish you all for what you have caused to happen to us. You made us stink in the nose of Pharaoh and also his rulers, and they have gotten tough with us."

Moses then went to the Lord and moaned, "Why, O Lord, did you get me into this mess? What's more, ever since I've come here there has been nothing but trouble and no deliverance, not even a tiny bit."

"Calm down, now, Moses. Wait and see what I will do in my own time. I assure you that Pharaoh will gladly release the Hebrews when I am finished with him. You forget, Moses, that I am the Lord. I am the God of Abraham, Isaac, and of Jacob. I am Jehovah. My promises will always be kept. I have heard the groans of my people and will give them Canaan, it will be so, for I am the Keeper of the Promises. I will redeem my people, and I will take them to me for a people, and I shall be their God."

Moses repeated these assertions to the people, but they would not listen.

God then spoke to Moses again and said, "Go see Pharaoh again."

"But, God," said Moses, "if the Hebrews won't listen to me, how do you expect Pharaoh to listen?"

"Remember who you are. You, Moses and Aaron, are descendants of my people down through years. Act like it!"

"I still don't think Pharaoh will listen," replied Moses.

"Now, Moses," said God, "I have caused Pharaoh to think highly of you. Aaron can say the words. Pharaoh will not be easy, but I will use his hardness of heart to demonstrate my power, so that finally even the Egyptians shall know that I am the Lord."

Moses and Aaron then did as God ordered and appeared before Pharaoh, who immediately asked that they show him a miracle of God. As God had instructed him, Aaron then threw his cane on the ground and it turned into a snake.

Pharaoh, however, called for some of his own magicians and they did the same thing, but the snake of Aaron ate up the other snakes. This just made Pharaoh mad.[1]

The Lord then told Moses the next day to go stand by the water pool where Pharaoh came to drink and take the rod and when Pharaoh came to say "The Lord God of the Hebrews says 'Let my people go!'"

Then the Lord instructed Moses to have Aaron stroke the waters with his cane, and as a result all the waters turned red and were polluted, and the fish died, and the river stank, but Pharaoh just

[1]Pharoah may have asked them to stay over a day and do the trick before Rotary

got madder. The Egyptians had to dig for fresh water as the pollution lasted a week.

The Lord then told Moses to go to Pharaoh and say again that he was to let the people go, and threaten him this time with frogs. Moses then told Aaron to stretch forth his cane and frogs began to arise from the rivers and the pools and the swamps so that there was a frog jubilee. The magicians claimed to be doing this same thing but Pharaoh got his fill of frogs and sent for Moses and told him that he would let the people go.

"Hurrah for me," said Moses. "I'll get the frog withdrawal going tomorrow." And the Lord heard the prayer of Moses and the frogs died out of houses, and the villages, and the streets.

When the frogs were gone, however, Pharaoh relented and cancelled the release of the people.

God then spoke to Moses and said, "Hit them with lice." Aaron, on the order of Moses, then struck the dust with his cane and lice began to get over everything everywhere.

Pharaoh's magicians could not handle this one, and they told Pharaoh that the lice touch had to come from God. Pharaoh was not impressed, as he still did not believe in God.

The Lord then waited a few days and spoke to Moses and said that it was now time to use flies on Pharaoh and the Egyptians, but that the land of Texas, where the Hebrews dwelled, would be spared. So the Lord released swarms of flies, and they covered the land, and the people, and the beasts.

Pharaoh then sent for Moses and said, "All right, tell your people to have their picnic, but have it here."

"No," said Moses, "it must be three days in the wilderness."

"All right, but don't go far," said Pharaoh, swatting flies as he spoke.

Moses then asked the Lord to remove the flies and He did so, but Pharaoh hardened his heart again and would not let them go.

The Lord then told Moses to go to Pharaoh and tell him that the hand of the Lord would be upon the cattle if Pharaoh did not let the people go, and there would be a terrible murain among all the livestock.

So the Lord struck the cattle and all over Egypt they began to die. The cattle of Israel had been separated and they did not get the disease.

Pharaoh just got madder and madder.

The Lord then told Moses and Aaron to prepare ashes and to cast them in the air in sight of Pharaoh and there would be boils and infections in the land. The magicians who were summoned could not stand still for the boils that were upon them, but Pharaoh would not turn from his resolve to hold the people.

After the Lord had seen again how bull-headed Pharaoh was, He told Moses that he would now smite the people with a tremendous hail, the worst that Egypt had ever seen. God said He wanted to teach the Egyptians that there was none mighty like unto Him.

On the next day, as the Lord had commanded, Moses stretched forth his cane and the Lord sent forth thunder and hail, and lightning ran along the ground, and hail rained down on the land of Egypt. The hail broke down trees and destroyed all of the standing crops.

Pharaoh this time sent for Moses and Aaron and said, "I quit. You win. I have sinned. The Lord is righteous and I and my people are wicked. Ask God to cut the thunder and the hail and I'll let your people go."

"As soon as I leave the city, I will spread forth my hands to God and the thunder and the hail will cease, but I doubt if you and your servants are really converted. I'm of the opinion that you're just scared."

Now when quiet had come and Pharaoh saw that only the flax and barley had been destroyed for the wheat and rye had not grown up, he sinned all over again, renounced his promise, and again hardened his intention to keep the Hebrews in subjugation.

Chap. 10

The Lord then told Moses that all of these things had been done to teach a great lesson, not so much to Pharaoh as to God's people, that down through the ages they might pass the word from father to son of the power of God and of His mighty acts.

This time, God told Moses, "Hit them with the locusts."

The servants of Pharaoh then implored Pharaoh saying, "How long will we have to put up with Moses and these plagues? Let the dog-gone people go!"

Pharaoh then sent for Moses and Aaron again and said, "You can go. I want to know, though, who will go with you and what you will take."

Moses said, "We will go with our young and our old, with our flocks, and our herds, for we must hold a feast for the Lord."

"No deal," said Pharaoh. "I will let the men go, but kids aren't needed for worship and you can leave the women and children behind. The interview is over!"

Moses stretched forth his hand as God had commanded and the locusts with an east wind began to swarm into Egypt and eat up every herb, and the locusts covered the land so that it was darkened, and anything that the hail had left the locusts ate.

Pharaoh summoned Moses in haste, confessed his sin, and begged for relief. The Lord then sent a strong west wind which drove the locusts away and again the heart of Pharaoh was hardened.

The Lord then told Moses to stretch forth his hand to heaven and he would bring a great darkness to the land of Egypt for three days and no one could see another person for the darkness, and everyone stayed at home during the big blackout.

Pharaoh then told Moses that the people could go, including the women and children, but that they could not take any livestock or any possessions with them.

Moses said, "No deal. You must give us sacrifices to take for burnt offerings and all our cattle go with us."

Pharaoh would not agree and called off the release again, saying to Moses, "Get out. I never want to see your face again. If you ever return I will see that you are executed."

"That suits me fine, Bub," said Moses, "because that means I'll never see your face again either."

Chap.
11

After this the Lord spoke to Moses and told him that one more terrible plague would be used against Pharaoh and that the last one would work.

First, Moses was to prepare all the Hebrew people for a sudden departure. Moses instructed the people to borrow everything they could from the Egyptians. By this time the name of Moses was important and the Egyptians were generous in their gifts and loans to the Hebrew people. There was much talk in the land, and Moses departed from Pharaoh in anger and Pharaoh's heart and head were hardened.

Chap.
12

"What I plan to do," said God, "is so important that from now on this shall be known as the first month of the year. For I will pass through the land of Egypt in the night and will smite the first born in every family, unless there be the blood of the lamb marked on the door, such houses I shall pass over. Let the Hebrew people carefully and liturgically mark their doors for this night, and if there be a family too poor to have a lamb, let them use the blood of a neighbor's lamb. Let it be remembered that this shall be a memorial day and feast day for my people forever."

"Years from now," continued God, "when your children shall ask why you observe this occasion, you tell them that it is the sacrifice of the Lord's passover."

And the children of Israel did as commanded. And it happened as the Lord said, for the angel of death passed through the land of Egypt and the eldest son in each place from Pharaoh's palace to the dungeons was taken by death, and also the eldest of the livestock. There was a great cry and sadness in Egypt, for there was no house in which there was not one dead.

The Lord told Moses and Aaron to get the show on the road, and they aroused the people, and the Egyptians urged them to leave, and they gave gifts and loaned articles, until the children of Israel had almost cleaned the Egyptians out of their possessions.

Now there were some 600,000 men plus women, children, livestock, vehicles that departed, after serving in bondage in Egypt for four hundred and thirty years.

The Lord spoke strongly to Moses regarding the keeping of the feast of the Passover, insisting that it be taught from generation to generation, for it should be a sign and a memorial for God said, "With a strong hand hath the Lord brought thee out of Egypt. Therefore keep the ordinance of the passover in its season from year to year."

On leaving Egypt Moses, as inspired by God, did not take the people the short route through the land of the Fascists, lest they encounter a warlike people and return to Egypt, but he led them through the way of the Red Sea.

Moses took the bones of Joseph with him for it was recorded by Joseph that eventually God would deliver, and that Joseph wanted his bones to make the trip.

Now the Lord led the children of Israel, using a cloud by day and a pillar of fire by night, and at no time did He take these away from the people.

The Lord planned that the Hebrew people should pitch camp by the sea, taking the long way so that Pharaoh would think the people lost in the wilderness. All this was done in order that the Lord could work His wondrous way on Pharaoh, and that he and all the Egyptians would know that there is only the one true God.

And so it happened that the Egyptians began to relent over the release of all their cheap labor and they encouraged Pharaoh to pursue the Hebrews, which he did with 600 chariots of high speed and all the mighty men of the army of Egypt.

When the children of Israel, camped by the Red Sea, saw the dust in the distance and the sun shining on the armor of the Egyptian army, they were terrified.

The first committee to immediately descend on Moses said sarcastically, "Were there no cemeteries in Egypt, was it for this that we were brought into the desert to die?"

The second committee appeared then and said, "Moses, we told you and we told you to leave us alone in Egypt. Now look what has happened. It would have been better for us to serve the Egyptians than to die in the wilderness."

Moses said, "Sit tight and don't be afraid, and you shall undoubtedly see the salvation of the Lord. You won't have to deal with the Egyptians any more after today for the Lord will fight for you."

Then Moses went and cried unto the Lord.

"Why cry unto me, Moses?" asked God. "Speak to the children of Israel and tell them to go forward!"

And God instructed Moses to hold his cane over the waters of the Red Sea as the people marched forward.

The angel of the Lord then removed himself from the front of the people to their rear and the pillar of fire moved behind them and the cloud came between the camp of the Egyptians and the Hebrews and it prevented the people from seeing each other and they were afraid saying, "The Lord fights for the Hebrews, let us flee."

As God had commanded, Moses stretched forth his hand over the sea and the wind began to subside in the night, and in the morning the tidal wave came down upon the main part of the Egyptian army that was in the sea, and the waters covered the chariots and the horsemen and they perished.

And Israel saw the great work which the Lord had done, and they feared and worshipped God, and believed God and his servant Moses.

Chap. 15

The children of Israel celebrated, and the folk song and ballad writers became very active and they put to music the "Red Sea Story". The songs all told of the greatness of God, the terrible destruction which fell upon the Egyptians, and everyone seemed to get into the act.

Miriam, sister of Aaron, led the women in a big dance scene, playing timbrels and singing the Ballad of the Red Sea, and there was feasting and rejoicing, and the praising of God.

After a few days the celebrating ceased and Moses began to lead the people through the wilderness. The Hebrews were no longer afraid, for they predicted that the people of Canaan would be afraid after they were told of the great victory over the Egyptians and so they followed Moses confidently.

The first major camping spot was selected for its trees and water. The water, however, was bitter and the people immediately began complaining. Naturally they appointed a committee to call on Moses and to gripe for the whole crew.

"Now we're in a terrible fix, Moses," the committee stated, "for the water is too bitter to drink."

Moses asked God for help and the Lord made it known to Moses that all that was needed was leaves from a sassafras tree. As soon as the leaves were put in the water, the water became sweet and the people quit griping for a few days.

Moses said to the people, "If you will obey God, and do that which pleases Him, you will have no health problems such as the sinful and wicked Egyptians have."

Chap. 16

Two and a half months later the food ran out and the supplies of flour, sugar, and staples from Egypt were all gone. The people immediately began to complain. Typical of the moans was the expression "Would to God that we had died natural deaths in Egypt rather than starving to death in this weird wilderness."

The Lord, the keeper of the promises, told Moses that he would provide food, but that the people would have to obey the rules of conservation.

Each morning following the heavy dew there would be small white pieces of ambrosia, which the Hebrews called manna, and each evening there would be quail, weary of flying, that could be caught on the ground.

The rules were simple. All the manna was to be gathered each day and on the sixth day of each week, a double portion of manna and quail were to be gathered in order that the seventh day be a day of rest.

Some of the people immediately goofed. First, there were some who would get tired and leave some manna on the ground, and it spoiled and smelled. Then there were some who went out to gather food on the sabbath day. The Lord was displeased with this.

The manna tasted like biscuit and honey and the people lived primarily on this for forty years.

The next hardship that brought forth major complaints was lack of water. Again they howled to Moses and Moses prayed to God saying, "What can I do with these griping people? They are ready to stone me because of the water problem."

And the Lord told Moses to go and assemble the people with their leaders and smite the rock Niagara,[1] and that he would cause water to fall out of it for the people to drink. Moses did as God suggested and water came and Moses snapped a bit at the people saying, "Is God with us or not? Where is your faith?"

Not long after this the Capone[2] gang came to harass the Israelites and Moses ordered Joshua, a strong young warrior, to gather up a few vigilantes and fight them. During the struggle the Hebrews did well as long as Moses kept his hands raised in encouragement; so they put stones under his elbows to keep his arms high, and Joshua prevailed. And the Lord said that this occurrence was to be remembered and that He would always hold this against the Capone gang, and that He would fight them and their kind from generation to generation.

Now back at the ranch in Midian, word came to Mr. Cartwright, Moses' father-in-law, about the great deliverance from Egypt and the trip that Moses was conducting for the children of Israel; so Mr. Cartwright decided to visit Moses when the pilgrimage approached his area, and to take Moses' wife and two sons to see Moses. The wife had returned home mad after Moses had gotten in a fight at the motel on the way to Egypt.

Moses welcomed his father-in-law and his family and had a big dinner in their honor. The next day Mr. Cartwright was amazed to see that Moses arose early and took the seat of judgment and spent all day and late into the evening judging the people, answering their questions, and settling disputes.

[1] Horeb   [2] Amalek

Mr. Cartwright spoke to Moses and said, "This has got to be the stupid way to live. You will not only wear yourself out, but you'll wear the people out and only trouble will result."

"Somebody has to make the rulings and explain right and wrong to the people," replied Moses.

"Yes," said Mr. Cartwright, "but what makes you think you are the only one that can do it? What will the people do when you have a stroke in the next few months?"

"What do you suggest that I do?" asked Moses.

"It will take a little organization," said Mr. Cartwright, "but you should choose the best possible men and make them the supreme court to rule over the many thousands, then set up a system of lower courts, down to a judge for as few as ten families or one row of tents. Let the lesser judge deal with small matters, and the next highest judge with more important matters, and so on until only the major matters of import come to your attention."

"Sounds like a great idea," said Moses, "I will try it."

As a result a system was inaugurated of courts and appeals. Mr. Cartwright had made a wise suggestion and Moses had been smart enough to accept the advice.

Mr. Cartwright then returned to the ranch.

Chap. 19

With a system of courts the need arose for specific laws and God spoke to Moses and said, "Tell the people again that I am God. Remind them of what I did to the Egyptians and assure them that if they will keep my commandments I will treasure them as a nation, and they shall be to me as if they were a nation of ministers and priests."

The Lord then further expressed the need for the people to be prepared for His revelation of law; so Moses instructed them to take three days of preparation, to bathe, clean their possessions, scrub their tents and lockers, and not to even have intercourse with their wives for this period in order that they might be ready in mind and body to be aware of the presence of God.

On the morning of the third day there came forth great thunder and lightning, the whole mountain of Sinai was engulfed in a dark cloud, and smoke came forth from the mountains. Moses climbed the mountain into the cloud and God told him to make certain that none of the others, save Aaron, should touch the mountain.

Moses said, "I had already thought of that, and put barriers up and blocked the trails so that no one would get too close to the mountain."

"All right," said God, "return to the people and I will speak from the mountain."

And God spoke and said, "I am the Lord thy God. I am the one that brought you all out of the house of bondage that you all had in Egypt."

43

"In the first place, be sure and know that I am the only one true God, and I must be considered unquestionably number one in all things.

"You are not, therefore, to make graven images in the likeness of any object or person to which you will bow down, or for whom you commit your whole being. I will not accept secondary service, for I do not hesitate to punish, even though it may affect one generation after another for several generations, and yet I am merciful in great plenty to the thousands who love me and attest thereby in their lives.

"Do not try to use my name for your own purposes. You cannot claim to speak or act in God's name unless I authorize you to do so.

"Observe Sunday. It is a different day. It is a day set aside in recognition of creation and the creator. You are not to pursue the regular work of the week. You are to acknowledge on this day that God is Lord, and this seventh day is to be for His glory, and for refreshment, and you are to influence your family and associates in this connection.

"Recognize and adhere to the basic scheme of man's development which is the concept of the family unit. Respect the family unit as this is the only way for a full and meaningful life.

"You do not personally have the right to decide whether another person shall live or die.

"Adultery is forbidden for it works against the basic family plan.

"To steal is a violation of the law of God.

"You do not have the right to give a wrong impression about your neighbor or repeat things about anyone that is not absolutely true.

"You also are not to desire the things or conditions that are not yours. You are not to desire your neighbor's house to the dissatisfaction of your own, or your neighbor's wife, or his golf clubs, nor his ranch, nor anything that he has that might appear preferable to what you have."

The people heard the mighty thundering, and saw the lightning, and the billows of smoke coming from the mountain, and they backed away and were afraid. The people told Moses that in the future let Moses speak to them anytime, but do not let God speak straight for it is too terrifying.

Moses said, "Don't get so fretful. God is just teaching you a good lesson; so that you do not sin."

God said to Moses, "Now tell the people that I do not want them to make any more images of silver and gold as objects of worship. If you wish to recognize God and worship Him, just build a small altar of stones, and do not even bother to cut or break the stones as the simplicity appeals to me."

Then through Moses there were established many detailed laws and rulings as a system of jurisprudence in order that the people might know how to relate themselves to their neighbors, and a person could thereby know what to expect of the law.

If a man hurt a woman who was with child and caused a miscarriage, the beating was to be left in the hands of the husband, but the judges would determine the fine.[1]

And God spoke again to Moses and said, "Come up near to me, bring Aaron and the elders and let them worship at a distance."

Moses told the people of the laws and of God's promises if they would obey and the people promised to obey. And Moses wrote all the words of the Lord and built an altar to God of twelve stones, representing the twelve tribes of Israel.

Then went Moses and Aaron and the elders up to the mountain, but only Moses went up on the mountain. A cloud covered the mountain for six days and on the seventh day God called to Moses out of the cloud. The sight of the glory of God appeared as a devouring flame bursting out of the top of the mountain and Moses disappeared into the cloud on the mountain and remained there in meditation for forty days and forty nights.

God spoke to Moses and said, "Tell the people to bring gifts of gold and valuables, as much as each will willingly give, and let the money be used to build the ark of the covenant, and this shall be a symbol of God's house, and here we shall regularly commune, one with another. There is also to be built a church[2] to house the ark.[3]"

The Lord then told Moses to take Aaron and his sons and set them apart as priests and ministers, to array them in special robes, and to train them in a proper liturgy of worship.

Moses was also instructed in special rites of ordination for Aaron and his sons and the special garment was designed saying 'Holiness to the Lord.'

"When all of this is done," said the Lord, "then in the tabernacle I will meet with the people, and I will sanctify the church with my glory and bless the altar and I will dwell with the children of Israel and will be their God and they will know that I am the Lord their God, that brought them forth out of the land of Egypt. I am the Lord!"

---

[1] A sample of the law   [2] Tabernacle
[3] Complete description Exodus 25, 26, 27

45

Further instructions were then given in the area of craftsmanship.[1]

Now the Lord had provided in the diversity of creation that there should be men with special talents and God called to Moses attention the fact that there were such among the people and that these talented persons were the ones to be named in charge of the construction of the ark and the tabernacle.

The people, however, began to get restless after Moses failed to return from the mountain in a few days and many rumors began to circulate about his going AWOL or dying or the like.

After a while the people came to Aaron and said they despaired of Moses returning and that they needed a new god and a new leader; so Aaron agreed to help with a false god, and acting as their new leader he assisted in the construction of a golden calf.

God beheld all this and He spoke to Moses on the mountain saying "You had better get back to camp. The people have corrupted themselves. I perceive that they are a stiff-necked outfit and have already forgotten me. I will completely destroy them and start a whole new nation from you."

"Please don't do that, God," urged Moses. "In the first place, the Egyptians would be pleased. Also remember your promise to Abraham, Isaac, and Jacob. Let me have a chance at them again."

The Lord agreed to this, and so Moses came down from the mountain with the two tablets of law in his hands and there he was met by a fine young man named Joshua.

"The noise the people are making," said Joshua, "sounds like the noise of war."

"No," said Moses, "it doesn't sound like people shouting for mastery, nor do I hear sounds of people being struck, but it sounds to me more like a bunch of drunks singing."

When Moses came to the camp he saw the people dancing and singing, full of wine, naked, and going wild around the golden calf.

Moses roared and he threw the stone tablets at the people and he threw the golden calf in the fire and he ground it to pieces and made the people drink it in their water.

Moses turned to Aaron and stormed, "What did the people do to you to force you to do this thing?"

"Nothing," replied Aaron, "they just asked me to do it and brought me the money. It was one of those 'boys will be boys' deals."

Then Moses stood forth before the people and cried, "Who is on the Lord's side? Everyone that is faithful come stand by my side."

[1]Exodus 30

Many men then came to stand by Moses, and Moses spoke to them, and told them to take swords to go through all the camp and to kill everyone that did not repent. Then Moses said that he might be able to go to God and seek His blessing again. So the men went forth and as a result something in the neighborhood of 3,000 men were killed before order was restored.

Then Moses came into the presence of God and spoke saying, "Lord, these people have sinned greatly. Forgive them. I am willing to sacrifice my own life for their sake."

"Thank you, Moses, but that is not necessary. I'll tend to the punishment. Start your trip again and I will let my angel again guide you, but I'm going to make the trip a tough one and I'm going to exercise reasonable punishment on the people."

Chap.
33

And the Lord told Moses to get the people together and to depart, but God also said that although He would be with Moses and the people when they arrived in Canaan, He would not be with them on the remainder of the trip, for they must suffer for their disobedience.

The news of this disturbed the people but there was nothing they could do about it. In fact, God instructed Moses to place the tabernacle well outside the camp and that at this location God would deal with his servant Moses, in whom God had great delight.

When Moses left the camp and entered the tabernacle in the distance, the people saw the cloud of God descend on the tabernacle, and they worshipped. The young man Joshua was present at the tabernacle with Moses, and God spoke to Moses as a friend speaks to a friend.

"You have told me, God," said Moses, "to bring this people to a new land. I want to know who is going to help me."

"My presence will go with you, Moses, and I will give you rest," said the Lord.

"All right, but agree to cancel the trip if you withdraw your presence, for it is your presence that makes us a people different from other people."

"I will agree to your request, Moses, for you have found favor in my sight and I even know you by name."

"Show me a sample of your presence, Lord," said Moses.

"All right," God said. "I will cause my goodness to pass near you, and I will pronounce my name. You cannot see me, for no one can behold God and live, but I will let you get in the crevice of a rock wall and I'll pass by and you can feel my presence and behold my departure, but my hand will cover you as I pass."

Chap.
34

"I'm ready," said Moses.

"First, however, you must hew me two tablets of stone in order that I might write on them the ten commandments exactly as they were on the tablets you broke when angry with the people. Do this by morning."

And Moses hewed the stone tablets and rose early in the morning and climbed Mount Sinai and the Lord descended in a cloud and stood there with Moses and proclaimed His presence and spoke saying, "The Lord God is merciful and gracious, long suffering, and abundant in goodness, showing mercy to thousands, forgiving iniquity and sin for those who repent, but visiting the unrepentant iniquity of the fathers unto the children for four generations."

Moses bowed his head and worshipped. Then Moses prayed saying, "Lord, I pray for your presence. Stay with us. I know the people are stiffnecked and sinful, but pardon us, and let us be thy people."

God spoke then saying, "I will make an agreement that I will do some marvels in sight of the people such as have never been done. I will drive out the Hippies, the gypsies, and the Russians from before you, but do not dare try to make side deals with any of them. Destroy their altars, break their images, and you people are to worship no other God, for I am a jealous God."

"Be very careful," God continued, "that you do not join with other inhabitants in strange worship, nor should you intermarry with them, and don't forget to tithe. The first fruits are mine. Observe the proper feast days and make certain that all the kids go to church at least three times a year. This is my covenant with my people."

When Moses came down from the mountain after visiting with God and carrying the ten commandments on the stone tablets, the face of Moses shone. The people were terrified and so Moses covered his face with a veil while he revealed the commandments of God and told the people of the covenant.

Chap.
35

Moses appeared again before the people and called for a thank offering. Moses urged that all the people who were moved in their hearts by the goodness of God to bring gifts of all kinds in order that the tabernacle, and the ark of the covenant, could all be properly completed.

The people did this and trained craftsmen were assembled and all were put under the care of Mr. Disney,[1] whom God himself had blessed with great talents. And Mr. Disney assembled other talented people and trained them, and then they set forth to do the building and the making of the garments.

Chap.
36

The people were moved by this great activity and continued to make gifts until Moses announced that enough was already on hand and no further gifts were needed.[2]

[1] Bezaleel

[2] They over-subscribed the budget

The building and the equipment, the garments and symbols were all set forth with great skill and in great detail[1] and all was approved by Moses and Moses saw that it had all been done in accordance with the will of God, and so Moses blessed all of those who had helped in any way.

God told Moses that now the tabernacle could be placed within the camp. It came about that all these things were completed after two years and Moses set up the bulletin board as the very last thing, and the tabernacle was finished. Then a cloud covered the area of the congregation and the glory of the Lord filled the tabernacle. From thenceforth the cloud of the Lord was in the sight of all during the day and the fire shown at night, and the people journeyed only when the cloud moved or the fire advanced.

[1]Read Exodus 37, 38 for details

LEVITICUS

Note: The book of Leviticus is a compilation of laws, liturgical procedures and admonitions. The following paraphrases are samples from the book and are selected passages.

Chapters 1-7 deals with the manner, nature and method of burnt offerings for peace as well as trespass offerings.

Chapters 8-10 set forth instructions for the garments of Aaron and his sons as priests as well as such admonitions as the prohibition of the use of wine or strong drink by the priest or minister before conducting the service in the tabernacle or church.

Chapter 11 made distinctions between the various animals to be eaten or sacrificed.

Chapters 12-15 expressed views on health habits and preventive medicine in specific areas of post-pregnant conditions, blood problems, leprosy, and purification or cleanliness cautions for travel in the wilderness.

Chapter 16 described procedures for priests in connection with tabernacle service and Chapter 17 emphasized the error of the eating of blood.

Chap.
18

At a later time God spoke to Moses and told him to remind the people that they were under the one true God and they must obey His admonitions. God stated the sins of the Egyptians had been their undoing and that the Canaanites were guilty of the same sins. The children of Israel must observe God's orders, or they too would encounter difficulty.

One of the prominent errors of the Egyptians was the matter of indecent exposure. God, speaking through Moses, reminded the people that careless nakedness and the intentional exposure of a person was prohibited. Man was not to participate in any act of a homosexual character, nor was he to attempt intercourse with animals. Women also were told this was forbidden. Respect for relatives and neighbors meant that a person did not have the right of free love and the exercising of such constituted wickedness.

Chap.
19

The Lord explained to Moses various other matters dealing with the behavior and attitudes of the people.

God said to Moses, "You are to be holy for I the Lord am holy."

This meant, God further explained to the people through Moses, that people were to respect the family unit as the basic structure or framework of life. Furthermore, that people were also to observe Sunday as a special day.

The people were also to make free will offerings, and to be

careful not to eat contaminated food.

The people were to remember the poor and to leave grain in the fields and grapes on the vine for strangers and for the poor to gather.

Moses said to the people, "You are to pay fair wages. You are not to verbally abuse the deaf simply because they can't hear, nor are you to take advantage of the blind by placing stumbling blocks in their way."

"You are to be fair in judgments and not consider whether a man be rich or poor. You are not to seek vengeance or carry grudges. Do not try to confuse nature by sowing mingled seed in one field or letting cattle get all mixed up with each other. You are not to take advantage of a woman who is not free to make her own decisions.

"Also you are not to debase your flesh with permanent markings or seek after wizards. You are to respect the elderly and be considerate to the stranger."

Chap.
20

The Lord spoke to Moses and instructed him to devise strict laws prohibiting all forms of human sacrifice with the penalty of death for those who violated and presented any human sacrifice to any god. In this section the law was set forth with the death penalty for homosexuality. Again Israel was reminded that intercourse between man and beast or woman and beast was forbidden as well as being a confusion of nature.

Chap.
21,22,23,24,25

Leviticus continued with a succession of further laws and restrictions, some repetitive, dealing primarily with the duties, dress, and function of the priests as well as innumerable arrangements pretaining to slaves.

Chap.
26

And the Lord promised the children of Israel many blessings, all conditional. The Lord told the people that if they would obey His commandments and worship only the Lord then there would be rain in due season, and good threshing and fine vintage, also that the enemies of Israel would flee and there would be peace in the land and furthermore God said, "I will walk among you and be your God and you shall be my people."

At the same time the Lord warned the Israelites that if they took His commandments casually and did not show enthusiam in their worship, then God would see that there would be terror and pain and frustration on every hand. God also promised to scatter the Israelites all over the world until they learned to serve Him and obey His commandments.

Always God offered, however, redemption. Even in strange lands and far away places if any repented and confessed their wrong and evil spirit, and humbly asked for restoration and help, God, the

51

keeper of the promises, promised to heal and restore, and God promised to never forget his covenant with Abraham, Isaac, and Jacob.

Chap. 27

No paraphrase.

NUMBERS

And the Lord prompted Moses to take a census of the people, according to families and tribes, and to take note of the men over twenty who were able to bear arms in order that an estimate for an army might be secured.

This was done and is recorded with the names of the leaders and the specialties of the tribes.

Time had elapsed and many months gone and the people became relentless, quarrelsome, and sin became commonplace. The Lord, as He had promised, began to further discomfit the people and they came to Moses and complained. The people said that they were tired of eating manna and they needed meat. The head of each house would stand at eventide in the door of his tent and gripe to Moses.

Moses then came to the Lord also complaining saying, "What have I done to be stuck with all these people? If you would do a real good deed for me you would kill me and get me out of this fix. The people want meat and I have no meat for them."

"Get the seventy elders together, Moses, and I'll meet you all at the Tabernacle," said God. "There I will pour my spirit on the seventy and you shall be able to share the burden of the people."

"Furthermore," God said, "you can tell the people to prepare to eat meat beginning tomorrow. In fact, you'll eat meat, a special meat, not for one day or ten days, but for the whole month, and you'll get sick of eating meat. This is what you'll get for all your griping."

"But, Lord," Moses said, "it can't be. We have 600,000 hungry footmen, not to count women and children, and we couldn't feed them meat if we killed all our livestock."

"Are you questioning my power, Moses?" asked God. "Well, just you wait and see."

As a result, Moses went out and told the people of God's promise and he assembled the seventy elders and the spirit of the Lord descended upon them and they began to prophesy.

Two of the men, however, who were called of God did not go into the tabernacle but remained at the camp and prophesied there to the people. Their names were B. Graham[1] and D. Moody.[2]

Almost at once a busybody came running to the tabernacle to

---

[1] Eldad   [2] Medad

report the matter, and Joshua suggested to Moses that Moses forbid the two to preach.

"Are you jealous, for my sake, Joshua? Don't be. I wish everyone would preach the word and speak for God."

There came forth then a wind from the Lord and the wind carried quail and dropped them by the hundreds all around the camp of the Israelites.

The people immediately began to gather all the quail that they could carry, although the Lord had forbidden them to take more than they could eat. The wrath of the Lord was kindled against the people for their disobedience and as a result, the quail eaters all got sick. Many died from eating too many quail.

It was not long after this had all settled down that Moses encountered domestic troubles in the fashion of Miriam and Aaron objecting to Moses' marriage to an Ethiopian. Miriam and Aaron began to poor-mouth Moses saying such things as "Does he think he's the only one to whom God speaks?"

Now Moses was a strong, humble but understanding man, and the Lord was displeased with the gossipy talk and he summoned Miriam, Aaron and Moses and asked them to meet at the tabernacle.

The Lord descended in a pillar of cloud and told Miriam and Aaron to step forth and they did.

"If there be a prophet among you," said the Lord, "I will make myself known to that one in a vision and will speak to him in a dream, but Moses, who is completely faithful, with him I speak directly, and I don't like your mutterings."

The cloud lifted and Miriam became a leper. As soon as Aaron saw this he said to Moses, "We were wrong and we admit we were foolish, but don't soak us this way."

Moses, with great compassion, then prayed to the Lord asking that God heal Miriam.

"All right," said God, "But if she had just been rebuked by her earthly father she would have been banned from the camp for seven days; so let her receive the minimum. Tell Miriam she is suspended for seven days and then she can return healed."

Some months or years later, as the children of Israel neared the promised land, the Lord urged Moses to send scouts into the land to seek information. It was decided that each of the twelve tribes was to appoint one man, an outstanding person, and the twelve scouts would return in forty days and report.

Moses instructed the scouts to examine the land, to meet the people, to learn of the population and the strength of the people, the fitness of the land for grazing and farming, and to bring back samples of the fruit of the land.

The scouts did as they were told and they returned in forty days and reported to the assembled people and in essence they said that the land was a beautiful land "flowing with milk and honey," but they reported that the people were strong and the cities well fortified, and that there were giants there.

Caleb, one of the scouts, however, stood up and said, "Let us go at once and possess the land for we are able to overcome the difficulties."

The other scouts, except Joshua, spoke up saying, "We cannot attack the people, for they are stronger than we are. In fact, they are giants. The country itself will swallow us and we sure saw a lot of big men. In fact, we felt no larger than grasshoppers in their presence, and so that's how we looked to them. The deck is stacked against us."

Chap.
14

Then the whole assembly cried out in dismay and the complaints began to pour in, most of them being directed to Moses and Aaron.

"If only we had been left to die in good ole Egypt," or "All this trip and now we will die in battle and leave our wives without a bus ticket home."

"How about all of us walking back to Egypt?" — all these moanings filled the air.

Joshua and Caleb then stood forth and pleaded saying, "The land we explored is beautiful and fruitful. It is a land flowing with milk and honey and if the Lord is pleased with us He will deliver it into our hands. There is no reason to fear the people for they do not have the protection of God as we have."

The people's response to this was to threaten to stone Joshua and Caleb to death.

The Lord said to Moses, "How much longer will this people continue being hard-headed and contemptuous of me? I am inclined to forsake them and simply make a great nation directly from your own personal family."

"Don't do that, please. What if the Egyptians hear of it? And what about the present inhabitants? It is known far and wide about the cloud by day and the pillar of fire by night, and of your many signs and wonders. If you destroy these people at one blow the enemy will say that the Lord tried to bring the people to Canaan and could not do it, and so he destroyed them rather than fail. Why not let your full power be known, true to your own words, 'The Lord, long suffering, ever sure and stable, who forgiveth iniquity and rebellion and punishes down through as many as four generations, but He does not destroy His own. You have borne with these people all the way from Egypt, do not forsake them now, even if they are acting like nuts."

"Your prayer is answered," said the Lord. "I pardon them. Yet as I live, shall the glory of the Lord fill the earth. I decree that not one of all those that have seen my signs and wonders shall cross into the promised land except Joshua and Caleb for none of those who flouted me shall see this land, only those who kept the faith. In fact, I will give the fertile and delightful area of Florida[1] to Caleb and his descendants."

The Lord further emphasized that everyone over twenty years of age who complained should die in this wilderness. "As for your dependents, about whom you suddenly seem to be so worried, I will bring them into the land of promise, a new generation in a new land. Actually the penalty is a year for each day that you needed. You could have come and possessed the land in forty days and I'll make it forty years. This may teach you something about what it means to defy God and to fail to trust me. In short, it is curtains for you faithless ones, you're going to die in the wilderness," said the Lord.

The ten scouts who brought an evil report to the people all died of a plague.

When all of this occurred and the people heard the word of the Lord from Moses, some of them repented and tried to get started some enthusiasm for an invasion, but Moses assured them that it was too late, that the Lord was angry and the chance to succeed in the immediate present was gone.

There were still some, however, who decided that they would go and establish themselves in the promised land anyway, with or without the help of God. This particular group thought the hill country was the most delectable and they moved into the mountainous region. The hill-billies simply came down and wiped them out promptly.

Chap.
15

Through Moses, God again reminded the people of the need for certain liturgical practices or a form for the worship or sacrifice time.

The observance of the Sabbath was exceedingly strict and a man who was caught gathering sticks on the Sabbath day was executed.

Chap.
16

A small revolutionary group began to form and was organized for the most part through the efforts of Frank[2], Dino[3], and Sammy[4]. Finally they assembled support in the amount of two hundred and fifty men and they went in a body to Moses and Aaron.

"Now look here," said Frank, the spokesman, "You two try to run everything and we're tired of it. You apparently think you all are above everybody else."

[1] Amalekite   [3] Dathan

[2] Korah   [4] Abiram

Moses was shocked when he heard these words. In a few minutes, however, he spoke to Frank saying, "All right, we'll just all appear before the Lord in the morning and see what He has to say about all this. Each of you bring an incense burner to the church tomorrow."

Moses then asked Frank to send for Dino and Sammy as he wanted also to reason with them, but they would not come.

In fact, Dino and Sammy sent a message to Moses saying, "It is a minor matter apparently that you have brought us from Egypt, a land of milk and honey, to get us all killed in the wilderness, and mainly to make yourself a prince over us. Furthermore, you were scheduled to lead us into the promised land and you haven't done it. We will not come at your call."

This really burned Moses and he immediately asked God to curse them.

Moses turned at last to Frank and said, "Bring the censers tomorrow, two hundred and fifty of them."

The next day all the two hundred and fifty gathered near the tabernacle in the presence of Moses and Aaron. The Lord spoke to Moses and said, "Step well away from these people as I want to consume them all at one time."

"Don't punish all of them because of the sin of one man. It is the fault of their leaders," pleaded Moses.

"Tell the people to stand clear of Dino and Sammy," said the Lord.

Moses told the people, "Get well away from the tents of Dino and Sammy, for they are wicked men and you'd better stand clear of them."

The people did as Moses orderd and Dino and Sammy came out and stood in defiance in front of their tents, with their wives and their children.

Moses then spoke to the people who had drawn apart and said, "Now you shall learn that the Lord is the one that sent me to lead you from Egypt, and I have not done these things on my own or because of my own choosing. Let this be a test. If these men standing in defiance die natural deaths then I am wrong, but if the Lord causes the earth to open and to swallow them then it should be fairly clear that the Lord is active and that these men have provoked Him."

When Moses had finished speaking the earth rumbled, and then the ground opened up and swallowed Dino, Sammy, their tents, their possessions and their families. Then there followed a fire which claimed the lives of the 250 men who had rebelled, and thus the rebellion came to a screeching halt.

Moses was then instructed by God to see to it that the incense burners were taken from the fire and that they were put on the altar as a remembrance of the occasion and a sign of the power of God.

The next day, however, some of the people began griping again, accusing Moses of killing a lot of good, honest people who simply differed with Moses. When the people gathered thus to complain again, God spoke to Moses and Aaron another time, and suggested that they stand aside and let the Lord smite the whole bunch.

Moses then instructed Aaron to rush immediately to the tabernacle and to intercede with God for the people in a worship service. By the time all of this was done, however, the plague had already started on the people and Aaron came and separated the dead and stood between the dead and the living, and lighted the incense, and checked the plague. The plague, however, finally killed over 14,000, including Frank, who had originated the whole trouble.

Chap.
17

God spoke to Moses later and told him that He would provide a sign in support of the priesthood of Aaron and that Moses should gather together the designated rod of each group, with the name of each leader on it, and the Lord would cause to grow the rod of the chosen one.

All of this was done, and the rods were all placed in the tabernacle and then one morning the rod of Aaron was found to have budded, and brought forth flowers, and finally almonds.

Then every man came and received his rod and each was plain. Then God told Moses to bring forth the rod of Aaron, which was blooming, and to show this to all the people to cause their murmurings to cease and to relieve the Lord from the use of additional punishment.

The people were impressed, particularly with the earth opening, but they also began to stand in awe of the tabernacle.

Chap.
18

The Lord then spoke to Aaron and his sons saying, "You will now be permanently in charge of the tabernacle and responsible for all the services and programs and functions of the church. For this you are due reasonable rewards. One tenth of all the productivity of Israel shall go to you all and the operation of the church."

Chap.
19

Ceremonial instructions were then given to the priests in connection with the preparation for sacrifice and the disposal afterwards.

Chap.
20

The children of Israel continued to wander in the wilderness and finally they arrived in Phoenix[1], where Miriam died and there was no water.

Naturally the people began to murmur and to go over the same old

---

[1] Kadesh

song and dance about leaving Egypt where there was food and water to wander and perish in the wilderness.

Moses then went to the Lord with his problem and the Lord instructed Moses to gather the people and then speak to the Big Rock and water would come forth.

Moses did as he was told but having listened so long to so many complaints and feeling a bit like hamming it up a little, Moses spoke to the people and said, "Do we have to even fetch water for you from a rock?" So saying, Moses struck the rock and water came forth in great abundance.

The Lord was displeased with Moses for his grandstand play and told him that as punishment Moses would never be allowed to set foot in the promised land.

Moses then sent messages from Phoenix to El Paso[1] telling the king there that he would like to lead the wagon train through the El Paso territory. In his message, Moses told of all the trouble that had been encountered, but also told of the Lord's blessing. Moses promised that the wagon train would not pass through the fields or vineyards, nor would the people even use the water wells, but the wagon train would stay on Highway 90 and would turn neither to the right nor the left until clear of the metropolitan area.

The King of El Paso said, "No deal."

"Suppose we agree to pay for the water our cattle drink," asked Moses.

"Still no deal," came the word from El Paso. To support the refusal, a large group of fighting men from El Paso came to guard the border; so the children of Israel turned and moved in another direction, journeying toward Santa Fe[2]. Upon arriving near Santa Fe, God told Moses that Aaron's number was up and to take him up to Cloudcroft[3] and divest him of his symbols and his frock and put them on his eldest son. This was done and Aaron died in Cloudcroft and the people mourned the passing of Aaron for 30 days.

Chap.
21

There was a southern king called Big Lip[4] who was upset when he heard that spies from Israel had been around and so he made a raid on one of the Israelite tribes and took some captives. Israel became incensed because of this and promised to destroy all the habitations of Big Lip if the Lord would be with them. The Lord therefore delivered the Canaanites into the hands of the children of Israel.

From Santa Fe the children of Israel began to take the long way around in order to avoid all the outposts of El Paso and the people again became tired, discouraged, and complaint ridden. The people

[1]Edom   [3]Mt. Hor
[2]Hor   [4]Arad

turned against God and Moses and lamented again the leaving from Egypt. The Lord replied this time by sending a great influx of serpents that began to bite the people.

The people then came to Moses and admitted that they had sinned and begged for deliverance from the snakes. Acting on instructions from God, Moses had a serpent of brass made and mounted on a staff and placed in a prominent place. Anytime anyone was bitten and then would come and look upon the brass serpent, then that person would not die.

The children of Israel continued their laborious wanderings from one place to another until finally it became necessary to pass through Kansas[1]. The people there would not agree to the passage and organized themselves to fight against Israel. The Lord was with Israel and they took complete possession of Kansas. This was a great boost to the children of Israel and they began even to make raids into other strongholds, such as Fort Knox[2], and still the people were not ready to cross the Jordan into the promised land.

Chap.
22

Now the King of Mississippi[3], Jack the Ripper[4], became greatly disturbed over the success of the children of Israel and his people had become quite afraid lest their own land be captured.

As a result, Jack wrote a friend in Mississippi and told him of their problem and asked him if he would come and advise them what to do. With this message Jack also sent some inducement money to encourage a favorable response. Now Stonewall[5], the Mississippi friend, was a devout man and he agreed to pray about the matter.

God told Stonewall to dissassociate himself from Jack and assured Stonewall that he could not do anything against Israel. As a result, Stonewall told Jack and his gang to leave, that he could be of no help.

When word of all this came back to Jack, he decided that the price wasn't right; so he sent new emissaries with more money to Stonewall.

Stonewall said, "I'm sorry, but if Jack would give me a whole house full of silver and gold, I could not go apart from the word of the Lord my God, but I'll at least ask him again tonight in view of the great interest you are showing."

God spoke to Stonewall that night and told him to go with the emissaries but not to promise anything for the Lord would show him in due time.

So Stonewall saddled his mule and went with the princes of Mississippi. God's anger was kindled against Stonewall, for he had

[1]Sihon   [3]Moab
[2]Bashan   [4]Balak
                    [5]Balaam

60

over-interpreted what God had said.

As a result, an angel of the Lord blocked the road as Stonewall came along on his mule, with two servants accompanying him also. The mule could see the angel, but Stonewall couldn't. The mule turned aside and went into a field; so Stonewall beat the mule to try to get him turned back. The angel then stood in the path in the vineyard, with a wall on each side, and the angel again appeared. The mule then bucked against the wall and mashed Stonewall's leg and he beat the mule again.

Again the angel of the Lord appeared in a narrow place in front of the mule and the mule sat down and Stonewall blew his cool real good and began to beat the mule hard. The Lord then permitted the mule to talk and she said, "Stonewall, what have I done that you have beaten me three times?"

"Because you've made a lousy cavalryman out of me. If I had a sword I'd kill you."

The mule replied, "Think a minute now. Am I not your mule? Have you not ridden me for years? Have I ever bucked before or spoken to you?"

"You're right," said the now amazed Stonewall. Then Stonewall could see the angel with his sword drawn in his hand; so he bowed down.

"What do you mean beating this mule?" asked the angel. "Your trip is not approved. The mule could even see that. In fact, if it had not been for the mule I would probably have killed you."

"I have sinned," said Stonewall. "I'll go home."

"No," said the angel, "go with the men as you planned, but don't open your mouth until you hear from me."

When Jack the Ripper heard that Stonewall had arrived he went out to meet him eagerly. When he met Stonewall, however, he said, "Why did it take so long? I sent for you several times. I can do a lot for you if you cooperate."

"I have come all right," said Stonewall, "but I haven't anything to say until God tells me what to speak."

That night there was a big welcome dinner and the next morning Jack showed Stonewall the city and the historical markers.

Chap. 23

Later that day Stonewall ascended to a high place, apart from the seven prepared altars, and there he sought to hear the word of God.

And God met Stonewall and spoke to him and told him to return to the place of the seven altars and to make a speech to the princes and the people.

Stonewall returned and stood by the altars and spoke to the crowd saying, "Jack the Ripper has asked me to pronounce a curse on the children of Israel, but how shall I curse whom God hath not cursed? How shall I defy whom God hath not defied? I foresee that the Israelites will dwell alone and will not be counted among the nations. Furthermore, they shall increase in number and they cannot be counted. This is true!"

"What have you done to me," yelled Jack. "I expected you to curse the Israelites and you've blessed them. I can't get my people going on this kind of jazz."

"I can only speak the truth," said Stonewall.

"Come on, Stonewall, try again. Maybe you were standing in the wrong place and you misunderstood the word of God. Maybe you can come up with a good curse on the second try."

As a result, Jack built seven new altars in a different place and Stonewall went apart again. Again Stonewall heard the word of the Lord and returned to the altar site.

"Listen, Jack, and all you people. God is not a man that He will lie nor the type that repents. God has spoken and that is it. There can be no change! For I have been commanded to bless Israel. The Lord is with Israel and the shout of a king is among them. God brought them out of Egypt and he'll see them all the way."

"How about just not cursing them or blessing them either?" suggested Jack.

"I'm sorry about that, Jack, but I can only speak as the Lord has commanded."

"Would you believe one more time, Stonewall? I'll fix another set of altars and we'll try again."

"All right. I am eager to please," said Stonewall.

Chap.
24

The whole procedure was tried again. This time, however, Stonewall viewed from a high place all the tribes of Israel, camped in orderly fashion and he returned and made another big speech.

"Blessed are the sons of Jacob. As the valleys are spread forth, as gardens grow by the riverside, as the trees of lin-aloes planted by God himself, as cedars beside the still waters, the buckets of Israel shall overflow, his seed shall be in many waters, and his king shall be above all kings. God brought Israel forth out of Egypt and God shall eat up the enemies. Blessed is he that blesseth Israel and cursed is he that curseth Israel."

Jack the Ripper was furious. "I went to a lot of expense to get you here and you've ruined me. I had planned to promote you and make a big man out of you, but your attitude toward your God has prevented you from amounting to something."

"Now listen, Jack. I told your messengers that I wasn't subject to price fixing. A whole house full of gold and silver could not make me go beyond the commandment of God. I'm leaving now, but before I go I'll tell you something extra. I'll prophesy for you."

So Stonewall spoke and prophesied saying, "Although it will not take place in my lifetime, there will arise a star of Jacob for the whole world. All nations will finally be under that one star."

The children of Israel continued to dwell in the wilderness and some of the men began to have affairs with some of the women of Mississippi, whose reputation for beauty was widespread. The men also began to attend the pagan rites with Mississippi women and follow the permissive plan of the god known as "little Baal."

And the Lord spoke to Moses as the wrath of God was great, and told Moses to eliminate all the men who had turned to Baal. Moses passed the word down to the tribes.

The practice of running around with the Mississippi women was so common that one man came with his foreign girl into the presence of Moses and in sight of the Tabernacle, whereupon J. Edwards[1], the son of Aaron, took a javelin and chased the man and woman down and killed them. After this incident the plague which had already claimed the lives of 24,000 was abated.

Now the name of the man who was killed was Sundance[2] and the woman was called Belle[3]. The Lord reminded Moses to continue to annoy the people of Baal for they had vexed the Israelites with their wiles and caused many to stray.

The Lord sometime after this told Moses that the time had come for another census; so every male from 20 years old upward was to be numbered. This was done by tribes and it was discovered that there was not anyone left from the original number except Joshua and Caleb, for the Lord had said these people would surely die in the wilderness for their disobedience.

Then there appeared before Moses the Gabor sisters[4] who wished to be recognized as lawful inheritors of their father's estate since there were no sons born into the family. Since nothing like this had ever been done, Moses went to the Lord for help, and God said let the Gabors have their inheritance. As a result, the laws of inheritance were changed so that in the absence of brothers, sisters were allowed to inherit, then the succession went to the brothers of the deceased, then to the brothers of the father of the deceased, and then to the next of kin, and this became the law from that day.

Then the Lord told Moses to get up and climb Pike's Peak[5] and look out to the promised land. God told Moses that when he had seen it he would die, for Moses had sinned in striking the rock and calling for water and his punishment was that he would not get to cross the Jordan into the promised land.

Moses then prayed to God saying, "Appoint someone to take my place for the people need a leader."

[1]Eleazar   [3]Cozbi

[2]Zimri   [4]Zelophehad girls

[5]Abarim

And the Lord said to Moses, "Take Joshua, for in him is the spirit of God. Lay your hands upon him, and set him before the high priest, and put some of your honors upon him, and give him rank, that the people of Israel may be obedient to him."

And Moses did as God commanded and placed his hands on Joshua in the presence of the priest and the people, and he gave him a charge.

Chap.
28,29

Information on sacrificial offerings.

Chap.
30

Moses assembled the heads of tribes and explained to them essentially the law concerning the binding of an obligation or a contract. If a man made a commitment his word was his bond and he was responsible for his vow.

Moses continued explaining by stating that a young lady who was living in her father's house and made a commitment in the presence of her father and the father made no contradiction; then the obligation became legal. If her father disapproved, however, she was not responsible for her vow.

If a lady was married and made a commitment or agreed to a purchase and her husband was present and did not object, then the agreement became legal. If her husband, however, objected, the agreement was forfeited or the obligation not binding. The husband, however, could change his mind and disapprove at a later time. It was on this type of basis that all sales, contracts, and agreements were based.

Chap.
31

The Lord then spoke to Moses and reminded him that he had only a short time left to live and the Lord wanted Moses to avenge the wrongs done by the Mafia and for Moses to be in charge. As a result, Moses asked each tribe to call out its National Guard, one thousand men from each tribe, and he sent the army of 12,000 to fight the Mafia. The Lord was with the army and they defeated the Mafia and the males and the leaders were killed, but the women and children and cattle were brought back as spoil.

When the victorious army returned with the captives of women and children and all the loot, Moses and J. Edwards went out to meet them.

Moses was mad because the soldiers had not killed the women, for they were the ones who had enticed the men and spread venereal disease through Israel. Moses then decreed that all the male children were to be killed and all women who were not virgins. The virgins could be kept by the man who captured one.

Moses further ordered that all this be done outside the camp and that the regular seven day period be observed of staying away until all the mess was cleaned up.

The cattle, jewelry and negotiable spoils were then divided among the National Guardsmen that went to war.

In appreciation to the Lord for their success and for not losing a single man in combat, the soldiers brought a valuable gift to the Tabernacle.

Chap.
32

The members of the tribes of Reuben and Troop were cattle people primarily and they came to Moses saying that now that the time was at hand to go into the promised land, they had decided that the wilderness was better range land and they wanted to stay with the grass.

Moses reasoned with them along the lines of their obligation to the whole nation and insisted that they could not secede as they were needed for the conquest.

After much discussion it was agreed that the fighting men of both tribes would march with the others in the conquest of the promised land, but that the women, children, and elderly men would remain in the wilderness and build habitations. It was also agreed that as soon as the conquest of Canaan was assured, then the men of Troop and Reuben would be free to return to the wilderness to their families and their possessions.

Chap.
33

Moses recorded in log form the trip from Egypt, tracing the journey all the way, with the multiple wanderings, and the encounters with the various tribes.

Chap.
34

The Lord outlined to Moses the boundaries to be respected in connection with the conquest of the promised land.

Chap.
35

The Lord spoke to Moses and said that he should tell the people of their responsibility for the welfare of their ministers. The people were told to provide housing and protection and to share some of their own possessions in accordance with the prosperity of each family. The Lord also told Moses to instruct the people to provide a special sanctuary area for criminals, where they might reside until provision had been made for their public trial.

The sanctuaries for criminals were to be at least six different places and they were to be used by the stranger as well as by the children of Israel.

If a man killed another man with an instrument of iron, that man was a murderer and should be put to death. The same applied if a man killed another with a stone, or with a weapon of wood. Such a murderer could be sought by the next of kin or a friend of the murdered man, and the murderer might them be killed in vengeance, not because of hatred.

The avenger, however, could not seek the murderer in the sanctuary area and the murderer could remain safe as long as the high priest lived who established the sanctuary. If the murderer left the sanctuary area, however, he might be legally killed by the avenger.

To establish the fact of murder there must be at least two witnesses. Moses futhermore instructed the people saying that the Lord warned the people not to defile the new land with blood, for a land could not be cleansed of bloodshed, and the Lord expected to dwell with his people in a land that was not defiled.

Chap.
36

Again there came before Moses for judgment the matter of the inheritance of the Gabor[1] sisters.

Moses agreed with the suggestion of the leaders of the tribe of Joseph and he decreed that the Gabor girls could marry anyone they chose as long as the man was connected with the tribe to which their father belonged. In this manner, the inheritance of each tribe would be intact and no one tribe would have an advantage of another. No inheritance, then, could be transferred from one tribe to the other, and to retain her inheritance, therefore, daughters must marry within their tribe or forfeit their inheritance.

All these things were spoken by Moses at the commandment of God and were told to the people as they stood in sight of the promised land.

[1]Zelophehad

Moses gathered all the people together in sight of the promised land, some forty years since he had started them from Egypt and he made a speech saying,

"The Lord has set before us the land and told us to possess it. The boundaries are clear. When the Lord first called me to this undertaking of leading you from Egypt to this new land, I knew that I would not be able to do it by myself.

"The Lord increased you greatly in numbers and I devised a plan of delegating authority and set responsible men over you and so a good system of leadership was instituted, with the better qualified men handling the more important matters.

"I charged all your leaders to hear the complaints and all the needs and strife that might arise. They are to judge righteously between every man and his brother and also the stranger that might be involved.

"They are not to consider persons in their judgment, whether they be important or not, and they shall not be intimidated by threats, for their judgment is to be of God. If the case is too hard for one of them, they simply refer it to me."

"You may recall," Moses continued, "how we journeyed through the great and terrible wilderness until we came in sight of the land of Canaan. You may remember suggesting that we send forth spies who would examine the land and report to us as to the best way to conquer the land. The spies returned and brought marvelous fruit from the land and reported that it was a good land, but you would not risk entering it, and you disobeyed the commandment of God.

"It was at this point that you made your biggest gripes and you longed to be back in Egypt in bondage rather than endure the hardships of conquest. I told you not to be afraid, but you were worried about giants, although God had nursed you through the wilderness, you would not trust him to deliver, in spite of the cloud by day and pillar of fire at night. Your lack of faith angered the Lord, and He decreed that none of those that refused to march would set foot in the promised land. Caleb and Joshua, the spies who urged immediate conquest, were the only two that God promised would walk into the promised land."

"I remember," continued Moses, "that after this you repented and some of you armed yourselves and were ready to go, but God did not approve for He felt you had blown your chance. I told you this, but pig-headed as you were, you did not heed and a whole bunch of you marched off to your death. The ones who survived returned moaning and again repentant."

Moses continued his review of the past forty years reminding the people that they had circled around Mt. Sinai until finally the Lord had told them to get a move on, to go North, to pass through the land that was originally Esau's and not to strive there with the people nor try to possess the land. We were to buy food and shop and get out, and this was done, and the next stop was the land of Mississippi.[1] The people of Mississippi were also not to be disturbed.

"In all, it took 38 years to cross the Delaware River.[2] It took this long for the unfaithful to die, and then the people proceeded to Ai, and through other lands, the Lord destroying the giants in front of them, and the Lord caused all nations to be fearful of the Israelites. Those nations which resisted the peaceful passage of the people were destroyed, and many cities were necessarily conquered.

Chap.
3

And Joshua was told "Your eyes have seen all that the Lord your God hath done unto the two kings who resisted; so shall the Lord do to all the kingdoms that you encounter in the new land. Do not fear them, for the Lord shall fight for you."

Then Moses prayed, saying, "Lord, you continue to show me your greatness and your mighty hand, for what Lord is there in heaven or earth that can do according to your works? I beg of you, let me go and at least see the land that is beyond Jordan, just to cross into the promised land."

"But the Lord was angry with me," continued Moses, "because of you and the smart alec stunt I pulled at the rock, and the Lord would not hear, and He told me not to bring the matter up another time. God told me to climb Lookout Mountain[3] and look in every direction and see as much and as far as I could see, but I could never cross the Jordan.

"God told me, however, to encourage Joshua for he would lead the people and enable them to inherit the land of Canaan.

Chap.
4

"Futhermore, my people," Moses continued, "recall the statutes and judgments which I taught you, observe them in order that you might live and possess the land which the Lord of your fathers will give you. You are not to add to the laws nor take away from them. You have seen what the Lord did in the case of the "Little Baal" worship stunt, how God destroyed this segment of our people, while you all that stuck with God are still alive. I have taught you the commandments of God, obey them, for this is your wisdom

[1]Moab   [2]Zered

[3]Pisgah

and your status in the sight of other nations. Other nations shall hear of these statutes and will think of you as a wise and honorable people. For what other nation has ever had God so close to them or so available to them?

"Or what nation is there that has statutes or judgments as righteous as the law which I have set forth before you?

"Only be careful, do not forget the things which you have read and seen, but teach them to your sons and your grandsons.

"Remember especially the day that the Lord came close upon the mountain, and fire burst forth from the mountain top, and a cloud encircled the mountain and the Lord spoke to you from the midst of the fire and He declared His covenant with you, and He presented to you the Ten Commandments on tablets of stone. It was at that time that God told me to teach you those commandments and to instruct you to obey them in the land of Canaan.

"Be very careful that you never corrupt yours and make graven images of any figure, male or female, or the likeness of any beast or winged fowl that flieth in the air, or the likeness of anything that creepeth on the ground, or of any fish that swims in the deep.

"Be careful also that when you look upon the heavens and see the sun, the moon, the stars, and the galaxies that you do not become so impressed that you worship them, for God has taken you as His people and brought you from the iron furnace of Egypt to be unto Him an inheritance.

"Futhermore, the Lord was angry at me, and it was mainly your fault,[1] and as a result I cannot cross over the Jordan into that good land which the Lord has given for an inheritance, but I must die in this land. You get to go, but I don't.

"Take heed that you forget not the covenant of the Lord and I promise you He is a strict God, and He means what He says.

"As the years go by, and your children's children grow in the promised land, and corrupt themselves, and stray from the commandments, I call heaven and earth as a witness against you, for you will not last in the land and you will utterly be cut off and scattered. The Lord shall scatter you among the nations so that there will be proportionately few of you in each heathen land, and in this situation you shall seek false gods, made of wood and stone, that neither see, nor hear, nor smell, nor eat.

"If, however, at any time you shall earnestly and sincerely seek the Lord thy God, you will find Him.

"If you are in great tribulation, and if you are living in the latter days of trouble, if you will turn to the Lord your God, and be obedient to Him, for God is merciful, He will not forsake you, nor destroy you, nor forget His promise.

"Inquire, ask anyone, from the far side of heaven to the ends of the earth, has anyone ever heard of a great thing as God speaking

[1] tut, tut, Moses

from the mountain?

"Has God ever previously selected a nation and rescued it from another nation, and with multiple experiences and signs and wars and wonders and the stretching of a mighty hand and with great terrors done what He has done with you?

"This was done that you might know that He is the Lord God, there is no other god except Him.

"Know therefore this very day and consider it carefully that the Lord He is God in the Heaven above and upon the earth beneath, there is none other; so keep His commandments."

At this point Moses set aside three cities of refuge on the wilderness side of Jordan, to these could the criminal flee and receive sanctuary.

Chap.
5

Again Moses called the people together[1] and spoke to them reminding them that God had made a covenant with them, "not with our fathers, but with us. All of us who are alive today." God spoke in our presence and said:

"I am the Lord thy God who brought you out of the land of Egypt, out of the house of bondage; you shall have no other gods before me.

"You shall not make any graven image or any likeness of anything that is in the heaven above, or that is in the earth beneath, or that is in the waters under the earth, you are not to bow down to them or serve them, for I the Lord thy God am a jealous God, passing the iniquities of the fathers on down to the children, on down to the fourth generation of those who despise me, yet showing mercy unto the great numbers that love me and keep my commandments.

"You are not to take the Lord's name in vain or use it disrespectfully, for the Lord will blame you for doing such.

"Keep the Sabbath Day, make it different, as the Lord thy God has commanded you.

"Six days is plenty for all the work you need to do, for the seventh is the special day of God, do not let it be a continuation of the other days, it is not for work, for you, or your son or your daughter or the people who normally work for you, nor for a visiting stranger, or any of your work animals.

"You just remember that you were servants in the land of Egypt and the Lord delivered you, and the Lord expects you to remember the day that He called the Sabbath.

"Respect the place of the family, through your mother and father, as God has commanded, for this is the system of continuing life.

"You are not authorized to take another person's life.

"You are not permitted to commit adultery.

[1]Probably after a coffee break

70

"You do not have the right to steal.

"You are not to testify falsely about your neighbor.

"You are not permitted to covet your neighbor's wife, nor his house, nor his field, nor his servants, nor his animals, nor anything that is your neighbor's.

"Now these are the words that the Lord spoke unto the assemblage, and He added nothing to these commandments, and they were written on two stone tablets, and delivered directly to me."

God was impressed with the reaction of the people, according to Moses, and it would be a great thing if the people would always fear God and keep His commandments. The people then withdrew into their tents and Moses received additional details in the area of law, with statutes and regulations in connection with health, liturgy and the rights of others.

Chap.
6

Moses spoke forth strongly at this point and proclaimed with a loud voice:

"Hear, O Israel, the Lord is one God, and you shall love Him with all your heart, and with all your soul, and with all your might, and the words which I have spoken are to be kept in your heart, and you are to teach them diligently to your children, and talk of them around the house, and when you are sitting around in groups, or on journeys, and they are to be constantly on your mind, and you should write them on the doorposts and on the gates to your place.

"Be on the lookout for prosperity, for when the Lord has brought you into the land which He promised to Abraham, Isaac, and Jacob, you will be receiving cities you did not build, houses full of good things you did not provide, and wells you did not dig, vineyards and olive trees you did not plant; so when you are full and contented be careful that you do not forget the Lord, who is the provider of all things.

"And in time when a son asks one of you 'What means the testimonies, and the statutes, and the judgments which the Lord our God has commanded?"

"Then you are to tell him that you were slaves in Egypt, not free, and the Lord delivered you with a mighty hand, and showed many wonders before your eyes, and brought you into the possession of this new land.

"Tell your son that the Lord commanded you to do all the statutes, to fear God, as He is the preserver of life, and that it shall be a great satisfaction to observe all the commandments of the Lord our God."

Chap.
7

Moses spoke further to the people saying "Now let me explain to you our foreign policy. You are going to encounter some powerful nations, and the Lord will deliver them into your hand and you are

71

to smite them and completely destroy them. You are not to make any deals with them, no treaties, and show them no mercy.

"Furthermore, you are not to intermarry with them, for this way they may be able to lead you to strange gods; so just tear down their idols, burn the wooden images, and whack away at their altars, for you are supposed to be a holy people, set apart to serve the one true God."

"If you obey God, and hearken to His voice, He will bless you abundantly in every conceivable way."

Chap.
8

"Observe and do all the commandments of God, for remember the Lord led you forty years in the wilderness to humble you, to teach you, and to prove you, and He fed you ambrosia that you might know that man doth not live by bread alone, but by every word that proceedeth out of the mouth of God.

"Again, be especially careful when you are prosperous, and your herds have increased, and you have much silver and gold, for you will be inclined to say in your heart that your own power and might has secured the wealth for you, but at this point particularly remember the Lord thy God, for it is He that giveth the power to obtain wealth. Remember this or you will lose everything, including your nation."

Chap.
9

"Now the time has come to move and you will encounter the giants, the Watusi[1], a people great and tall, and you have heard it said 'Who can stand before the Watusi?'

"Do not be concerned, for the Lord thy God will go with you and with a consuming fire shall He destroy them. Be careful though that you do not develop a conceit because of this, for it is not for your goodness that the Lord does this, but because of the wickedness of the other people, and because of His promise to Abraham, Isaac, and Jacob.

"You are a stiff-necked, irksome people, and it is not for your righteousness that the Lord does this wonderful thing for you.

"I remember how wishy-washy you birds were, and how you made a molten image of a calf while I was on the mountain for forty days. In fact, the Lord was so angry about this that if it had not been for my intercession He would have destroyed all of you. I did this knowing that you have been a stiffnecked and rebellious outfit ever since I've known you.

Chap.
10

"I don't know why, but the Lord chose your fathers and you and your people, you are selected of God. Please quit being so

[1]Anaks

stiffnecked and scrape the barnacles off your hearts. The Lord your God is the God of gods, and Lord of lords, a great God, and mighty, and at times fearsome, one who plays no favorites in justice, nor is He subject to bribes. The Lord is just in caring for the fatherless and the widows, and He believes in aiding the stranger who is in need.

"Fear the Lord, serve him, and cleave to His name, do not stray!

Chap.
11

"Your children have not seen all the acts of power which the Lord performed, but you have seen them, therefore you keep God's commandments that you may be strong and possess the new land.

"The land where you are going is not like Egypt where you sow seed and have to nurse its growth yourself, but the new land is one of hills and valleys, and it drinks from the rain of heaven, and the eyes of the Lord are always upon this land.

"If you will listen to the admonitions of God and obey His commandments, God will give you rain for the land in due season, with a gap between rains so you can gather your corn and make your wine, and the cattle will have plenty of grass. Do not let this prosperity go to your head, and be careful not to wander off to strange gods. Lay these words up in your hearts.

"Actually, today I set before you a blessing and a curse, a blessing if you obey the commandments of God, and a curse if you don't."

Chap.
12

Moses repeats a previous part of his speech.

Chap.
13

"If there arise among you," continued Moses, "a prophet or a dreamer who gives a sign or performs a wonder, and then attempts to lead you to the worship of other gods, just be sure that the Lord is only testing your faithfulness. Kindly put that prophet to death!

Chap.
14

"Remember you are a holy people. Do not mark yourself or in any way deface yourself because of grief.

"Among other things, do not eat anything that you find dead, which has naturally died. The animal may be diseased and it is not healthy to try to eat it.

"Be absolutely certain that you care well for your preacher. Care well for the fatherless also, and the widow, and the stranger that is in need, and the Lord will bless you for it.

Chap.
15

"The seventh year is a year of release, of forgiving indebtedness and the restoring of property. Do not take advantage of this and plan

73

to gyp your neighbors by the strategic use of the seventh year, for the planning of this is a sin in the eyes of the Lord.

"When you give to the needy or return property during the year of release, do so gladly and with good heart.

"Keep the Passover. This is a great occasion for the remembrance of the power of God. At least three times a year every male must go to church, and must give as he is able.

"You are to establish Judges at the gates of the cities to run the cities justly. These judges or officers are not to accept favors, nor are they to show partiality to any person.

"When you finally come into the promised land and possess it, you will no doubt start bellowing for a king so you can be like other peoples. If this occurs, let the Lord choose the king from among you, and he must be no stranger.

"The king must be careful not to take advantage of the position to acquire for himself horses or other possessions, nor should he become rich through the office,[1] or take advantage of his position to chase women.

"The king should read this admonition regularly, as he should regularly read all these laws and statutes, that he may go straight and be a credit to his people and humble before God.

"The Lord has spoken to me and He said, "I will raise up a prophet someday from among these people, something like you. Moses, and I will put my words in his mouth, and he shall speak the things that I will command. It will go hard with anyone who refuses to listen to him when he comes.

"The false prophets, however, shall be in for great trouble. How can you tell the good prophets from the bad? It is easy. The prophets who are mine speak and the things come true, but not so always with the fakes and the guessers.

"Don't forget," Moses repeated, "to set aside three cities as refuges, or sanctuaries. For instance if a man is in the woods chopping wood with his neighbor and the axe head accidentally comes off and chops his neighbor's head, let the man flee to one of the refuge cities and remain there until everyone has calmed down and the matter is peaceably settled.

"If a man ambush another man, however, and actually murder him, and then seeks refuge in the sanctuary city, the law can go and

[1]Recommended reading for politicians

get him and bring him to trial.

"It is not acceptable for one witness to testify, but it must be an established testimony of two or three witnesses before a punishment may be applied. If a false witness is discovered he shall receive the punishment of the guilty party, thus evil may be put from among you.

"All people should then hear of the consequences, and fear, and put evil away from themselves.

"There is no place in this particular type of operation for pity, but life shall go for life, eye for eye, tooth for tooth, hand for hand, and foot for foot."

Chap.
20

"Let me remind you", continued Moses, "that when you go to do battle and you discover that your enemies have better equipment and that there are more of them than you thought, do not be afraid, for the Lord thy God will be with you. In fact, the priest will speak to you of these things before you go to battle and he will re-impress you with the availability of the power of God.

"There should be deferments for some of you, however, as everyone does not have to go to war. If you have built a new house and have not dedicated it, you are deferred, or if you have planted a vineyard for the first time and never eaten of its fruit, you should get a temporary occupational deferment, or if you are engaged to be married, you are deferred until you have been married for a short time.

"In fact, if you are fainthearted and have a tendency to be a coward, you should be deferred.

"After the army is assembled, however, and you have appeared before your enemies, the head of your army should at least offer conditions of peace. If the enemy refuses to make peace, declare war, and kill every male, and take the women and children for yourselves.

"Another thing, when you besiege a city and need wood for poles or pick handles, do not cut down fruit bearing trees as you will need the food before it is all done.

Chap.
21

"As a matter of balance and justice, if you find a man slain and lying dead in a field and there is no way of knowing who killed him, make the town that is nearest to the body present a sacrifice.

"If you capture a city and one of you manages to snag a beautiful woman and you develop a great desire to possess her, then bring her home, shave her head, cut her fingernails, and let her mourn the loss of her family until her hair is grown, then marry her. If, after all this, you decide that she did not measure up to her looks, simply turn her loose, but you can't sell her.

"Another matter of justice needs to be stated in connection

with a man who has two wives, and he loves one and hates[1] the other. The hate is not to be transferred to the children, but if the hated wife bears for the man his first son, that son shall receive a double portion of the inheritance.

"If a man have a stubborn and a rebellious son, and the paddle has been ineffective, as a last resort the man should turn the son over to the elders of the city and they should take him outside the walls of the city and stone him to death.[2]

"If a man be put to death justly by hanging, cut him down before night fall and bury him, don't let him clutter up the scenery.

"If you see a loose goat or sheep, get them and return them to their rightful owner and don't let them wander off, nor should you try to pretend that you didn't see them.

"Don't mix up the dressing of men and women, but let the men dress like men and the women like women.

"If you're in the woods and find a bird nesting, don't disturb the mamma bird. If you can't resist, you can take the young and raise them at home.

"When you build a house be careful to fix the roof so no one will fall from it and spill blood on your ground.

"When you plant seed, don't mix the seed and raise a conglomeration, and don't try to plow with an ox and an ass at the same time.

"Another matter of justice concerns the case of a man who takes a wife and then decides later that he doesn't want her. As an excuse, he claims that she was not a virgin. If this report is false, and the husband spreads it around town, the father and mother may appear before the elders of the city with the tokens of virginity, state their case, and if the elders believe them, then the husband is to be given a good beating, and fined $100, which will be given to the father, and the man must also retain the girl as his wife.

"If, however, the girl was lying and she was not a virgin, then she shall be stoned to death.[3]

"If a man be found having intercourse with another man's wife, then both shall be put to death.

"If a man visiting in the city locates a girl engaged to another man and he goes to bed with her and she doesn't protest, then if the two are caught, both are to be put to death. However, if a man forces himself on an engaged girl, and she cries out for help, then only the man is put to death.

"If a man find a girl that is a virgin and not engaged and he lies with her and is caught, then he is to pay the father a fine and is forced to marry the girl. A man is not permitted to be free with his

[1]This no doubt means "Cares less for"   [2]Delinquent Control Program
[3]Very Few Cases reported

stepmother nor his father's mistress.

"A man who has lost his testicles should not enter the tabernacle, nor should a bastard. It is permissible for such an Egyptian to enter the tabernacle, for you were strangers in the land of Egypt.

"If a man has to go to the bathroom at night, let him leave the camp taking with him his weapon with a shovel top on it, and when he has emptied his bowels, he is to dig a hole with the shovel head and bury his excretion. Keep the camp clean!

"You are not to charge your brother excessive interest rates, in money, food, or possessions. It is all right to use high interest rates on strangers.

"Your word must be good. If you speak in agreement on anything, it is binding. It is permissible to pick a few of your neighbor's grapes or an ear or two of his corn, but you cannot put the pickings in a container and carry them off, but you can eat some on the spot.

"If a man becomes dissatisfied with his wife, then he should write her a bill of divorcement and turn her loose, and she is then free to re-marry. If she re-marries, then under no circumstance can she ever return to her first husband.

"When a man takes a new wife he should take a year off, and he should not go to war or enter business, but spend the year getting acquainted with his wife and bringing her good cheer.

"The penalty for stealing should be death.

"If you loan a man something don't nag him for it, especially if he be a poor man.

"You are not to take advantage of any hired servants, yours or anybody else's.

"The fathers are not to be put to death because of the children nor children because of the father. A man is to be put to death only for his own sin.

"Remember that you were once slaves; so do not take advantage of the unfortunate.

"When you gather your grain or beat the olive trees for their fruit, be sure and leave some on the ground or in the field for the poor. You are also to leave some grapes in the vineyard.

"If two men appear before the judge because of a controversy, the judge shall rule at once and cause the man in the wrong to be beaten immediately, a licking not to exceed forty blows.

"If two brethren dwell together and one of them dies without having a child, the wife shall be another wife unto the remaining brother. If the new wife then have a son, the son shall be counted as the first born of the dead brother and shall receive his inheritance.

"If the remaining brother refuse to take the dead brother's wife, the elders of the city shall send for him and rebuke him and confer with him. If he still refuses after this, then the lady in question shall come and in the presence of the elders she shall loosen his shoe and spit in his face, and he then shall be called "Foot-loose" by his friends.

"If two men are fighting and the wife of one, in an attempt to help her husband, grabs his antagonist by the testicles, she shall have her hand cut off as punishment.

"You are not to possess equipment for fraud, such as wrong weights, unbalanced scales, and loaded dice.

"Once again, don't forget the Capone gang[1]. They are an abomination to the Lord.

Chap.
26

"When you come into the promised land and possess it, do not forget about the offering to the Lord. Bring the first fruits to the place designated to be a church.

"And when you bring these first fruits, present them to the Lord, and make mention to Him your gratitude for the deliverance from Egypt, and acknowledge His mighty acts.

"When you have fulfilled the giving of your tithes in the regular third year of tithing, then you may seek of the Lord a blessing. The Lord has assured you that you are a special group of people and to those that obey His commandments, He has promised to make of them a great nation, in praise, in name, and in honor, in order that you might become a holy people unto the Lord thy God."

Chap.
27

Moses, supported by the elders of the people, instructed the people to build an altar as soon as they had entered the promised land. In addition, tablets were to set in the ground, and all the commandments of God as explained by Moses were to be written in plaster and made permanent as a record and as a landmark.

The Levites, the priestly group, were then to pronounce the following curses:

Cursed be the man that maketh any graven image and puts it in a hiding place.

Cursed is the one who makes fun of his mother and his father.

Cursed is any man that moves his neighbor's boundary line, or misleads the blind, or misinforms the stranger, the fatherless, or the widow.

Cursed is the man who makes love to his stepmother, or tries to lie with a beast, or lieth with his sister or half-sister.

[1] Amaleks

Cursed be the one who has intercourse with his mother-in-law, or who ambushes his neighbor, or takes money to kill someone.

Cursed also is anyone who opposes these laws.

If, however, you shall obey all the laws of God and hearken to His voice, blessings in abundance shall come to you.

You shall be happy in the city and in the country, and you shall be blessed in your children, and in your planting, your store will prosper, and the Lord will smite your enemies.

The Lord shall also open to you his good treasure to give you rain, and you shall be a lender rather than a borrower, and you shall be the head and not the tail.

If you don't obey the commandments and do not hearken to the voice of the Lord, then the following curses will come your way:

You will be uncomfortable in the city, in the country, and in your store; your kids will be a constant source of trouble, and nothing that you try will work very well.

You will get the shingles, sometimes fever, and the Lord will withhold rain. Your enemies will overcome you and leave you to the buzzards. You are also apt to get hemorrhoids and the itch, some of you will go mad or blind. You will court a girl and another man will take her to bed, you'll build a house and never live in it, and plant fields and vineyards and never harvest the grain or pick the grapes. Your ox will drop dead in front of you and you will lose your ass.[1] Your sheep will be stolen and you won't recover them. Your sons and daughters shall be captured and you will be powerless to prevent it.

A strange nation shall devour your land and oppress you. You will have trouble with arthritis and your knees will hurt, and the king who you have selected will be defeated by another nation and you will be scattered. You will become a byword and people will make sport of your name.

All the good things promised will be reversed and you will get the little end of every stick. All because you fail to serve God and worship Him.

The Lord will bring a nation from afar off, one that operates like an eagle, a nation whose language you do not know. It will be a fierce nation, and it shall be merciless to old and young. This nation shall lay siege to your cities and you shall become depraved because of hunger. All these things will happen unless you obey the laws of this book and stand in awe of the glorious name, the Lord thy God.

If you are disobedient, you shall become few in number, you shall perish from sickness, and the Lord will scatter the remaining few throughout the nations of the world, and you will have no ease or real home among the nations.

[1]donkey or beast of burden

You will be so miserable that each morning you will say, "Would that it were already evening." Often you will be put up for sale and there will be no buyers.

Chap.
29

Moses called forth then even more vehemently. "You know of all the mighty acts of God, the signs, the wonders, the miracles, yet you seem unimpressed. I have led you forty years in the wilderness. You are well prepared, yet you stand this day before the Lord, you, your wives, your little ones, the hewers of wood and the drawers of water, and you are to enter into a covenant with the Lord thy God on this day.

"Do not for one minute think that you can deceive God. Lip service will not be sufficient. You cannot say one thing and do another.

"There are some unknown things, and they belong to God, but His revelation belongs to us and to our children, if we obey his law.

Chap.
30

After you have gone through the periods of blessing and cursing, and you remember all the things that I have told you, and you decide to return to the Lord and obey Him, then the Lord will deliver you from captivity, and have compassion on you, and bring you from all the nations whereto you have been scattered, even if there are some on the moon, God will fetch them, and bring you again to your native land, the land promised to you. The Lord will bless you in this.

"This commandment and this pronouncement which I make to you today is clear. It is not on Mars so that you might wonder about it, nor is it beyond the sun, but the word is clear and at hand and you can hear it.

"I have placed before you today life and good or death and evil.

"I commend you today to love God, to walk in His ways, to keep His commandments and His statutes and His judgments, and the Lord thy God will bless thee. If you turn away, however, and do not heed so that you wander off and worship strange gods, then I denounce you this day for you shall surely perish. I call heaven and earth as a witness this day, for I have set before you life and death, blessing and cursing. Therefore choose life, for the children's sake; decide that you will love the Lord thy God and that you will obey his voice, for He is your life and the controller of your days, and then you may dwell in the land that the Lord promised to Abraham, Isaac, and Jacob.

Chap.
31

Moses continued, saying, "I am an old man. I am no longer nimble and barely mobile, also the Lord has told me that I can't cross the Jordan, but the Lord will go with you, and he will not fail you."

Moses then summoned Joshua and spoke to him saying, "Be strong and of good courage for you must go with these people into the land promised by God, and you will help them take the land, and God will be with you, He will not fail you nor forsake you; so fear not, and never be discouraged."

And all this was written and handed to the priests for safekeeping.

The Lord then spoke to Moses and reminded him that the time was short and told him to appear with Joshua in the tabernacle to receive the Lord's blessing. Then Moses and Joshua presented themselves, and the Lord appeared before them in a cloud that hovered above the door of the tabernacle.

The Lord spoke to Moses and said, "Your time has come. You will pass away and the people will in time forget and wander into strange religions. They will forsake me and break my covenant, then I shall be angry with them, and I will leave them to their miseries. Write this now in a song, to be recorded, as a witness against them. This song shall testify against them when they have found a home in the land flowing with milk and honey, and when they have forgotten me." Moses that day wrote the song.

Moses then gave Joshua, the son of Nun, a charge and instructed him to lead the children of Israel.

When all of this was written in a book, Moses had the writing placed in the ark of the covenant, that it might be there as a witness.

"I know you," repeated Moses, "You are a stiff-necked and rebellious people and when I'm dead you are going to forsake God. You even did it with me around; so I know you'll do it after I've gone." Thus Moses spoke to all of them and told them again of the punishment of God in the latter days for those who disobey.

Chap.
32

Moses decided to speak again, pleading, and saying, "Listen everyone, everywhere, my teachings are coming down as the rain, my speech like the still dew. It is as soft water to the grass, because I proclaim the glory of God, to God I ascribe greatness. He is the Rock, His works are perfect, all His ways are full of understanding, a God of truth, just and right, while the people are a perverse and crooked generation.

"O you foolish people, is God not the father that saved you? Didn't he make you and put you here?

"Remember the olden days. Ask your fathers, ask the elders. From the very beginning you have been the Lord's portion of the people.

"Jacob is a good illustration. God found him in the desert, in a howling wasteland. God kept him and instructed him. As an eagle wing sweeps the nest, and flutters over its young, and spreads its wings so the young may ride on the broad wings; so the Lord did with Jacob, and there was no following of strange gods for Jacob.

"Jacob rode on the high places and was abundantly blessed, but some of you are just fat slobs, who have forsaken God.

"What a shame that you act as a nation without common sense. It would be wonderful if you were wise and understood. How could it be that two could chase ten thousand, except the Lord were handling the matter? The rock of our enemies is not like our Rock, their grapes, even, are grapes of gall.

The Lord shall judge His people. The Lord shall ask of the people, "Where are your gods now that you are in all this trouble? Why don't you get them to help you?"

"You should know that there is only one God. He kills and He makes alive. He will avenge himself of the enemies and He will have mercy on those who love Him and keep His commandments."

Moses spoke all these things also to the people, and it was a new day.

That day God told Moses to climb Mt. Nebo and look over the land of Canaan which would be given to the children of Israel. God told Moses that the climb would kill him and he would then be gathered to God's home among his people.

"You can see the land, Moses," God said, "but you can't enter it."

Moses then blessed the people before he departed. Moses blessed each of the tribes in turn and he added, "May the shoes of all of you be of brass and iron, and may you retain your strength as long as you live. There is only one God, who ruleth the heaven, and he is your refuge, and underneath are the everlasting arms. God shall thrust forth your enemies, and Israel shall be at peace. Happy you should be, O Israel, a people delivered by God, who is as a shield for all of you."

Chap.
34

Then Moses ascended Mt. Nebo to the top of Lookout Mountain,[1] in sight of Jericho. The Lord said to him, "Moses, there she is. As far as you can see. This is the land that I promised to Abraham, Isaac, and Jacob."

Then Moses died and was buried in land where he had ranched, but no one knows the place. Moses was still in possession of all his faculties when he died, and his eye was clear. The children of Israel mourned for Moses the full thirty days.

Then Joshua took Moses' place, for Moses had laid his hands on Joshua and blessed him, and taught him wisdom, and the people listened to Joshua.

There never was a prophet like Moses, one to whom God spoke mouth to mouth, and knew face to face. Through Moses the Lord performed tremendous signs and wonders and did mighty things through his servant Moses.

[1]Pisgah

82

JOSHUA

After the death of Moses the Lord spoke to his assistant minister, Joshua, and told him to get up and go, to cross the Jordan and to conquer the land promised by the Lord through Moses, and the Lord reminded Joshua that no enemy would be strong enough to prevent his success. The Lord said "As I was with Moses so shall I be with you. I will not fail you nor forsake you. You be strong and of good courage and observe the law as I explained it to Moses. The book of the law of God should never depart from you, speak from it, let it be your guide, and there will be no problem."

"Have at it, Josh, but tough and strong, for I am with you all the way!"

Joshua then had the word passed among the people that they had 3 days to pack.[1] To the tribes that had voted to remain in the wilderness, Joshua reminded them that all the able-bodied men were to remain in the Army until the promised land was secured, and then they could return to their chosen homes and cities. The men agreed to do as Joshua ordered, for they said they would adhere to Joshua as well as they had to Moses[2], and would execute anybody who rebelled.

Chap.
2

Joshua then selected two men to go to Jericho and spy for him and bring back a report. The spies entered Jericho and lodged in the only desegregated boarding house available, which was run by a lady named Sophie[3].

Word was passed to the Mayor of Jericho about the strangers, however, and he sent word to Sophie to bring the men to him for questioning as he suspected that they were spies.

Sophie, however, didn't care much for City Hall and so she hid the men and sent word to the Mayor that the men had been there and left and failed to leave a forwarding address. Sophie did report, however, that she had seen two similar looking men slipping out of the gate of the city only a few minutes before dark and she thought that the Mayor and the Vigilante Committee could catch them by heading north. This was a great opportunity for action so the whole posse went north in mad pursuit of two men.

Sophie, who had hidden the spies under some straw on the roof top, came to the two spies and said "I know you men are from the camp of those under the Lord God and I know that this collection of yellow-bellies here in Jericho are absolutely terrified. Everyone has heard of the Red Sea incident, and what happened to the Mafia, and

---

[1]Some housewives no doubt mentioned that it couldn't be done in 3 days.
[2]which fell short of 100%

[3]Rahab mentioned as harlot, but this also could simply mean an early Lib movement girl.

the Capone Gang, and the hearts of the people in this area are just plain melted. We know that the Lord your God is the real God, both in the heaven and on earth. Now promise me, under oath to your God, that in exchange for the kindness that I have shown you that you will return the favor and that when your army comes to capture Jericho that you will not destroy this my father's home, nor will you kill my father, my mother, my brothers, or my sisters."

"It's a deal, Sophie", said both the men together, and they shook on it.[1]

Sophie then let them over the wall by use of a rope and she said to them "Go south to the mountains so you won't run into the vigilantes that I sent north and hide for about 3 days, for that's about as long as a posse lasts in this county."

The men were highly appreciative and they suggested that in order that no mistake be made, Sophie tie a red ribbon in the window of her house and promised to deliver her people, but warned them not to go out the front door into the street when the fight started as they would very likely get clobbered, but that they should all escape down a rope from the same window even as the spies were escaping."

Everything then being arranged they left and Sophie tied a red ribbon to the window. Just as Sophie thought, on the third day the posse returned worn out and most of them went and got boozed up for their trouble.

The spies hid during this three day period as Sophie had suggested and then they returned to Joshua and reported.

"The Lord has already delivered those people into our hands," reported the top ranking of the two spies, "for the people there are already scared to death."

Chap.
3

Joshua got up early in the morning and ordered the people to assemble near the edge of the Jordan and here began the three days of preparation for the crossing[2] and the appointed leaders went all through the camps passing the word that when the ark of the covenant crossed over the Jordan, then to break camp and get going.

"Do not get too close to the ark of the covenant for the ark is to be your guide and you can watch. Furthermore, prepare yourselves for the trip, no wild parties or the like, but thought and prayer, for the Lord will begin the very first day working wonders through you," said the leaders.

Joshua then told the priests to pick up the ark of the covenant and begin the trip.

The Lord then spoke to Joshua and said "This day I will begin to increase your importance with your people that they may be

---

[1] or kissed her, depending on Sophie   [2] No doubt with a few more complaints

certain that I am with you as I was with Moses."

The Lord went on to say to Joshua that he should tell the bearers of the ark to stand still when they entered the Jordan. When this was done Joshua addressed the people again and said "Now you will know why you should enter the promised land without fear and you can be sure of your victories for the ark of the covenant of the Lord of all the earth shall proceed you."

Joshua then had each tribe select a man to be present as a witness, for he said the Lord will cause the waters that fill the Jordan to cease when the bearers of the ark enter the waters, and the tribes of Israel would cross the Jordan on dry ground. The sources of the waters of the Jordan dried up and the river bed was dry until the tribes of Israel had crossed the Jordan, and it was witnessed and the glory of God was there.

Then the Lord made a suggestion to Joshua that he require one man from each of the tribes of Israel to lift a stone from the Jordan and to place the twelve stones together in a pile on the bank of the Jordan river close to where the crossing occurred. This would serve as an historical marker and when the children down through the years would ask their fathers for the meaning of these stones then the fathers could tell them of how the flow from the sources of the Jordan was stopped in order that the ark of the covenant might pass over the Jordan and that these stones would serve as a memorial for this occasion.

The representatives of the tribes each did as he was commanded and Joshua saw to it that the stones were properly placed and they are there today.

After this was done, and all the people had crossed the Jordan, and the ark of the covenant was safely secured across the Jordan, then Joshua prepared an army of 40,000 select men who were to march onto the plains of Jericho and besiege the city. At this very time, the Lord magnified Joshua in the eyes of all the people so that they respected him as they had respected Moses.

When the priests carrying the ark of the covenant had come forth from the trickling waters and secured the ark on dry land, then the Lord released the waters again from the sources of the Jordan and the river returned to its natural flow.

Joshua then made a brief speech[1] to the children of Israel and spoke to them saying "As the Lord your God did to the Red Sea as you entered the wilderness so did he to the Jordan River as you left the wilderness in order that all the people of the earth might know the power of the Lord, and that He is mighty, and that you must stand in awe of the Lord thy God forever."

[1]He was never as long-winded as Moses

When news of the drying up deal of the Jordan had spread through the various towns and cities in Canaan[1], then all of these people became faint hearted and feared greatly these same people who some few years earlier had seemed to be as grasshoppers in their eyes.

During the wilderness wanderings and the constant mobility of the whole nation, none of the children born in the wilderness had been circumcised. As a result, Joshua ordered every male to be circumcised and this was a painful and time consuming operation, and Joshua ordered the people to remain in camp until everyone had healed and some of the gripping had died down.

The children of Israel then observed the feast of the passover and on the next day there was no manna, nor did the children of Israel ever have to eat manna again, for they began to eat of the fruit of the land of Canaan.

Now Joshua decided to go and have a look himself at the city of Jericho to plan his attack and as he came in full view he was confronted by a man with a sword in his hand, as if he were ready to do battle. Joshua spoke to the man and asked if he was for Israel or against Israel.

"I am the captain of the host of the Lord" said the man, and Joshua bowed his head to the ground, and asked what he should do.

"Loose your shoes and take them off your feet, for you are on holy ground," replied the man. Joshua did as he was told.

The city of Jericho had been put under martial law and there was no coming and going through the gates of the city and commerce was at a standstill.

The Lord said then to Joshua "See, the people of Jericho, even the warriors already know that they've had it. They are terrified. Use some psychological warfare on them and get all your men of valor and march around the city for six days, parading, and taunting them. Let the priests with the ark of the covenant lead the parade, and let them sound forth their trumpets, and let it be a joyful, triumphant type of march, then on the seventh day march around the city seven times and at the end of the seventh time around the city on the seventh day let the priests give a mighty blast with rams' horns and then instruct the people to shout with a great triumphant shout, and storm the walls of Jericho, for the walls will be flattened before them."

Everything was carried out exactly as the Lord said, and Joshua only reminded the people of Israel to preserve the house of Sophie and the family of hers that were there, and also to bring all the loot

[1]no doubt with added touches.

to the synagogue.

Joshua explained that this was the Lord's victory and that all silver, brass, gold, and precious things were to be brought to the Lord's house.

So when the people shouted at the final blast of the rams' horns, the mighty warriors of Israel, 40,000 strong charged the walls, and they were flattened before them and they took the city, and destroyed everything in the city, men and women, cattle and cats, and Joshua sent the two spies to protect Sophie and her household and they delivered her safely with her family.

Finally the warriors set fire to the city and burned it to the ground, but gold and silver and valuables were brought to the treasury of the church. Joshua then turned upon the smoking city and pronounced a curse on any man that should attempt to rebuild it.[1]

And the Lord was with Joshua and his fame was spread throughout the land.

Chap.
7

As might be expected, there was one fellow named Fingers Lasky[2] who took some of the silver and jewelry from Jericho and hid it in his tent. No one knew of this, but the Lord, and the Lord was angry because of this.

The next city to be captured was the city of Abilene[3] and Joshua sent a few of his officers to survey the city and report back on the prospects.

The committee returned and told Joshua that Abilene was a small place with only a few warriors around and that it was not necessary to worry with sending the whole army against the city but that 2 or 3 thousand men could handle the capture easily.

As a result, Joshua sent 3 thousand men to attack Abilene and the warriors of Abilene poured forth and began to beat the stew out of the portion of the army that Joshua had dispensed. By the time about 36 men had fallen under the Abilene blows the remainder panicked in fear and became track men, and ran wildly to the safety of the camp.

Joshua was horrified, and immediately fell on his face before the ark of the covenant and prayed to the Lord saying "Why did you let me bring this pack of yellow bellies over the Jordan? I wish we had never crossed the Jordan. I cannot stand to see my army unwilling to stand up and fight. What is more, everyone in the country will hear of this, and they shall no longer fear us and will even lose respect for thy great and holy name."

[1]The archeologist are still not exactly positive about the exact place, though I was shown what might have been when I visited the Holy Land.

[2]Achan   [3]Ai

87

Then the Lord spoke to Joshua and said, "Get up and get with it. Quit your own moaning and groaning. The failure is due to sin, for you have among you one who has stolen from the treasury of the church and has hidden it. Naturally, the children of Israel cannot stand up and fight unless the spirit of the Lord is with them, and I have withheld it because of this sin. Find the offender and punish him."

Immediately Joshua ordered a tent and locker search, tribe by tribe, and the searchers were given a tip that Fingers Lasky had the loot from Jericho, which belonged to the synagogue.

Joshua sent for Fingers and said to him, "Confess."

"I have sinned against God," said Fingers. Then Fingers began to give a big explanation about his need for money, his sick children, his chariot needing repairs, and the high cost of living. Fingers then told Joshua that all the money, jewelry, and garments were hidden in his tent.

Joshua sent men to check his story and they returned with the loot. Then Joshua called an assemblage of representatives from all the tribes and had Fingers and his sons, and all his possessions, and the loot all placed on public view and Joshua said, "Why did you all do this to us? Now the Lord will trouble you for the trouble you have caused."

Then Joshua ordered the people from all the tribes to stone the Lasky family to death and to pile a heap of stones upon the bodies and to make the stones a historical marker and to let the place be known as "Death Valley Days."[1]

Chap. 8

The Lord then encouraged Joshua to again do battle against Abilene, for now that the sin against God was punished, the Lord would be with the army of Israel.

It also occurred to Joshua that Abilene might have been poorly judged by his scouts and he was not going to take the second attempt lightly.

As a result Joshua selected 30,000 of his best men and instructed them to hide themselves during the night behind the walls of Abilene on the opposite side of the city. Joshua explained to them that the remaining group under his command would approach the city from the front and entice the warriors of Abilene out as had been done before. Joshua then said that after a brief encounter this section of the army would again flee and the soldiers then of Abilene sensing a great victory would pour forth from the city to capture the entire fleeing army. When this occurred Joshua told the leaders of the 30,000 crack troops to go into the open gates of the city and to capture it and burn it to the ground, doing to it as was done to Jericho.

[1] The valley of Achor

88

The plan worked even better than Joshua thought it would, for when the people of Abilene saw Joshua retreating with his army they ran out of the city, every able-bodied man left and there was no one to defend the city when the main army suddenly came from behind the city and entered the open gates. All this was done by pre-arranged signal from Joshua.

When the army of Abilene looked back and saw that the city was lost they were demoralized, and the small portion of the army left with Joshua turned again upon the enemy and smote them right and left. The Mayor of Abilene was taken alive.

There were killed that day about 12,000, some of them women who didn't want to be left out of the action.

The Mayor of Abilene was given special attention as a warning to other mayors and he was hanged by the neck from a tree and his body placed at the entrance to Abilene. Another historical marker was placed there.

Following this victory Joshua built an altar to the Lord, and the stones were placed in proper array, and the commandments of Moses were inscribed on the stones, and the priests and the rulers of the tribes, and the people worshipped God. During the service, Joshua read to the people all the words of the law, the blessings and the cursings, and there was not a word recorded in the law which Joshua did not read.[1]

The word of this second victory created great alarm among all the other mayors and governors of the various places in Canaan and they decided to have a summit meeting and combine their strength to war against Israel.

There was one place called Brooklyn[2], which decided that there might be a slicker way of doing things than war against a highly successful army. As a result they selected a few of their men skilled at deception and dressed them in garments from a faraway place, put old, worn-out saddles on their donkeys, antique wine bottles[3], put worn-out shoes on them, and equipped them with mouldy bread and provisions. These bedraggled looking Brooklyn Dodgers came into the camp of Israel saying they had come from a faraway land and would like to arrange an agreement of peace.

The chief of the C.I.A. of Israel immediately said, "How do we know that you are from a far country. You might be from close at hand and next on our list of places to capture?"

Joshua then spoke and said to them, "Who are you? Tell us from where you came?"

The ambassadors then said, "We come from a far away country of which you have never heard. We consider ourselves your servants, for we have heard of the name of the Lord thy God, the fame of

[1]The service definitely lasted well beyond 12 o'clock   [2]Gideon
[3]Sorry, ladies, but we don't know where they are now.

89

Him, and what happened to the Egyptians, and all that He did to your enemies on either side of the Jordan. When the rulers of our country heard all these things, they gave us beasts of burden and provisions to seek peace with you."

The ambassadors made a point of showing their old bottles and worn saddles, and mouldy provisions.[1]

Joshua then made peace with them, and agreed to spare their lives and the lives of the people they represented.

About three days later one of the C.I.A. boys decided the ambassadors were phony[2] and reported the matter to Joshua. An immediate investigation revealed that the ambassadors had only come from 12 miles away and represented the next group on Joshua's kill and burn schedule.

Joshua and the rulers of Israel, however, had sworn to a treaty of peace, and even though it was because of deceit, Joshua and the rulers would not violate their word. .

In spite of the murmuring of the people and the political pressure, Joshua ordered that the Brooklyn people were to be spared.

Joshua said, "We will let them live, but since they came to us declaring that they were our servants; so shall they be. They shall then be our servants, and they shall be hewers of wood and drawers of water."

Joshua called the ambassadors into conference and asked them why they had tried to deceive him.

"The answer is simple, General Joshua," replied the ambassadors, "for we know that the Lord had promised the land to Moses and we know that you are a "kill 'em all" type of general, and we were afraid for our lives. We are now in your hands and we must submit, but at least we will all live."

Joshua immediately began to assign them to the cutting of wood and drawing of water, and even made them build for Israel a church.

Chap.
10

Now Alex[3], who was mayor of Jerusalem, heard about all these happenings and he was particularly concerned about the treaty with Brooklyn for there were mighty men there and it was a great ctiy. As a result Alex called a meeting of nearby mayors, Sarge from Baltimore[4], Ollie, from Pittsburg[5] Lindsee from Albany[6], and George from Montgomery[7], and entreated them to all join forces and attack Brooklyn. Alex felt that the whole crowd could easily defeat Brooklyn with a portion of its people off working for the children of Israel and not permitted anyway to retain an army.

[1]This would have never fooled Nero Wolfe   [2]Too Late
[3]Adonizedec   [4]Hoham of Hebron   [5]Piram of Jarmuth
[6]Japhia of Lachish   [7]Debir of Eglon

As a result, the mayors all got their armies together and went and encamped around Brooklyn.

Some of the men from Brooklyn then slipped out at night and went two days journey to the camp of Joshua and told him what was happening. The men pleaded with Joshua for instant help.

As a result Joshua immediately gathered all his mighty men of war. The Lord encouraged Joshua in this and told him not to fear the combination of mayors and the cities as the Lord would help deliver them into his hands.

Joshua, always a careful strategist, moved his army silently in the night and suddenly came down upon the gathering of the men surrounding Brooklyn and slew them with a great slaughter. Shortly after the assembled armies began to flee the Lord sent a tremendous hailstorm that struck the warriors down as they fled, and more were killed by the hailstones and the landslides than were killed by the men of Israel.

Then Joshua[1] called upon the Lord to let the sun stand still so his army could keep killing the enemy a few more hours, and the Lord held up the sun for forty minutes[2]. This had never been done before nor would it ever happen again.

The five mayors of the cities involved had not counted on having any trouble, but as soon as the battle started the five of them hid in a cave. A private, bucking for corporal, had spotted them, however, and relayed the information to Joshua. Joshua ordered that the cave be closed with stones until the battle was over and then he would treat mayors as part of the victory celebration.

In a couple of days the remnants of the defeated armies had sought refuge in one of the sanctuary cities and the children of Israel all returned to base after a great victory.

Joshua then ordered the opening of the cave and brought the mayors out before the assemblage of a large crowd.

Joshua then ordered five of the top ranking men of his army to each put a foot on the neck of a mayor. Joshua then said to the heads of his army, "Never be afraid, for the Lord will do to all our enemies as you are doing to the mayors."

As soon as this message had soaked in, Joshua said, "Kill them, and hang their bodies on a tree until dark, then throw the bodies in the cave where they hid, and close the cave." This is exactly what was done.[3]

Then Joshua set forth with his army and began to knock off systematically a number of smaller places, such as Ripley[4], Savannah[5], and Jersey City[6]. Then a rather brash mayor of Chicago[7], named Monthly[8], came with his crowd to fight Joshua and

[1]He didn't think much of enemies
[2]There is some evidence that the earth's rotation slowed or stopped at one time.
[3]This may have dampened some election enthusiam in Jerusalem that year
[4]Makkedah [5]Libnah [6]Lachish
[7]Gezer [8]Horam

the children of Israel and Joshua cleaned out his whole army.

Joshua felt that his army had impetus and he immediately moved quickly to knock off Lexington[1], Rochester[2], and even Muleshoe, Texas[3].

Joshua continued his policy of killing everyone that opposed him as he apparently did not have facilities for a POW camp.

Joshua continued to smite and conquer each village and hamlet until he had subdued the whole surrounding area, and then he returned to base camp.

Chap.
11

Word of all this began to spread everywhere and mayors from everywhere became alarmed and finally organized what might be called a grand alliance and brought another army to do battle with the children of Israel, and Joshua brought his highly organized troops against them and the Lord delivered these also to Joshua and there was great slaughter. Joshua then went forth and destroyed by burning all the cities represented against him, but those towns and cities that had not joined the alliance Joshua left standing. The warriors of Israel were now allowed to keep the things captured for themselves and this was a morale booster.

Joshua conquered all the land and the hills of the south country and in every direction, and war took a long time and Joshua was relentless in his conquest as he had been commanded to do by Moses.

Brooklyn was the only place that made peace with Joshua and it alone was spared.

Finally all the kings and mayors were dead and all the cities conquered and Joshua took the whole land according to all that the Lord had said to Moses and he gave all the land as an inheritance to Israel and divided it among the tribes, and the land rested from war.

Chap.
12

A list of the cities, towns, mayors, and kings which were recorded as conquered.

Chap.
13

Now Joshua was getting old and there were still left many areas that were originally promised by the Lord to the children of Israel. The Lord suggested to Joshua that he assign remote areas to the different tribes and to let each tribe as it developed its own army to move and possess new territory until all the land of Canaan was possessed by the children of Israel. This was done, and the property decisions were decided by casting dice and the children of Israel went forth into the land by tribes and increased their possessions and overcame all that opposed them.

The tribe of Levi was not given an inheritance, for these were

[1]Eglon [2]Hebron [3]Debir

the priests of God, and it was the responsibility of all tribes to see that the priests of God were provided for properly in every way.

Chap.
14

During all these many decisions and discussions of land there came to Joshua his old companion who had joined him in the favorable scouting report to Moses, good, faithful Caleb.

"Joshua, in spite of my years, I am still strong and a sturdy fighter, I feel no loss of strength from the time I was young, and you remember I am sure that Moses promised me all the great land and streams, and mountains in Colorado[1]. No doubt, Joshua, you remember how everyone was afraid of this area, but if you will deed me this area and if the Lord be with us, I will take the territory." It was done.

Chap.
15

A description of the cities and areas assigned and conquered by the tribe of Judah.

Chap.
16,17,18,19

The dice were continued to roll in selection of land for the various tribes, which are named in these chapters.

Chap.
20

The Lord then spoke to Joshua and reminded him to set aside the cities of refuge so that a slayer who was simply guilty of manslaughter, or self defense might have a safe place to dwell until things cooled down and justice could be done. "The wanted man is to have refuge until the judge who would have tried his case is dead, and then he may return to his house a free man," said the law.

Chap.
21

Then Joshua ordered each tribe to assign a portion of their possessions to the tribe of Levi, who were priests of the Lord.

Chap.
22

Then Joshua called to him the leaders of the tribes of Reuben and Troop and praised them for staying with their agreement to fight with Joshua until all the land was conquered and told them that they now could take their possessions and their booty and return to their families and their cities that they had left on the other side of the Jordan.

Joshua then reminded them saying, "Take diligent heed to hold to the commandments of God, to love the Lord your God and to serve Him with all your heart and all your soul." Then Joshua blessed them and sent them away.

[1]Land of the Anakims

When the tribes reached the Jordan River and were prepared to cross it, they built there a huge historical marker. Word of this returned to the other tribes and they rose in great indignation, saying one historical marker is enough and we put one there first and now they have built a bigger one and it is sacrilegious.

As a result of this the tribes gathered together a mighty army and went near to the spot of the placing of the big, new historical marker and accused the tribes responsible of turning against God.

A spokesman from the tribe of Reuben said to the leaders of the other tribes, "You are wrong in what you say, this marker is an altar to God. For the previous one is one that you can show to your children and say to them 'see this is the sign of our obedience to God', but what can we say to our children? Our children will not believe we obeyed God, and so this marker is placed here so that we can tell our children that we did as the Lord commanded, we fought with you all at our sides as we agreed, and this marker shows that we crossed and returned, it is to teach our children to obey God."

The speech pleased the leaders of the tribes very much and they shook hands and had a big party instead of a fight.

Chap.
23

There followed then a long period of rest in Israel from all their enemies and Joshua became old and near the time of death. As a result Joshua called for a convention of all the leaders, elders, judges, and officers of all the tribes of Israel and he made a speech to them saying "I have had it. My days are numbered. You have seen all that the Lord has done to your enemies, for it is the Lord your God who has fought for you.

I have divided unto each of your tribes an inheritance of land according to the casting of lots and the Lord will see that you are able to complete the possession of all that has been assigned to you.

Keep your courage. Observe all things that are written in the book of Moses, do not waiver to one side or the other. Be exceedingly careful in the mingling with people of other nations that you do not even mention the names of their strange gods or participate in any of their observances, but cleave unto the Lord your God.

No man has been able to stand before you because of the strength of the Lord and for this reason one man of you is better than a thousand of the enemies of God.

Take heed therefore that you love the Lord. If you begin to get careless, and go astray with some of the women of these nations, or marry them, the Lord will not support you, and these minglings will be snares and traps for you and you will eventually lose this land.

I am about to go the way of all that dwell on the earth and I testify that not one thing has failed within the promises of the Lord, the great keeper of the promises. Even so as all good things have come to you because of your obedience so shall all things turn against you if you transgress the covenant of the Lord your God. If you serve other gods and bow yourselves to them and let other matters become more important to you than the Lord your God, then shall the anger of the Lord be stirred against you and you will lose this land."

Following lunch, Joshua called the convention to order again and he said, "I have a message from the Lord God of Israel. The Lord has reminded me to tell you that your ancestors go all the way back to the father of Abraham, and God took Abraham into the land of Canaan and gave him Isaac, and Jacob and Esau as grandsons, and gave them lands. God sent Moses and Aaron to deliver the children of Israel after they had been enslaved in Egypt, and God brought your fathers out of Egypt, and destroyed the army of Pharaoh at the Red Sea, and brought your fathers through the wilderness, and brought you across the Jordan and delivered into your hands the men of Jericho and Abilene, and Chicago, and Ripley, and Savannah, and many others. The Lord, has given you a land for which you did not labor, and cities which you did not build, but in which you now live, and vineyards and olive orchards from which you do now eat."

"Now, therefore," continued Joshua, "stand in awe of God, serve him in sincerity and truth, put away from you any thought of the strange gods that some of your ancestors served in Egypt and other places, and serve the Lord.

But, of course, you can choose, you can choose this day whom you will serve, whether you serve strange gods of some of your ancestors, or the gods of the gypsies, but as for me and my house, we will serve the Lord."

The people answered and said, "We will not forsake the Lord, for we know that it was the Lord our God that delivered us, that saved our fathers from the bondage in Egypt, and who has preserved us unto this day. We will serve the Lord, for He is our God."

"Do you really mean this?" asked Joshua. "For the Lord is a jealous God and he does not take these things lightly."

The people again shouted, "We will serve the Lord."

Joshua then said to them, "You are witnesses yourselves that you have chosen the Lord, to serve him."

"We are witnesses", cried the people.

As a result, Joshua had minutes of the meeting recorded, and wrote all these words in the book of the law of the Lord, and marked the place of the testimony with a historical marker under an oak tree, and Joshua reminded the people that the marker was a reminder of their covenant, and then he dismissed the convention.

Not many days later Joshua died and they buried him near Mount Vernon [1].

[1] Timnathserah

After the death of Joshua the children of Israel prayed to the Lord for guidance, for there was no leader to unite all the tribes. The Lord instructed the tribes to each pursue and conquer the enemies within their own areas, the portions which had been assigned to them by lot.

Judah was the first tribe to make its move and the leaders of this tribe asked the tribe of Simeon to join them on a reciprocal agreement, that Judah would then join Simeon in helping with their territory. The plan worked and both tribes completed the conquest of their territories.

Caleb was having some trouble in his area with the Scarlotti[1] gang and he offered as a reward his beautiful daughter Raquel[2] to any man who would lead a successful raid against this mob. The sheriff of Cade County[3] decided to try it, and he succeeded.

Raquel flashed a bit of her charm on her father, and suggested that since the sheriff was poor but honest that it would help matters considerably if Caleb would give her a couple of sections of land that had running water. Caleb consented and all worked well in this matter[4].

Not all of the tribes, however, carried out the injunctions of the Lord. The tribe of Benjamin allowed the Rotarians[5] to remain in Jerusalem, and they are there to this day.

Some of the other tribes, for one reason or another, did not bother to pursue their enemies and they allowed them to remain in their land. The general feeling was that Israel had become so strong that there was no point in further pursuit of frightened people. The enemies of Israel simply interpreted this as weakness, and began to think in terms of rebuilding their own strength.

A man full of the Spirit of the Lord, speaking for the Lord, came to the children of Israel after they had enjoyed many years of prosperity. Joshua was long since dead, and the elders and rulers that Joshua had trained were dead, and new generations had grown up, and they were enjoying themselves too fully to be concerned with the word of the Lord.

The man from God then spoke to them and reminded them of

[1]Kirjathsepher   [2]Achsah   [3]Othniel
[4]Particularly for the Sheriff   [5]Jebusites

the covenant of old and warned them about their iniquities, for they were making free with women and worshipping Baal, and following the strange gods of selfishness and greed.

The anger of the Lord was stirred against them and the enemies of Israel began to entrap them and create multiple difficulties for them.

The Lord, however, remained the great Keeper of the Promises and so he began to raise up righteous men, judges in Israel, that were representatives of God's help and his love, and these judges began to deliver the people.

The trouble was that when one of the great judges died, the people would gradually return to evil ways and their enemies would again oppress them. Somewhat in disgust the Lord then decided to let Israel fend for itself for awhile, and He did not drive out their enemies or discomfort them as He had in times past.

Chap.
3

The children of Israel began to degenerate rapidly and they began to intermarry with the enemies of God and they began to violate all the commandments of God, and they became a decadent and deteriorating nation.

As always, there were those few who faithfully worshipped God and began a reform movement and they prayed earnestly to God to help deliver them from their enemies. As a result, the Lord let his spirit enter into the heart of the sheriff of Cade County and he went to war in the name of the Lord, and led the people of Israel to great victories, and delivered them from their enemies, and restored the worship of God. As a result, there was forty years of peace and prosperity in Israel.

Then the sheriff of Cade County died. It wasn't long before sin began again to take its toll and the people wandered from sanctuary habits, and worshipped strange gods, and pursued selfish enterprises. As a result, God stirred up the evil king of New Orleans[1] who gathered together some support from neighboring cities and towns and they swept down upon Israel and conquered their strongholds and subdued the people.

The Israelites had been under this satellite arrangement for 18 years when one of their number, Mac the Knife[2], decided that he would try to do something about the problem. First, he made for himself a special dagger with two edges, and a long thin blade, and he concealed it carefully by sticking it to his thigh with scotch tape.

Now the king of New Orleans was an exceedingly fat man and

[1]Eglon   [2]Ehud

98

enjoyed flattery and recognition. Mac the Knife was admitted into his presence on the basis of bringing the king a very fine present, and the bearers of the beautiful gift[1] made the presentation and then excused themselves. Mac the Knife told the king that he also had a bit of secret information[2] and asked the king to dismiss his guards so that he might whisper his secret without fear of anyone hearing. The king then ordered the guard to leave him and he remained alone on the summer patio with Mac.

"Great king, I have a message from God for you," said Mac the Knife, whereupon he took his left hand and drew the dagger from his right side and thrust it all the way into the king's stomach, so much so that the fat of the king came over the handle of the dagger and hid it.

Mac the Knife then left the enclosed patio, closed the doors and locked them. When the servants of the king came a few minutes later and found the doors locked they assumed the king was taking his afternoon snooze and did not wish to be disturbed.

Finally, some two hours later, the servants became alarmed and broke down the doors and found the king dead. In the meantime Mac the Knife was long gone.

A couple of days later, Mac sounded the trumpet on a faraway hill to assemble the remaining faithful people of God, and he told them the king was dead and that New Orleans was in great turmoil and that they could win a victory if they attacked immediately. The people responded and descended on New Orleans and its surrounding area with great force and subdued it, killing some ten thousand people in the process. Following this there was sixty years of peace.[3]

Chap.
4

The memory and influence of Mac faded and the children of Israel again did evil in the sight of the Lord and returned to their old tricks of strange gods and foreign women, greed and neglect of the obligations to the church.

There was a strong leader among the people of the hill country named Jesse James[4] and he had accumulated a collection of chariots of iron and the people of Israel stood in great fear of him and were strictly under his thumb.

The children of Israel then began to cry again in their prayers to God and to promise to reform, and the Lord raised up for them a female leader named Carrie[5], which was a big switch in policy[6].

[1]possibly a hand carved couch
[3]Wouldn't it be nice if our nation under God-fearing leaders would commit ourselves to Him?
[2]intimated it was a stock tip
[4]Sisera   [5]Deborah
[6]You've come a long way babies

Carrie sent word to the so-called leader of the army of Israel, a man named General Maybe [1] and told him to bring his army of 10,000 men and she would sic them on Jesse James and that the Lord would deliver Jesse with all his iron trains into the hands of Maybe.

General Maybe then sent a note to Carrie saying that he would do this if she would go with him and hold his hand [2]. Carrie said she would at least walk along with him, but that because of his sissy tendency the honor of killing Jesse James would be given to a woman [3].

Carrie set a trap or some inducement of loot down near the Pecos River [4] bottom and Jesse James and his iron chariots fell for the bait. When the iron chariots were in the river bottom Carrie sent General Maybe and his army down from the hill and they thoroughly defeated the James gang.

Jesse fled and sought refuge in the nearest friendly area he could find. As Jesse was running a lady named Mae East [5] called to him and invited him to come and hide in her tent, as her husband was not at home.

Jesse was pooped out from running and laid down in the tent and Mae covered him with a blanket. Jesse was also thirsty and asked for water, but she gave him milk as she said milk would help him more.

Jesse then said, "Mae, honey, please stand in the door of the tent and if any man comes and asks if there is a man hiding in your tent tell him there isn't."

"Okay, Babie", said Mae. However, as soon as Jesse was fast asleep, Mae slipped quietly up beside him and took a huge hammer and a railroad spike and nailed Jesse's head to the ground.

When General Maybe came puffing along a little while later and asked if anyone had seen Jesse James, Mae stepped forth and said, "Sure. I like to deal with winners only; so I have Jesse nailed to the ground in my tent [6]".

Chap.
5

Following this mighty victory, Carrie called for a celebration and she made up a ballad to sing for the people and she sang a mighty song to them, she composed it herself, and it was long, but she sang and they listened [7].

[1] Barak
[2] Not much of a general
[3] This meant no medal, which hurts a general very much
[4] Kishon [5] Jael [6] Mae got the medal
[7] This will help prepare us for a woman president

"Praise the Lord", she sang, "His truth is marching on, the people responded to His call, praise the Lord, all of you. The Lord is wonderful indeed, for the Lord shakes the earth, and He causes rain, and great landslides, and then there was the great depression, the villages were empty, travelers walked only on the byways for fear of Jesse James, and then I came along, a great Mother of Israel. I came at a time when there was no army and no enthusiasm, but I bestirred the men, and no longer do the drawers of water at the wells have to worry about the gunslingers of the James gang. How can I help but sing? Didn't I gather together the leaders of Israel and didn't we do a great job?

What a beautiful sight to see the James gang floating facedown in the Pecos River. Curses be on all those of Israel who did not get in the action.

Blessed above all women is the great Mae East. Jesse James asked for water and she gave him milk, she even slipped him some bread with butter on it, and then when he went to sleep she nailed him to the floor. Like wow! she just put her left hand to the nail and the right hand to the hammer, and that ended him. Talk about dead, he was as dead as they come.

Meanwhile back at the gang's ranch in the hills, the mother of Jesse kept wondering why he had not returned.

'What is holding him up?' moaned Jesse's mother. 'What's wrong with his train?'

What happened? The James gang is gone, it is defeated. It is as nailed down as Jesse.

So let all the enemies of the Lord perish, but let those that love the Lord be as the sun when it goes forth on its mighty journey."

The song ended, and Israel had peace for forty years.

Chap.
6

Then comes again the same old story, selfishness, greed, and the strange gods of material things being worshipped instead of God. As always, this meant trouble, this time in the form of the Dalton gang, who dwelt in Midland.

It took the Dalton gang seven years to take over the children of Israel, but they finally subdued them and made of them an impoverished satellite nation.

Then the people cried again to the Lord. Then the Lord sent a prophet unto the people to speak to them and to remind them that God had delivered them from Egypt, and cleaned out the land of Canaan for them, but that the people had disobeyed God and followed after the gods of Wall Street[1].

[1] Amorites

101

The people repented and prayed again for deliverance.

An angel of the Lord appeared unto a man named Gideon and said to him, "You are a man of great courage."

"Who, me?" asked Gideon in surprise.

"Yes," said the angel, "and the Lord wants you to lead the children of Israel against the Dalton Gang."

"Well, if the Lord is so much for us, why are we in this mess in the first place?" [1]

"Gideon," said the Lord, "All you need to know is that I am with you."

"But, Lord," argued Gideon, "how in the devil can I save Israel? I am a nobody. In fact, my whole family is a poor family, and I am the poorest one in the crowd."

"I will be with you", replied the Lord.

"This is a new thing for me, Lord, and just so I won't think I'm imagining things, show me evidence of your support."

"All right," replied the angel of the Lord. "Bring an uncooked TV dinner and place it on the rock before me."

Gideon did this, and the angel of the Lord stretched forth his staff and fire came out and cooked the TV dinner as if by laser beam.

Gideon was astounded and began to think that because he had seen an angel of the Lord he would be cooked also, but the angel told him to calm down. Gideon then gathered together a few stones and built there an altar to God and worshipped.

That night, Gideon being inspired by God [2] went to town in the middle of the night and took two of his father's oxen and used the oxen to pull down the statue of Baal and the trees around it, right in front of the Dalton Gang's headquarters [3]. Gideon had ten men helping him cut down the trees.

Two bums sitting in front of the country store saw it all and told the Daltons who had done the mischief.

The head of the Dalton Gang was a pretty bright man [4] and he reasoned that there had been no loss of money and no one had touched any of his gang. In fact, he said, "Gideon attacked Baal. If Baal is a real god, let him get up and do something about it. What's the point in worshipping a god who can be defeated by ten men and two oxen." [5]

Gideon then began to send messages out among the tribes announcing the possibility of a revolution, and the unfriendly gangs who supported the Daltons began to gather together and plot,

[1] Some questions just don't get answered
[2] And probably a little bit impressed with himself
[3] The Daltons being at the saloon at this time of night.
[4] Had finished Jr. College
[5] So they went back to the saloon

including a big bunch from Odessa[1].

Gideon began to get a little nervous about this time, as it occurred to him that tearing down a statue and attacking a mighty army were two different things.

As a result, Gideon prayed to the Lord saying, "I will put a rug in front of my door tonight, and if in the morning the rug is wet with dew but the ground all around is dry, I will know you are still with me and I'll get with the army deal."

In the morning Gideon arose and was able to wring a bowl of water from the rug, but the ground around was dry, and Gideon was excited.

That night, however, Gideon prayed again and said, "Lord, don't get mad at me, but I had a science teacher that told me about fleece rugs drawing the moisture out of the air and just so there will be no misunderstanding between us, tonight let the rug remain dry and the ground around it wet.'

And the patient God of all did as Gideon requested, and in the morning the ground was wet, but the fleece was dry.

Chap. 7

The whole personality of Gideon now changed. No longer did he feel himself the poorest of a poor family, but he was General Gideon, leader of the army of the Lord. The first thing General Gideon did was to draft everybody, with no deferments, and ordered them to assemble at Lamesa[2].

The Lord then spoke to Gideon and said that he had too big an army to manage and most of them weren't much help in trying to slug it out with the Daltons anyway.

As a result, General Gideon assembled the army and announced that anybody that wanted to quit and felt that he had a good excuse, or who was afraid, any such could go home. As a result 22,000 left and Colonel Gideon had an army of 10,000.

The Lord spoke to Gideon again and said that there were still too many, that there was a lack of real enthusiasm on the part of many, and that only dedicated, committed men were needed when the power of God was available.

So God inspired Gideon to wisely test his army at the next water hole. Those men who were so dedicated and determined for victory that they walked through the water, lapping the water with their tongues as they passed through were to be kept, while the lukewarm who sprawled out on the ground yelling "coffee break, coffee break" were to be sent home.

[1]Amalekites   [2]Harod

103

On the other side of the water hole Captain Gideon and his 300 men departed to encounter the Dalton gang and their allies. The Lord told Gideon that with the 300 the Lord would see to the defeat of their enemies.

Gideon arrived with his 300 men and viewed the vast army of the assembled gangs in the valley.

The Lord suggested to Gideon that he go down in the night, with a private going in front in case of booby traps, and that he listen near the tents to hear what the Dalton boys had to say and maybe learn their strategy.

That night as he listened to the Daltons talking he learned they were afraid, for they had heard of the power of the Lord God of Israel, and one of them had dreamed of the crushing of their tents from the landslides that the Lord sometimes used.

Gideon returned and reported to the small group that the whole army was terrified and so he planned the first Halloween. Gideon divided the men into companies of one hundred each and placed them on the hill tops on the 3 sides of the army camped in the valley. Each man was to make an earthern jar, and equip himself with a bamboo trumpet and a torch of fat pine.

Every man had his instructions, and in the middle of the night, when the camp fires were burning low and the bewitching hour was come, Gideon sounded an eerie note on his bamboo trumpet, and then all the others all around did the same, and then they broke their earthern jars and threw them down the hillsides as if the mountains were crumbling, and then they set fire to their torches and came running down from all 3 of the surrounding hills, shouting, "The sword of Gideon and of the Lord has fallen upon you."

The Dalton gang and their allies went to pieces, and in their tremendous eagerness in the darkness to get out of the valley the gangsters began to kill each other in their panic, and they killed more among themselves than were killed by the 300 men of Gideon.

The next day as the terrified gangsters fled helter-skelter, the self-deferred draftees began to come out of the neighboring villages and they joined in the chase and in the slaughter. The Dalton boys themselves, the two leaders, had their heads removed and brought to Gideon's trophy room. Again Israel had called upon the Lord, and deliverance had come.

Chap.
8

The people of Lubbock[1] then became a little jealous of Gideon and his success and they complained to him saying, "Why didn't you

[1]Ephraim

104

tell us that you were going to make a move against the Dalton gang and the ruffians from Odessa and we would have helped you and been included in the glory?"

Gideon had apparently become a very wise man for he replied to them, "What I have done is nothing compared to what you have been doing in your area. While I was working on the Dalton gang and their allies you did a marvelous job of irrigating and planting, and there is more glory due to you than to me." This made the people of Lubbock satisfied[1].

When Gideon called his original 300 men together he found them hungry, thirsty, and worn out from chasing bandits. As a result he asked the mayor of San Angelo[2] if he would see that his men were fed and given proper rest and treatment.

The mayor said, "Nuts to you. We don't feed stray armies."

Gideon replied, "All right, Mac, we will move along for we have to consolidate our victory and move further north, but on the way back as we come marching through with our whole army we are going to stomp your little city into the dust, and just to add to your worries we will bring thorns and briers and scratch you to bits personally."

The next town was Sterling City[3] from which Gideon received the same reply when asking for food and shelter. Gideon then said to the leaders of Sterling City, "When I come back through with my army you can say goodbye to that big new water tank you have built, for we will pull it to the ground."

After Gideon had consolidated his army and finished the complete defeat of all the Dalton gang and all their allies he returned as he had promised and he tore down the water tower of Sterling City and when he came to San Angelo he sought out the City Council Members and one or two from the school board who had all been designated as the ones responsible for the unwillingness to feed his 300 men, and he captured these persons and took them out on the edge of the city and used briers and cactus thorns to scratch them until they had thoroughly agreed that they had learned a good lesson.

After all these things had happened the people of Israel came to Gideon and asked him to be their ruler and upon his death for his son to be their ruler.

Gideon replied, "I will not rule over you, neither will my son, but the Lord God of Israel will rule over you. However, I will represent him. First, however, I want every man to bring some gold to be put

[1]Recommended reading for congress   [2]Succoth
[3]Penuel

in the treasury of the church." It was done. This became a great source of trouble for Gideon as he made no attempt to have this money used, and though his intention was good as an act of worship, the temple funds became a great temptation for thieves.

Gideon had many wives and many children from them, and also a few children from some ladies that he did not quite get around to marrying, but he ruled Israel with justice and there was peace in the land for about forty years, and then Gideon died.

Chap.
9

Again the children of Israel did evil in the sight of the Lord and they were without a great leader for among the many sons of Gideon none had arisen in a godly fashion to lead the people.

Finally one of the sons of Gideon[1], a man named Kaiser[2], called a family reunion and made a little speech to all the other male kinsmen and reminded them that it was impossible for all of them to rule Israel and that he knew it was a tough and dangerous job, but if none of them wanted to do it, he would do it himself.[3]

The family decided that maybe this was best and Kaiser passed his hat among the crowd and collected enough money to get his program going.

After everyone had returned to his own home, Kaiser employed a small band of hoods[4], and contracted with them to go and kill all his uncles and the remaining grandsons of Gideon so that there would be no problem as to which of Gideon's descendents would rule[5]. The hoods killed all on the list except Aesop[6].

Kaiser was then officially made king and began to rule over a large portion of the children of Israel.

Aesop came out of hiding and gathered a big crowd and told them a fable saying, "The trees were doing nicely but they felt that there should be one of them to establish rules and be their king, so they went first to the olive tree and the olive tree said, 'I am sorry, but I don't care to leave my fatness, which honors both me and God.'

Then the trees went to the fig tree and the fig tree said, 'Should I forsake my sweetness and good fruit just for a little recognition?'

The trees then went to the grapevine and said, 'come reign over us', but the vine said, 'why should I leave my wine, which cheereth God and man, just to get promoted and cheered a bit?"

Finally then the trees went to the bramble bush and said, 'what

[1]Probably a grandson   [2]Abimelech
[3]He also was the only one who came to the reunion with a sword
[4]Hit men   [5]Also another family reunion would not be necessary.
[6]Jotham

about you reigning over us?'

The bramble replied, 'I will, but if you allow me to reign over you, put your trust in me and agree to live in my shadow, I warn you, that if you turn against me and try to destroy me with fire all the trees will burn along with me.'

"Just think about this," continued Aseop, "for you have put the Bramble Kaiser as your king and he has already choked his own family to death except for me. I tell you now, that when the fire starts, you'll all burn along with ole Bramble Kaiser."[1]

After making this speech, Aesop fled to the hills and stayed hidden in faraway caves.[2]

Needless to say, the people began to fret under the reign of the evil Kaiser and various plots began to develop to overthrow his rule.

The first leader of a rebellion was a man named Big Mouth Lee[3] and he gathered a half-pint sized army and moved into the city of Rochester.

Big Mouth made several speeches saying primarily, "Would to God the people would elect me king instead of ole Bramble Kaiser." Now the mayor of Rochester wasn't real sure how all this would work and he decided to play it safe and sent word to Kaiser about Big Mouth and suggested that he bring his army and then fight Lee's outfit on the plains in front of the Rochester gates.

The mayor of Rochester on the appointed morning[4] stood in front of the gate of the city with Big Mouth Lee when the army of Kaiser began coming down the mountain sides.

"What are those people doing coming down the mountain?" asked Big Mouth.

"I think those are shadows," said the mayor.

"Here come a company of soldiers down the valley. They ain't no shadows," said Big Mouth.

"Where is your mouth now, Lee?" asked the mayor, "didn't I hear you say 'who is ole Bramble Kaiser that we should serve him?' Aren't these the soldiers you despise? You wanted to fight you said, so now is your big chance."

Bramble Kaiser and his well organized army defeated Big Mouth and killed many people in the process.

Bramble Kaiser then decided that the Mayor of Rochester[5] was not to be trusted and he attacked the city and leveled it to the ground. Some of the leaders of the people who had been opposed to the Kaiser anyway hid in a tower and Bramble learned of this; so he went and cut down a tree and told his followers to do the same and

---

[1]The basic problem in our own politics   [2]Probably writing fables
[3]Gaal   [4]Kaiser had sent him a time schedule
                                             [5]Zebul

107

then he placed the logs at the foot of the tower and had a big bonfire featuring toasted mayor and councilmen.

Kaiser heard of another place that was rebellious called Houston[1] and he stormed the walls of this city and the people fled to a high tower in the middle of the city. Bramble decided that this would be a good place to have another bonfire. As he was standing at the foot of the tower thinking about this matter, Belle Starr[2] took a large stone and dropped it four stories down for a direct hit on Kaiser's head. It knocked him down and he was flat on his back looking bug-eyed at the laughing girl and so he turned to his trusty armour-bearer and said, "Take your sword and kill me. I couldn't stand to be killed by a woman."[3]

The armour-bearer obeyed immediately.[4] The army then disbanded and everybody went home. The wickedness of Bramble Kaiser had brought his own violent end.

Chap.
10

There then came into the leadership position of Israel a man named Cool Cal[5] and he ruled Israel under God and in peace, and he practically said nothing, and there was peace during the twenty-three years of his reign. Then came Woodrow[6] and he was a good man and judged Israel well for twenty-two years, and then he died.

Following this time, the children of Israel did evil again in the sight of the Lord, and began chasing foreign women and worshipping Baal, and putting the Lord further and further from their thoughts. The anger of the Lord was again aroused and he caused them to fall into the hands of their enemies, who oppressed the Israelites mightily for eighteen years.

Finally, the children of Israel cried again unto the Lord and admitted their sins.

The Lord spoke to them and said, "Did I not deliver you from the Egyptians, the James gang, the Dalton boys, and countless others, yet you always turned back to strange gods, such as Baal. Why don't you pray to them? See if the strange gods will deliver you."

"We deserved that, O Lord," cried the Israelites, "we have sinned and we repent. Please help us." After this prayer they put away the strange gods and served the Lord. The Lord was impressed and he grieved for the afflictions of his people.

The Moscow Muggers[7] gathered together and decided to take advantage of Israel and they camped with their army near Israel. The

---

[1]Thebez   [2]Actually we don't have the girl's name
[3]The disgrace would kill him   [4]Kaiser was known as a poor tipper
[5]Tola   [6]Jair   [7]Ammonites

children of Israel then said, "Who will lead us against the Moscow Muggers? Anybody who will lead us we will make a judge of Israelites in this area."

There was born in Baldwin[1] county in Israel a man named Big Jake[2], who was a mighty man of valour, strong and courageous, but he also happened to be an illegitimate child. As a result, the brothers and sisters all began to shun him and he was deprived of his portion of the inheritance from his father and the county officials and local gendarmes had him driven out of the county.

It came to pass in time that the Moscow Muggers became active again and began to harass and threaten to take over Baldwin County. The county leaders finally swallowed their pride and went to find Big Jake and asked him to come back and help them.

Big Jake said, "What goes on? Didn't you hate me, and expel me from the county, why come to me now?"

"We've changed our minds. We want you to be our leader for the Moscow Muggers are about to take us to the cleaners."

"All right, but it must be understood that if I come and the Lord delivers the muggers into my hand, then I shall be the new chairman of the county."

"With God as our witness, we agree."

Big Jake then returned and organized for himself a tough outfit and then he presented his cause to the Lord God of Israel at the holy place of Mt. Wesley.[3]

Big Jake then sent messengers to the muggers asking them why they were trying to make war against him. The muggers wrote back saying that they were merely trying to take again the land that was originally theirs[4]. All you have to do is restore our land and we will be happy and peaceful.

Big Jake then wrote back a long letter explaining about the whole trip from Egypt and how Moses had asked the people of Baldwin County to let his people pass through and he would not harm them or take their land, but the county commissioners would not allow this and Israel had to take the long way around Baldwin. Big Jake also said that Moses at the time had said that one day they would pay for this and their refusal of peace at the beginning meant that one of these days Israel would come and capture the land. This was done and God ordered it. The land is ours by order of the Lord, and so what claim can you possibly make? Why didn't you do like good neighbor Sam[5] and let Israel alone and live in peace with the people? Instead of that you chose war and lost, and I strongly suggest that

---

[1]Gilead   [2]Jephthah   [3]Mizpeh
[4]Makes you think about the Indians   [5]Balak

you don't try war again."

But Marx[1] would not listen to this reasoning and made preparation for war against Baldwin County and Big Jake.

Big Jake then prayed to the Lord and made a promise to God saying that if the Lord would grant him a great victory over the muggers that when Big Jake returned in peace to his home town that he would sacrifice whatsoever living thing he first met in sight of his home.[2]

So Big Jake and his band engaged in battle with the muggers and the Lord delivered them into his hands and they chased the muggers as far as Pensacola, Brewton, Atmore, and Greenville, and about 16 more places.

Then Big Jake returned, and to his horror and amazement his daughter came running to meet him, singing and dancing and welcoming him home as a hero, and she was his only child.

When Big Jake saw her he came to pieces, and began to tear his clothes and to moan and lament. Big Jake said, "I have opened my mouth unto the Lord and I cannot relent."

"Father", said the daughter, "If you have made a promise to God about me, you must put God first and fulfill the promise."

Big Jake explained to her what he had promised God and she said, "All right. I will be sacrificed willingly, but first let me go and have a couple of months in the hills to pray and prepare myself, and let me take a couple of my young girl friends with me so that we may lament my fate together."

Big Jake agreed. At the end of the two months she returned and Big Jake sacrificed her to the Lord, according to his vow to the Lord.[3]

Chap.
12

There was a big tribe of people many miles south of Big Jake in his county who heard of his victory over the muggers and they became very angry for not being included, for they could have been in on the plunder, and the money confiscated, and the women captured.

As a result, they brought their forces near to the camp of Big Jake and filed their complaint.

"Your memories are too short," said Big Jake. "In the first place, you never raised a hand when I was thrown out of my own family. What is more, I sent word that we could use more help against the muggers but you thought we'd get a licking; so go jump in the lake."

[1]Chief of the muggers [2]Naturally he figured on one of his cows
[3]This is one of the tough parts to explain. Big Jake was no doubt miserable the rest of his life. What about the mother?

After a few more exchanges like this the armies engaged in battle. The army of Big Jake was victorious and they captured the crossing places along the Jordan. Since there were no uniforms for identification, Big Jake's men guarding the crossing places had difficulty identifying fleeing members of the army until one of the smart boys gave them a good plan. At each crossing place, the representatives of Big Jake would say to every man that came to cross, "What number follows thirteen?"

Those who said "fourteen" were allowed to cross but those who said "foteen" were killed, for their accent betrayed their home county.

Big Jake then judged Israel for six years in peace before he died. Following him were a number of judges of no particular consequence, but they were men of faith and they kept the people mindful of their responsibility to the Lord and his commandments.

Chap.
13

The children of Israel could never make it apparently for more than about 50 or 60 years on the right path, for again they began to do evil in the sight of the Lord, and succumb to greed and worship false gods. As a result the Lord delivered them into the hands of the Fascists[1] and the Fascists controlled them and kept them in submission for forty years.

Again the prayers of some of the faithful touched the heart of God and he sent an angel to appear before a woman named Jean who had no children and was married to a man named Dempsey[2].

The angel said to Jean, "I know you are barren and without child, but you shall soon be pregnant. Take good care of yourself, do not drink any wine or strong drink and be very careful about eating. Your child shall be a boy, and you are not to cut his hair, for this is to be a sign and symbol of the power which God is going to bestow on your son, for he shall deliver Israel."

That night Jean told Dempsey about the man from God and what he had said; so Dempsey then prayed to God and asked the Lord to send the man back to talk to him, as he wanted some instructions about rearing the child.

The angel of the Lord again appeared to Jean, and she ran and got Dempsey and said to him, "Here's that man again."

Dempsey came and spoke to the man and said, "Are you the fellow that talked to my wife?"

"I am," replied the man.

"How about some instructions," said Dempsey.

[1]Philistines   [2]Manoah

111

"There are no further instructions. Just let Jean observe the things I told her."

"Fine. Now will you stay for dinner. We will kill a goat and I'll barbeque some delicious cabrito."

"No, even if I stayed I wouldn't eat. Any offering you make must be to the Lord."

Now Dempsey was not at all of the opinion that this man was an angel; so he said to him, "We really haven't officially met. My name is Dempsey, what is your name?"

"Sorry about that, but my name is a secret."

Dempsey then took the goat and offered a sacrifice to the Lord and as this was taking place the words and expressions of the angel were impressive on Dempsey and Jean. Then as the flame from the fire ascended toward the heavens the angel of the Lord entered the flames and ascended out of sight. Dempsey and Jean then fell on their knees and worshipped and the man did not appear again, and they both knew that he was an angel of the Lord.

Dempsey was really shook up, and said to Jean, "We will surely die, for we have seen God."

"I don't think so, Demps", said Jean, "for I think if the Lord was going to kill us he would not have accepted our worship service. The funeral always comes after you die, not before."

Shortly Jean became pregnant and in the normal time had a son and they named him Samson, and the child grew, and the Lord blessed him, and the spirit of the Lord made him a restless one.

Chap.
14

Young, powerful, restless Samson wandered about the country, and he saw a beautiful girl in Atlantic City[1]. When he returned home he told his father and mother that he had seen the most beautiful girl in the world and he wanted his folks to go and get her for him. [2]

"There are some real sweet girls here near home, daughters of some of our friends, why don't you let us talk to them? This girl you want is a Fascist," complained the mother and father.

Samson said, "Get the Fascist girl for me."

Now the mother and father did not know that this affair was the working of the Lord, for the Lord was seeking a way to get carefree Samson turned against the Fascist.

After some more huffing and puffing on both sides, the father, mother, and Samson all started to Atlantic City to make arrangements for Samson to marry.

Samson moved a great deal faster than his parents and he was a

[1]Timnath   [2]Parents made the proposals in those days

112

couple of miles ahead of them when he encountered a young lion in the path. The spirit of the Lord came upon him, and he was also pretty full of himself, and he killed the young lion with his bare hands. He did not tell his parents of this, but went ahead and found the girl and had a big time with her.

Arrangements were made, and some weeks later Samson returned for the formal wedding services, which would be under the Fascist system. Enroute this time to Atlantic City Samson saw the carcass of the lion he had killed and the bees had made a hive and there was honey in the carcass; so Samson took some of it and ate and then gave some to his parents to eat, who were going with him to the wedding.

The father and mother of Samson visited with the girl and her people and discussed the wedding plans while Samson went to the bachelor dinner. Since none of Samson's friends had come with him, about thirty friends of the bride came to the feast.

Samson stood up at the feast and said, "I am a betting man. I'll bet you 30 to 1 that I can propose a riddle you can't solve, and I'll give you seven days to get the answer. If you solve the riddle I'll give you each a new suit of clothes and a shirt, and if you can't, each of you must give me one."

"It's a deal. Tell us the riddle," said the companions.

"Out of the eater came forth meat, and out of the strong came forth sweetness."

The Fascists were completely baffled and finally it came down to the seventh day, six days after the wedding and they went to Samson's wife and said, "Entice your husband. Find out the answer to the riddle and tell us, or we will burn you and your father's house to the ground. We can't stand to pay off the bet."

So Samson's wife was on the spot, and she came to Samson and began crying and saying, "You don't love me anymore. You have put a riddle to my friends and you have not told me anything about it."

Samson said, "I haven't told it to my father and mother either and I love them, what's so important about a riddle?"

Samson's wife continued weeping and begging. At last Samson told her just to shut her up, and she told her friends and they came to Samson with the answer, "What is sweeter than honey or stronger than a lion."

Samson said, "You got your information from my wife."

Samson was extremely furious and the spirit of the Lord then descended upon him and accentuated his strength, and he went forth on the board walk at Atlantic City and everytime he came to a fascist he knocked him down and choked him to death, then he took off his

suit and his shirt, and he continued until he had slain thirty men and
had the pay-off for his bet. Then he took the clothes to the friends
of his wife and he left Atlantic City in a rage and returned to his own
home.

The father of Samson's wife was frantic[1] and he gave
Samson's wife to the best man at the wedding, claiming desertion by
Samson as the equivalent of divorce.[2]

Chap.
15

Sure enough, about nine months later the Atlantic City Belle
had a baby and Samson heard about it and decided to visit his wife.
When Samson knocked on the door, however, the old man wouldn't
let him enter and said, "When you left here so mad I didn't think
you would ever come back, I gave my daughter to one of the local
lads. However, the younger sister is still single and she's a beaut and
I'll be glad to let you marry her."

Samson left again mad, saying to himself that now the trick
he planned to play on the Fascists would be justified. After this
Samson began to set snares for fox and after some months he had
finally caught 300 of them and kept the foxes all penned up and well
fed.

At harvest time, when all the standing grain of the Fascists
was ripe and dry and almost ready for gathering, Samson took the
foxes in pairs, tied their tails together with firebrands and set the
torches on fire, turning the foxes, 150 pair of them, loose in all the
grain fields around the country, with each pair furiously dragging a
burning torch. As a result, all the corn, and vineyards, and olive
orchards of the Fascists were completely destroyed.

It did not take Nero Wolfe to find out who was responsible
and the Fascists then blamed one of their own, the father-in-law of
Samson, for causing all the trouble by giving away Samson's wife.
For vengeance then, they came and burned the father and the
Atlantic City Belle and their house. Samson heard of this and came
to town and killed every Fascist he could find for a couple of weeks,
and then departed feeling that he had evened things us a bit.

The Fascist then became greatly worried about return visits
from Samson, as no three or four men were a match for him and his
tremendous strength.

As a result, the Fascists organized a big posse and went to the
area where the tribe of Judah lived.

"Why do you come with a posse into our area?" asked the
men of Judah.

"We have come to get Samson, but if you don't turn Samson
over to us we'll turn on you."

The men of Judah then voted to turn Samson over to the

---

[1]Odds are he figured she might turn up pregnant
[2]Legal with the Philistines

Fascist.

The men of Judah went to Samson's hideout on Old Smokey[1] and told him of their problem.

"I have only evened things up with the Fascists. They did a few things to me and I did a few things to them," said Samson.

"We are sorry, Samson, but we must bind your hands and turn you over to the Fascists."

"All right," replied Samson, "but promise me that if a fight starts you won't be on the Fascist side. Also don't bind my hands too tightly."

"Agreed. We will bind you and deliver you, but we will not harm you," said the men of Judah.

As a result, Samson came down from Old Smokey and came near to the Fascist posse. At this time the spirit of the Lord came upon Samson and cords binding his wrists seemed only as threads, and he broke them easily, and seeing a hockey stick lying near the roadside he seized it and began killing Fascists as fast as he could get to them. Samson kept his weapon and he continued for several months killing Fascists everytime he could catch one, until he had killed one thousand, which was his goal.

After this he threw away his weapon and went to a beach resort for a little rest praying to God and saying, "You have done a great thing for me and given me a great victory, but I'm tired and thirsty and I have no energy left."

God then caused a healing water to spout forth from the weapon which lay where he had dropped it and he drank from this, and rested and was revived.

For the next twenty years he ruled and judged Israel without any trouble from the Fascists.

Chap.
16

The Fascists were always trying to get Samson but they knew they would have to catch him alone in their territory. Samson's weakness for women gave the opportunity as he had a lady friend in Reno[2] and the Fascists decided to lock the gates of the city while Samson was courting and then catch him in the morning. Some of the girls heard of this and slipped word to Samson; so instead of staying all night, he left his girl at midnight and tore down the gates of the city as well as the posts holding the gates and carried the debris to the top of the nearest hill.

Samson next began to court a lady named Delilah. Delilah was no green kid and Samson was in hog heaven with this affair.

The Fascists, however, came to Delilah and offered her some choice diamonds to do a little sabotage work for them and learn of the source of Samson's strength. In a few minutes she got them to add $5,000 in cash.

[1]Etam   [2]Gaza

As a result, Delilah asked Samson about his strength, and if there was anyway that he could be captured[1].

Samson said, "Come to think of it, if I were bound by green grapevines that had never dried, I'd be as weak as anybody else."

Delilah naturally passed the information along and was given seven green vines. At the first opportunity[2], Delilah let Samson go soundly to sleep and then she tied him with the green vines. Arrangements had been made for men to be in hiding in the house at the time, and Delilah came and awakened Samson saying, "The Fascists are here, wake up."

At this juncture the Fascist came running out of the closet, and Samson broke the green vines as if they were light string and laid out a Fascist or two before they could escape.

Delilah then began to tease Samson and to put on the pout act for his not telling her the truth about his strength.

"Well, I had to have a little fun, but if I'm bound with new rope, I can't do a thing."

The same song, second verse; Delilah bound him when he was asleep, men were hiding in the closests, and when she said, "The Fascists are here", Samson broke the new ropes and banged on a few Fascists.[3]

Delilah was really hot about this, as she was getting in trouble with the Fascists and she didn't like Samson having fun at her expense; so she pleaded with him again.

This time Samson told her to tie his long hair to the beam supporting the house and he would be helpless.

This time the Fascist decided to wait outside and not show up unless the trick worked. Needless to say, Delilah gave Samson the usual treatment of food, wine, and love, and then when he was asleep she tied his hair to the pin beam at the corner of the house. Again she cried, "Samson, the Fascists are here." Samson jumped up and pulled the pin and the beam out and went looking for Fascists, but found only tracks this time.

Delilah did not give up a minute as she really wanted the bonus money. In fact, she kept nagging Samson for the truth, and daily worked on him until he couldn't stand it any longer.[4]

Finally, Samson broke down and told Delilah that his strength came from God, and that the symbol of his strength was his long hair, for it had never been cut as a sign of his faithfulness.

Delilah realized that this was the real thing and she sent word to the Fascist rulers and told them they could come safely.[5] After

[1]Delilah could purr
[2]Indications are that Samson may have actually been living with Delilah at this time.

[3]Fascist volunteers were beginning to have to be appointed.
[4]It never occurred to him to give up Delilah

[5]And to bring the money

116

Delilah had given Samson the full treatment and he had fallen asleep she let his head rest against her knees and then signaled to the barber to come in and cut off Samson's hair.

Delilah herself then began to push on Samson to test his strength and she realized that his power was gone; so she called for the Fascist and they entered the house when she said, "Samson, the Fascist are here."

Samson thought that he would go out as before and knock a few heads around sideways, for he did not realize that the Lord had departed from him. The Fascists seized Samson, bound him, and then burned out both his eyes, and took him to the outskirts of Reno and tied him to a grist mill in place of a donkey and he began to grind grain all day in the grist mill.

During this time, however, the hair began to grow again on Samson's head, and he became thoughtfully repentant.

Meantime, the Fascists decided to have a giant Fiesta to celebrate their victory and to dedicate the celebration to Dracula[1], who was their favorite god at the time. The Fascists all rejoiced saying that their god had delivered Samson into their hands and they began to build a large covering supported by two huge central pillars, and under this cover they were to stage the big celebration, with drinking, dancing and merry making.

After about 3 years the building was finished and during this time Samson had been regaining his strength and had sought forgiveness from God.

The day of the celebration the people insisted that Samson be brought to the Sport's Center in order that they might mock him.

Samson was led into the center by a young lad and Samson said to him, "Lead me to the center of the arena in order that I might hold on to the pillars in the middle on which the whole structure is built."

Now the place was full of men and women and the leaders of the Fascists were there, and there were three thousand men and women on the roof[2].

Then Samson called upon the Lord saying, "Remember, O God, I pray you to strengthen me this one more time. I know I'll die, but give me strength to avenge myself and defy the Fascists and their false god."

Then Samson took hold of the two middle pillars, one with his right arm and one with his left, and he cried, "Lord, let me die with the Fascists," and he pulled with all his strength and the house began to shake and it came tumbling down upon all the people so that in his death Samson killed more people even than he had during his lifetime.

Samson's family came and found his body and gave him a christian burial.

[1] Dagon   [2] This helped

There was a man who grew up in Israel named Mickey Creep[1] and his mother had $1,500.00 hidden, and it turned up missing. The mother did a great deal of cursing about this, and was very suspicious that Mickey might be responsible.

One day Mickey came to his mother and said, "Mama, I took the $1500.00. I've decided that I shouldn't have done it and I'm returning it to you."

"You're a fine boy, Mickey," said his mother. "Actually, I had saved the money to use some of it for some idols to put around the house, and the rest was in appreciation for you as a son; so I'm giving you the $1500 back." Mickey would not take the money, however.

His mother then took $300 and went to a sculpturer who made her a graven image for her house, which became the house of Mickey shortly, as the mother passed away.

Mickey then began to collect idols so that his house was a house of graven images, and in those days there was no leader in Israel, but every man did his thing just as he thought was proper in his own way.[2]

It so happened that a young seminary student was wandering around the country and he stopped by the house of Mickey to see all the idols.

"Where are you from?" asked Mickey.

"Austin Seminary[3]," replied the young man, "and I'm just looking for a pastorate or the like."

"Well, just stay here," said Mickey, "you can be a father and a priest to me[4] and I'll give you room, board, and $4,000 a year."

"You just secured a father and a priest," said the preacher.

The arrangement worked well, and the preacher made a favorable impression on Mickey and Mickey decided things would go well with him, and that the Lord would bless him for having a priest in his home.

There was no king or judge in Israel at this time and the tribe of Dan decided to expand a bit and they dispatched five brave men to go on a scouting expedition and to meet together after their wanderings at the house of Mickey Creep on top of Nob Hill[5].

When the five arrived finally at Mickey's house they recognized the priest and began to question him about what he was doing and why he was living here in Mickey's house.

"Mickey offered me a job and I'm here as his father and pastor," said Phil[6] the priest.

"Father Phil, tell us if the Lord is with us on our endeavor

[1]Micah   [2]It just won't work   [3]Bethlehem—Judah
[4]I think Mickey needed both   [5]Ephraim   [6]I never did learn his name

and if we are doing the right thing."

"The Lord is with you and you will succeed," said Father Phil.

The five men noticed the people in the surrounding area, how careless and free they seemed to be, without any law and order, and they returned to their tribe and reported saying, "Let us get up and move against the people of Lazyburg[1] for the land is good and we can take over the place without difficulty."

As a result, they gathered a vigilante type outfit of 600 men and started on the march to Lazyburg. On the trip, they came fairly close to Nob Hill and Mickey's house. While chatting at a coffee break one of the five original spies said, "Do you fellows know that in a house near here there are great treasures. Mickey Creep has been assembling all kinds of valuables, including antique jewelry, not to mention a few graven images. Don't you think we ought to do something about this?"

As a result, they marched the 600 men by Mickey's house and they spoke to Father Phil and then the five scouts went into the house and began to remove all the treasures.

"What are you doing?" asked Phil[2].

"Now Father, just calm down. Mickey isn't home and all you need to do is cover your mouth with your hand[3] and join us as our priest. Isn't it a big promotion to move from a church with only one in the congregation to one that has 600?"

This suited Father Phil fine and he even helped to carry the graven images and some of the loot.

After they had departed some of the neighbors of Mickey Creep got together and came with Mickey to regain his possessions. When they caught up with the 600 men of Dan, the men of Dan turned to Mickey and said, "What's the matter with you, you look pale and angry?"

"You have taken my gods, stolen my treasure, and gone off with my preacher, what more can I say? You ask me what is wrong, you must be nuts."

"Now calm down," said one of the leaders of Dan, "for if you and your friends get noisy some of these 600 men might just start a big killing."

When Mickey realized that they were too heavily outnumbered he returned in sorrow to his house.

The 600 men of Dan proceeded to Lazyburg and smote it with the edge of their swords and burned out a great portion of it, capturing most of the people. Then they established themselves there, and renamed the town Dan.

They set up here the graven images that had been stolen from Mickey.

---

[1]Laish   [2]Fairly silly question   [3]high class way of saying "shutup"

There was still no king or judge in Israel, but there was a circuit riding minister who had a woman with him who was his common-law wife, and her name was Lullabelle[1].

Lullabelle became a bit weary of the tent meetings and she ran away and went back to her father. The minister went after her in a few days to talk her into joining him again.

When Sig[2] arrived at his so-called father-in-law's house he was welcomed by the father of his girl. In fact, they enjoyed each other so eating and drinking and telling jokes that the father of Lullabelle kept Sig around for over a week, but finally he left, and Lullabelle went with him.[3]

After a long journey they came near the city of Saigon[4] and the servant said, "Let us go into Saigon and spend the night."

"Not a chance," said Sig, "for it is no place for a stranger and it is not a city of Israel. We will go to Tel Aviv[5], for it is a city of Israel."

As a result, the servant, the donkeys, Sig, and Lullabelle entered Tel Aviv, but no one would give them lodging for the night.

Finally, an old man came and saw them sitting on the curb and he said, "What's the trouble, Mac?"

"We can find no lodging," said Sig, "even though this is a city of Israel."

"Come stay at my place. I'll be glad to have you," said the kindly old man.

After they were settled in the old man's house, however, some of the local hoodlums who had been drinking came knocking on the door. They called out to the old man saying, "We know you have some strangers in there. Send the man out as we want to chase him up and down the street and have a little sport as we don't want strangers around here."

"I will not do it." said the old man. "This man is under my care by law. I know you are a wild bunch though and if it will keep the peace, I'll let you have my daughter and this visitor's traveling girl friend and you can frolick with them."

The men claimed there were plenty women they could chase.

Sig, however, figured they hadn't seen anybody as desirable as Lullabelle; so he pushed her out the door, reluctantly, but to save his life and the old man's. As a result the men began to abuse Lullabelle, and they took turns, continuing all through the night.

At dawn, when Sig opened the front door, Lullabelle was lying on the threshold, dead from mistreatment. Sig carried her into the old man's house. Then Sig took a knife and cut Lullabelle into twelve pieces and sent one piece to each of the twelve tribes of

[1]Tribe of Bethlehem-Judah   [2]A Levite, I'm not certain about the Sig
[3]no indication of enthusiam reported   [4]Jebus   [5]Gibeah

Israel[1]. It was generally agreed that this was the biggest news story of the year. The message with each body piece said "Think about this happening in Israel."

This incident caused a great furor and the representatives and many others from all the tribes from Maine[2] to California[3] gathered together and held a great convention with 400,000 men carrying swords present[4].

Then Sig stood before the whole crowd and told the grisly story and said, "All Israel is disgraced by this. What shall we do?"

The people shouted with great fury and they took a pledge saying that no one would go home until the matter was settled and the wrong avenged.

It was decided to take ten men out of every hundred, using the lottery system, with a thousand selected to provide food for the trip, and all the people of Israel were united for this cause.

As a result, a message was sent to the tribe of Benjamin saying, "Send us the men who were guilty of this crime that we may put them to death and take such evil out of Israel."

The tribe of Benjamin refused to do this, and so they gathered themselves together to do battle with the other tribes. The other tribes had agreed to take vengeance one tribe at a time and the Lord[5] chose Judah to go first.

Now the tribe of Benjamin and all the people from Tel Aviv made a big army, but the tribe of Benjamin had trained 700 left-handed experts with stone slingers[6] and when the armies engaged there was a mighty battle, but the victory went to the tribe of Benjamin.

The children of Israel gathered themselves again and prayed to the Lord, asking if they should go against their brother tribe of Benjamin and the Lord said, "Go."

The second day of battle was another victory for the tribe of Benjamin and that evening the armies of Israel again appeared before the Lord and wept and fasted and prayed earnestly, again asking if they should try another time.

This time the Lord said, "Go up against Benjamin, and I will deliver them into your hands. This time the command of the army of Israel was given to Patton[7]. Patton first placed soldiers in ambush during the night close to the city of Tel Aviv and when in the morning the army of Benjamin came forth to do battle they were overconfident. As Patton had instructed, the first line was to begin fleeing in various directions and as Patton figured the Benjamin outfit scattered in their chase.

[1]This may be where obscene mail started.   [2]Dan   [3]Beersheba
[4]Sounds worse than used car salesman convention
[5]Possibly through the lottery   [6]This was like using a secret weapon
[7]Phinehas

121

Then when the army of Benjamin was scattered in every direction chasing the fastest runners of Israel, the organized army of Patton arose from close to the city and the Lord was with Israel and while this was happening the original ambush group moved into Tel Aviv and set it afire. When those left fighting for the tribe of Benjamin looked back and saw the burning city they knew they were doomed and defeated.

What men were left of the tribe of Benjamin fled into Mexico[1] and about 600 men made it safely across the border.

Meanwhile, the army of Israel under Patton, since it was already doing well, destroyed a few more cities and made a few more conquests before going home, and for kicks they set fire to all the cities they passed on the way home[2].

Now at the big convention in Israel another pledge which the people made was that they wouldn't let one of their daughers marry a member of the tribe of Benjamin.

After everybody had cooled down and had been home, some of the people began to lament that on the present basis there would never be 12 tribes of Israel again and this meant changing the flag and other things. The people presented the matter before the Lord and they worshipped God and began to bemoan the loss of the tribe of Benjamin, all because of Lullabelle.

Since everyone had sworn not to let a daughter marry a Benjamite, one of the men of Israel came up with a bright idea. The man's name was Ford[3], and he spoke saying, "I have a better idea than lamenting. There is a town about forty miles from here that has a lot of fine women in it and I suggest that we send 10,000 of our best troops under Patton and let them go and capture 400 young girls and bring them safely to us. Then we can take these girls to the 600 men of Benjamin hiding in Mexico[4] and the tribe of Benjamin can be started again and this will help heal the bad feelings among us."

This motion was seconded and passed unanimously and was done.

Word was sent to the 600 men and the time was set at one of the regular feast days and the plan was to turn the 400 girls loose to dance in the vineyards and the men of Benjamin could come and any girl a man caught he could marry.

Everything worked according to plan and the people all returned to their homes. There was still no king or judge in Israel, and the people operated on a basis of doing whatever seemed right to each man in his own way.

---

[1] Rimmon
[2] Their mothers said "boys will be boys"
[3] Not sure about this name
[4] 600 girls would have been an even better idea

RUTH

Years rolled by under various judges and then there came a great famine in the land. There was a sheepherder named Sim[1] and his wife Nan[2] who had two sons, Charles[3] and Walter[4], and they took what sheep they had left and went to Mississippi[5] where they had been told that there was land and grass.

It wasn't long before the boys fell in love with a couple of the Dixie Belles, named Pamela and Ruth.

Not long after this Sim died and then a couple of years later the two sons were killed in an accident[6], which left Nan with two daughters-in-law and no property rights.

Word had also come that the famine was over back home and so the three ladies started to travel back to Judah.

Nan then turned to the two girls and said, "I think it would be better if each of you returned to your mother's house and I will give you my blessing. You were good wives to my sons and you've been good to me, but there is no reason for you to leave your home state. I hope you will find new husbands and a happy home and I hope the Lord will bless you both."

At this point all three began to cry.

"We will see you safely to your own country," said both of the girls.

"It just isn't sensible. I have no more sons for you to marry. I'm too old to find another husband and if I did and became pregnant next week with twins it would be twenty years before you could marry them. It grieves me, for I love you both as if you were my own flesh and blood, but I cannot have you waste your life on an old lady."

This brought on another short period of shedding tears.

Pamela then kissed her mother-in-law, thanked her, and headed home, but Ruth stayed with Nan.

"You'd better go to your own people and your own way of life," said Nan.

"Please don't ask me to leave," said Ruth, "for wherever you go I want to go, where you live I want to live, your people I want to have as my people, and your God as my God. Where you die, there I want to die, and I want to be buried in the same cemetery with you, and I pledge before God that nothing but death shall ever separate us."

Nan realized the sincerity of the statement and she argued no further, so the two of them headed for Bethlehem.

When they arrived in Bethlehem some of the old friends gathered around and said, "Are you really Nan, Sim's wife that left here so many years ago?"

[1]Elimelech   [2]Naomi   [3]Mahlon
[4]Chilion   [5]Moab   [6]chariot drag?

"Yes," said Nan, "but don't call me Nan anymore, call me "Bitterweed",[1] for the Lord has been rough on me. I left here with a full family, husband and two sons, and I return broke and tired and old, with my family dead in Mississippi."

It was harvest time in Bethlehem when Nan and Ruth arrived.

Now Sim, Nan's dead husband, had a cousin whose son had become very wealthy and owned many fields. His name was Bobo.[2]

Ruth said to Nan, "Let me go to the fields and begin to pick the corn and grain that the rich are required to leave for those who will work for it."

"Good idea," said Nan.

So Ruth went and stayed well behind the harvesters as she was required. She picked grain and by chance she chose to work in fields that belonged to Bobo.

Bobo came out from Bethlehem one day to check the work and he said to the harvesters working for him, "Howdy, and may the Lord bless you."

"Same to you, boss," they replied.

Bobo then spied Ruth bending over picking grain and he said to one of his servants, "Whose the doll on welfare?"

The head reaper said, "She is a Mississippi girl[3] and she asked properly for permission to pick the left overs. She came from Mississippi with her mother-in-law, Nan, after her husband was killed."

Bobo then went to Ruth and said, "Do not go to any other fields. Stay in my fields to do your picking. Stay also with the other girls that are reaping here."

Then Bobo turned to the foreman and said, "See to it that none of the young harvesters make any passes at that cute Ruth."

Then Bobo turned to Ruth and said, "When you are thirsty, drink from the barrels that are for my workers."

Ruth then did a little bow with a wiggle and said, "Why are you so kind to poor little ole me?"[4]

Bobo said, "The word has reached me about how hard you work and how good you have been to your mother-in-law. I also am told you have accepted the God of Israel and I hope that the Lord will reward you properly."

"I am anxious to please you for your kindness and for the great comfort that you and your words have brought me. You have been friendly to me even though I am not one of the regular girls, and I am deeply grateful."

Bobo then said, "Not only are you to drink from my barrels, but come to the chuck wagon and eat with my paid workers."

[1]Mara   [2]Boaz   [3]Even in those days some Mississippi girls were real beauties.   [4]Life is just like that for pretty girls.

Ruth did this and left for home that evening feeling fine.

The next day or so Bobo had a few more looks at Ruth, who was a real knockout, and he told the regular harvesters to let her gather grain anywhere and not just to pick up the left overs. In fact, Bobo told them to deliberately throw some grain her way and make it easy for her.

At the end of the day, Ruth had a record supply of grain to take home. Nan was tremendously impressed.

"Where did you scrounge for grain today?" saked Nan. "May the Lord bless any man that leaves that much for the poor."

"Well, Nan," said Ruth, "I worked in a field belonging to Bobo, a fine looking man."

"Hot ziggity-dog," squealed Nan, "The Lord has started giving us some breaks. The man is a kinsman and we just might get something going here."

"Well, Nan, he did tell the young men not to chase me around the field and he told me to stay with his regular girls who worked and not to mix with the men or go to other fields."

So Ruth continued working in the fields of Bobo until the harvest time was ended.

Chap.
3

Nan then said to Ruth, "It is time for me to do a little coaching as I want the best for you and I know the ways of dealing with men in this country, the customs, and the rights of the kinsmen."

"I'm all ears," said Ruth.

"Well, tonight is the big celebration of the harvest ending, when they have the eating, drinking, and dancing. First, we are going to give you a tip-to-toe bath, the right kind of perfume, and your snazziest dress, then off to the party."

As soon as Ruth was ready to go Nan said to her, "Now you stay in the background and don't let Bobo see you until he has fininshed eating and had a fair amount of wine. Then you watch when he goes in the big barn to lie down and snooze. Then you go and lie down beside him, take off his shoes, and lie up close to him. When he begins to wake up he'll know what to do."

"I'll do just like you say," replied Ruth.

Off to the party went Ruth and all worked according to plan. After ole Bobo had eaten and had a good bit of wine and was very merry with wine, he went into a corner of a corn bin and laid down among the shucks. Ruth came in and slipped off his shoes and lay close to him.

Bobo awoke about midnight and began to stir and was flabbergasted to find a woman with him.

"Who are you?" asked Bobo, a bit shakily.

"I am Ruth, one of your working girls. I'm the one from Mississippi and since we're sorta cousins you can spread the blanket over the two of us."

Bobo said, "Hurrah for you. You are a remarkable girl. I'm glad you didn't go off with one of the young harvesters tonight. Don't be afraid either of this circumstance, for everybody knows what a virtuous girl you are. Now it is true that I am remotely kin to you, but it so happens that there is a second cousin alive and I think I'm your third cousin; so according to our law the second cousin has first choice."

"We don't play that way in Mississippi," said Ruth.

"I know." said Bobo, "but I must first offer you to Clutch Midas, and if he will not marry you as next of kin, then I will. In the meantime, though, honey, just stay here with me until just before daylight and leave in the dark so no one will know that a woman has been with me all night."

"Just as you say, couz," replied Ruth.

As requested Ruth slipped out of the barn before it was light enough for anyone to see. She also took with her a sack of feed which Bobo gave her as a keepsake.

When Ruth came home Nan could hardly wait to hear all the details. When she saw the sack of grain she said, "You've got him for sure. I bet he will not rest until he has seen the next of kin and figured a way to keep you, but at least you'll get a husband one way or the other."

Chap
4

The next day Bobo went early down to the courthouse square near the gate of the city and sat until he saw Clutch Midas. Bobo called to him and asked him for a conference, and he requested ten men to listen as witnesses; so there would be no misunderstanding.

"Clutch," said Bobo, "our cousin Sim left years ago and is dead and his widow has returned and claimed the small piece of ground that was Sim's. As you know, it must be offered to the next of kin, which is you, or then to me, before it can be offered publicly."

"Well, I'll buy the land," said Clutch.

"Of course, in fairness to you Clutch, I think I ought to tell you that when you buy the land you also get Nan, the widow. Furthermore, you get a girl she brought from Mississippi, and you'll have to support both of them for the rest of their lives."

"Yow!" cried Clutch. "Of all the things I don't need is a couple of more expensive women. You redeem it, Bobo. You aren't even married and it wouldn't hurt you to support a couple of women."

It was the custom in Israel at that time, that when a contract was made, the party of the first part took off his shoe and gave it to the party of the second part.[1] Clutch gave Bobo his left shoe.

Bobo then turned to the witnesses and said, "You are my witnesses. I have now accepted the responsibility of all that belonged to Sim, Charles and Walter. Furthermore, I have purchased Ruth

[1] Same as "OK it's a deal, let's shake."

126

for my wife."

"We are witnesses," said all the crowd standing around the gate.

"Good luck, Bobo," said one of the witnesses, "and I hope the Lord makes this Mississippi girl as good as Rachel and Leah, the two who really produced the tribes of Israel."

After this Ruth and Bobo were married and she gave him a son in the proper time.

The friends of Nan congratulated her on becoming a grandmother and told her how this would put new life in her. Nan was elated and she constantly looked out for the baby and kept him when Ruth and Bobo went on trips.

The Lord blessed this marriage and the devotion of Ruth and through her son came the lineage that brought forth King David and it was through this same descendancy that there was born Christ, the Lord.

There was a certain man from Birmingham whose name was Toby[1] and he had two legal wives, one was named Hannah and the other was named Penny.[2] Penny produced several sons and daughters[3] but Hannah had no children. Toby, however, particularly loved Hannah; so when he distributed the monthly allowances he gave freely to Hannah, though normally this would not have occurred in most families.

Penny, however, began to put the lip on Hannah and teased her about being childless, calling taunts to her and saying such things as "had any children today?"

This kept up year after year and finally Hannah could hardly eat because of her inferior feeling and the idea that she was good for nothing.

"What is the matter, Hannah?" asked Toby. "It is ridiculous to worry about not having kids. I treat you better than if you had ten sons. Lay off the moaning and groaning."

Actually, this made Hannah all the more anxious to have a son for her husband's sake; so she began to eat and drink again, and then she went to the temple and prayed earnestly to the Lord for help.

Father Eli, a grand old priest of the church, saw her enter the temple and observed her lips moving as if she was mumbling. Actually Hannah was making an arrangement with the Lord, agreeing that if the Lord would bless her with a son she would turn him into the church at an early age and let him grow up as a priest for the Lord.

Father Eli stopped Hannah as she left the temple, for he had observed her mumbling and her tears, and he said, "Hannah, you've got to quit hitting the bottle. How long have you been going too strong on the wine?"

"You are mistaken, Father Eli, I have touched neither wine or strong drink, but I have poured my problems out to the Lord. I have been speaking out of my sorrow, and not from drinking."

Then Father Eli said, "Peace to you. May the Lord God of Israel hear your prayers and grant your request."

"Thank you, Father," said Hannah, and she returned home refreshed and she began to eat and drink normally, and she was no longer a sour puss.

This change in attitude and brightness re-awakened Toby's interest and he again began to have intercourse with Hannah and she became pregnant, and in due time delivered a son and she called him Samuel.

When the time came for one of the regular occasions of going to

---

[1]Elkanah   [2]Peninnah   [3]A real status symbol

church[1] Hannah would not go and said to Toby, "I will stay and nurse the baby, for I will not go to church until he is old enough to be given to the Lord, and to live in church."

"All right," said Toby, "do what you think is right in the eyes of the Lord."

When Samuel was old enough to walk and talk and go to the potty by himself, Hannah took what she had been saving from her allowance and when the time came to go to church she took Samuel and her offering.

When Hannah presented Samuel to Father Eli she said, "Do you remember me? I am the woman who stood in the temple here a few years ago praying, and it was for this child that I prayed. The Lord has answered my prayer, therefore, I am doing as I promised and I bring him now to the temple, to turn him over to the Lord, for he is to grow up as a man of God."[2]

Chap.
2

Hannah then prayed a prayer of thanksgiving saying, "My heart rejoices. I have been blessed because I trusted in the Lord. There is none holy as the Lord, neither is there any rock or support like our God. Don't ever let me speak arrogantly again, for the Lord is a God of knowledge and of actions. The Lord knocks people down and raises them up, he helps the poor and the beggars, the very pillars of the earth are the Lord's and he has built the whole world.

No man will prevail by his own strength, for the Lord will light the path of the righteous and make dark the way of the wicked.

The opponents of God don't have a chance. The Lord shall rule the whole earth, and in his time he will thunder down upon the wicked."

So Hannah left Samuel at the church with Father Eli, and Samuel began to work around the church, helping with the sweeping, and looking out for Father Eli.

Father Eli had two sons of his own, both grown young men, and they began taking advantage of the people who brought offerings to the church, and they were actually stealing a portion of the offerings. This was a great sin, and the Lord was displeased.

Samuel, however, behaved himself and he grew and he learned as a child of God. Every time Samuel's mother came to church[3], she brought Samuel a new coat.

Father Eli also had a special kind word to say to Toby and Hannah and thanked them always for Samuel. After this Hannah had 3 sons and two daughters.

Now Father Eli began to become old and he was disturbed about what was happening with his grown sons, how they were

[1]Three times a year was all you went to church-how about that?
[2]Hannah may be No.1 in the kingdom
[3]Never more than 3 times a year, usually at the yearly feast.

taking from the offering, and how they were making love to various women in the congregation and said to them, "Why do you do these things? The word is that you are living in sin with some of our church women and taking advantage of teen-age girls. Now when you break one of man's laws you simply have to deal with man, but when you break God's law you must deal with God."

The young men paid no attention to their father.

Samuel, all the while, continued to grow in favor both with God and with the people with whom he came in contact.

There came then a man sent from God to Father Eli who said to him, "The Lord is displeased with your house. You have been faithful and a good priest, but your sons are hellions. God is still the Lord, it is the same Lord that delivered the people from Egypt, and this same Lord is a living Lord, and he will not have his offerings stolen and his house abused. As punishment, therefore, you are the end of the line as far as your family name is concerned. Your two sons, Snatch[1] and Wolf[2] shall both be killed at once, and I will raise up a new priesthood and the illegitimate grandsons of this house will have to come and beg bread in the welfare line at the church, and get the needy baskets at Thanksgiving."

This was an ungodly time in Israel, and the word of the Lord was rarely studied and observed, but Samuel worshipped God. Now Eli was getting old, and his eyes were dim, and Samuel slept nearby to the old man on a cot so that he could be sure that the lamp of the Lord in the temple did not go out, as well as be an aid to Eli.

One night Samuel heard a voice saying, "Samuel."

"I am right here," answered Samuel, thinking that Eli had called, and he went to Eli's side.

"You called me, what do you want?" asked Samuel.

"I didn't call you, boy, go back to bed," said Eli.

"Samuel," came the voice again a little later.

Samuel again went to Eli and said, "Here I am. What do you want?"

"I didn't call you son. Just go on back to bed."[3]

Again, for the third time, came the voice, which was the voice of God, "Samuel, Samuel."

For the third time Samuel went to Eli and insisted that he had heard him call.

Father Eli then finally understood that it was the call of God to the boy, and so he said to him gently, "Go lie down, my boy, and if you hear the call again, do not come to me but say, 'speak, Lord, for thy servant heareth.'"

Samuel returned to his cot and laid down and again the Lord

[1]Hophni   [2]Phinehas
[3]Samuel was about 12 years old and probably took
a dim view of this situation.

called as He had before, "Samuel, Samuel."

Then Samuel said, "Speak, Lord, for thy servant is listening."

Then the Lord spoke to Samuel and said, "I will do a great thing in Israel and it will put a tingle in the ears of the people, and scare the willie-nillie out of some of them. I will destroy the family of Eli for I know of their many sins and will bring them to a violent end."

Samuel lay and pondered on these things and then opened the doors of the temple in the morning, but he did not want to tell Eli of his vision.

"Samuel," called out Eli.

"I'm coming, Father," answered Samuel.

"What is the thing about which the Lord talked with you last night. Do not hide it from me, for I am a man of God, and the words of God should not be hidden from me."

Then Samuel told Eli all that the Lord had said and he did not hold back anything.

"It is truly the word and way of God." said Eli, "Let God do what seems best to Him."

Now Samuel grew into manhood and the Lord was with him, and Samuel wasted no time in idle talk.

The word gradually began to spread everywhere, from Maine to California[1] that Samuel was being recognized as a prophet of the Lord and the Lord appeared again to Samuel in the inspiration of his words.

Chap.
4

The Fascists[2] had again organized themselves and then set themselves up and moved against Israel and its army. Israel could not stand before the Fascist army and was defeated, losing 4,000 men.

When the leaders of Israel gathered together they wondered why they had lost, and why God had forsaken them. One of the elders suggested that it would be a good idea to get the ark of the covenant, and this would be a rallying banner for them.

The people went to Westminister Abbey[3] for the ark of the covenant and when it entered the camp there was great rejoicing and the army morale was raised.

Now the Fascists heard all the shouting and the celebrating and they could not understand how you could celebrate a defeat. As a result they sent spies who returned and said that the ark of the covenant of the Lord had arrived in camp.

The Fascists then were terrified and they said, "Our goose is cooked, for God has come into their camp. What can we do? Who can deliver us from the God that destroyed the army of Pharaoh?"

"We don't have any choice. We've got to fight," said one of the

[1] Dan to Beersheba   [2] Philistines   [3] Shiloh

Fascist leaders. "When the going gets tough, the tough get going [1]. If we lose we'll be servants to the Hebrews. Tomorrow we fight like mad."

On the next day the Fascists again engaged in battle with Israel and beat them, and the slaughter was great, and the Israelites fled every one in his own direction, and the Fascists captured the ark of the covenant.

There was a man from the tribe of Benjamin who was one of the better track men and ran all the way to Montreat and told Father Eli that the children of Israel were defeated, that 30,000 had been killed or scared away, that Father Eli's sons, Snatch and Wolf, had both been killed and that the ark of the covenant had been captured.

Upon hearing this news Father Eli had a heart attack and died [2].

About this time Penny was in labor and she heard that her lover [3] had been killed and she died giving birth to a son; so the neighbors named the son Vanish [4] because glory was gone from Israel and the ark of the Lord had been stolen.

Chap.
5

The Fascists then took the ark of the covenant and set it in the place where they kept their idol, for they worshipped a god they called Iron Mike. [5] The next day the statute of Iron Mike had fallen to the ground and been broken in pieces; so the people said, "What will we do with the ark of the covenant, for it is more powerful than Iron Mike?"

Now this occurred in San Antonio [6], and the people began to develop virus trouble, diarrhea was everywhere, and most of the people began to suffer with hemorrhoids and when the men realized all this they decided that it was because of the power of God in the ark of the covenant.

As a result, they appointed a study committee of leaders to deliberate on the matter, and they decided to carry the ark of the covenant to Austin [7], and the hand of the Lord began to disturb these people and they began to have hemorrhoids and rawness in their secret parts.

As a result they sent the ark of the covenant to Waco [8] but the people of Waco protested and said that they didn't want the ark of the covenant in their city as they had enough trouble as it was. The men of Waco said, "Send the ark of the covenant back to Israel, and let them have sore tails, but we are sick of this, and dying with our disorders."

---

[1] A statement not originated by Darrell Royal
[2] Probably a coronary occlusion of the myocardial infractory type.
[3] She apparently was a mistress of Snatch or Butch
[4] Ichabod
[5] Dagon
[6] Ashdod
[7] Gath
[8] Ekron

All this took about seven months, going from one place to another, and the Fascists then went to the fortune tellers and the soothsayers and said, "What shall we do?"

This group suggested returning the ark of the covenant to Israel, but added that it should be conveyed with gifts, some of them being images representing the diseases. "Don't change your mind or get hardhearted about it, but remember what the record says about what happened to Pharaoh and his army when he changed his mind," one said.

"We suggest," said the spokesman, "that you make a new cart for the ark of the covenant, and get the best milk cows to pull it, and put the jewels and images in a box by the side of the ark, and then turn the cows loose and see what happens. If the cows go to Israel we will know it was the Lord plaguing us, but if they don't but stay around here, we will figure that the miseries just came to us by chance."

This was done. It also happened that the Israelites were reaping their wheat at this time and the cows came toward their fields and the people lifted up their eyes and were overjoyed to see the return of the ark.

Now the cart came into the farm of Old McDonald[1], in Scotland[2], and the priests there and the people looked into the ark of the covenant and handled the jewels in the box attached, and the Lord smote them with diseases and a great plague, until they cried to people of England[3] to come and get the ark, for they knew they were not permitted to touch the ark or look into it, and they were sick and afraid.

So the men of England came and took the ark and brought it to Westminister Abbey and it stayed here as a symbol of the people's return to God, and there were years of peace again for the people, though still under the Fascists.

Then Samuel spoke to the people and said, "If you will return to the worship of God with all your heart, and give up your selfish ways and the strange gods you put before the Lord, then the Lord will deliver you from the Fascists and you will no longer be a satellite nation."

The children of Israel listened to Samuel and they put away their phony antics and returned to the Lord.

Then Samuel said, "Gather all the representatives of all the people at Mt. Wesley[4] and I will pray for you to the Lord."

The representatives gathered and they confessed their sins and repented and they worshipped God and brought gifts to the church.

[1]Joshua   [2]Bethshemesh   [3]Kiriathjearim   [4]Mizpeh

The Fascists heard about this gathering and they assembled an army and decided to come to Mt. Wesley and break up the meeting, and the people of Israel were afraid.

Samuel stood before the Lord, he worshipped and he prayed, and he also instructed the men to arm themselves for battle. As the confident Fascists approached the Lord caused a great storm to descend, with howling winds, and driving hail, and the storm terrified the Fascists and scattered them, and the army of Israel pursued them and won a great victory.

Then Samuel placed a historical marker at Mt. Wesley as a memorial to this event. The Fascists were subdued by this battle and the hand of the Lord was against them, and many of the cities were restored to Israel. During this time Samuel acted as a judge and a prophet and a circuit rider going from place to place in Israel.

Chap.
8

As Samuel became older he appointed his sons as judges[1], and the name of one was Hoppa[2] and the other was Grafter[3] and they took bribes, and were money seekers, and were warped in their judgments.

As a result a committee of citizens called on Samuel and told him that his sons were ruining the country and that they thought what they really needed was a king.

Samuel did not like what they had to say, particularly the part asking for a king. Samuel, however, was a man of God, and he prayed about the matter and sought council with God.

The Lord said to Samuel, "Let them have a king. It might teach them a lesson on taxation, at least. These people are not protesting your rule or rejecting you, they are rejecting me. In spite of the multitude of times that I have delivered these people, they still waiver and falter in their duty and devotion. Tell the people, however, what a king is like and the way a king rules and then appoint them a king."

Samuel then said to the people, "I have prayed about this and the Lord has consented to let me appoint a king. First, however, let me remind you what a king will do. He will draft most of your sons and make foot soldiers and chariot drivers out of them, some even will have to run beside the chariots, and some he will put in his fields. Furthermore, he will take the daughters that are pretty and he will put them to work around the palace as cooks, pastry makers, and cocktail waitresses, he will also select some of your best land and declare it government property for parks, and he will take everything you earn, taking at least 10%[4] and then when all these things befall you and you begin to worry about your freedom, you will cry and gripe to the Lord, and the Lord will not hear you."

[1] I've always been dubious about nepotism   [2] Joel
[3] Abiah   [4] Not so bad. Presidents run higher.

The people were not impressed. Some of them said, "Everybody else has a king, why can't we have one?" [1]

Some said, "We want a king. We want somebody who will take the responsibility, and fight our battles for us."

Samuel then repeated all this junk to the Lord. Then God again said to Samuel, "Go get them a king, and maybe they'll learn."

Now there was a man of the tribe of Benjamin who had properly fed his son vitamins, aside from being a big man himself, and the son grew to be 6 inches taller than the fellows around him, and he was strong, and a good man, and his name was Saul.

Saul's father came one day and reported losing a bunch of donkeys and he sent Saul and one of his servants out to find them. Saul went to Nob Hill [2], and Brownwood [3], and as far as Clovis, New Mexico [4] and he couldn't find them. Saul then said to his servant, "We had better go home. Daddy will begin to worry more about our being lost than the donkeys."

"The fellows at the tavern told me that there was a very wise man staying not far from here and that he might be able to help."

"It's O.K. by me, " said Saul, "but I'm broke. What can we give him for his advice?"

"It just so happens," said the servant, "that I picked up 10 bucks at the dice game last night, and we can give him that."

"That's fine" said Saul, "let's go to the city and find the man."

As they approached the city they encountered some young girls drawing water and they inquired of them if the prophet was still in the city. The girls told Saul that if he went in a hurry he could find the prophet as he was conducting special services and it would be easy to find him today.

Now the Lord had moved Samuel the day before to believe that on the next day he would encounter a young man who would make a good king. God had instructed Samuel to anoint him and had promised that he would help in the troubles with the Fascists who were getting active again.

When Samuel saw Saul approaching the city he knew this was the man of whom God spoke, also the biggest he'd ever seen.

Saul approached Samuel who stood at the gate of the city and said, "Where is the prophet's house, as I would like to see him?"

"I am the so-called fortune teller that you seek. We will eat together today and tomorrow I will tell you all you need to know and send you on your way."

"Incidentally," said Samuel, "the donkeys that were lost are found. Your house is blessed."

"I am a member of the smallest tribe and my family is unimportant even in our tribe, why are you so gracious to me?"

[1] Very familiar   [2] Ephraim   [3] Shalim   [4] Zuph

135

Samuel then took Saul to dinner and had thirty guests, all key men in the city. It was a special meal, and Samuel said it was particularly in honor of Saul, and Saul ate one whole shoulder of beef to show his appreciation.

Samuel and Saul continued in friendly conversation the next day, and then as time for leaving came Samuel told Saul to send his servant on ahead as he wished to remain in private with Saul and to pass on to him the word of the Lord.

Then Samuel took ceremonial oil and put it on Saul's head and said, "In the name of the Lord, I annoint you to be the head man over all the Lord's people. As a sign that I know what I'm doing, when you leave here you will find two men by the cemetery near Adamsville[1] and they will say to you that the donkeys have returned home and that your father is now worrying about you. From Adamsville you will go on to Glen Rose[2] and there you will meet three men who will give you a couple of loaves of bread for food, and from there you shall go to a place where there is a revival being held, and the spirit of the Lord will descend upon you at that place and you will become converted and be a new man. When these things occur you will then know that God is with you. Then in a week or so I'll come to you and tell you what to do next."

Everything occurred exactly as Samuel had said, and Saul had a new attitude develop within him, and Saul himself prophesied and spoke forth for God and the people wondered saying, "Is this not the son of that fellow who is the big blacksmith? Has he suddenly become a prophet?" The people talked much about this man Saul and the new circumstances surrounding him.

Upon arriving near his home Saul met his Uncle Ned who said, "Where in the devil have you and your servant been all this time?"

"Well, we went after donkeys," said Saul, "but we couldn't find them. Then we ran into a fellow named Samuel."

"What did Samuel say to you?" asked Uncle Ned.

"He said that the donkeys were found," replied Saul, but he did not tell him the rest of the story.

Samuel then called the people together again at Montreat and said, "In God's name, I remind you that I brought you from Egypt and I have delivered you often, yet in my place you want a king, now therefore present yourselves in the Lord's meeting place here, representatives from all the tribes and I will show you your king."

When all the tribes were gathered, Samuel said, "Where is Saul?"

When they looked for him, they couldn't find him, for he was embarrassed and had hid himself. It wasn't long, however, before they found him, and when he came where the people were it was

[1]Zelzah   [2]Tabor

136

seen that he was a head taller than anyone there.

Then Samuel said, "This is the man the Lord has chosen. Have you ever seen a finer looking fellow?"

And the people shouted, "God save the King."

Samuel then recorded the meeting, and made the selection of the king official.

Saul went home and with him went a bunch of men who were moved of God to join him. The anti-godly element were not pleased and booed him, but Saul held his peace.

Chap.
11

Then a man named Fisty, head of the old Bass Gang,[1] encamped with his raiding party type of army outside of Louisville[2] and threatened the city. Fisty sent a messenger into the city to say that unless every fighting man in the city would let his men blind each one of them in the right eye, Fisty and his raiders would capture the city and kill every man, woman and child.

The city council asked for seven days to think the matter through and appoint committees. Immediately, however, they sent a messenger in secret to Saul and told him of the situation and begged for help, and all the people that heard of this were horrified.

Now when Saul heard of this terrible threat the spirit of the Lord came upon him and he took a yoke of oxen and killed them, and sent a piece of oxen to all the villages, and down all the coast of Israel with the message that any man who failed to report immediately for duty in Saul's army would have his own oxen fixed as the sample indicated.

The fear of the Lord then fell upon the people[3] and then all came to the summons of Saul and he assembled thereby a tremendous army and Saul sent word to Louisville that help would arrive by noon the next day.

So the men of Louisville sent word to Fisty that the next afternoon they would start sending their men out to get their right eyes removed.

Saul divided his gigantic army into three sections and before noon the next day they poured down on the Bass Gang and defeated them easily and scattered the remnants so that no two of the gang left together.

Then the people shouted in gratitude to Saul and they said, "Where are those crummy characters that voted against Saul for king, let's find each one and hang him."[4]

Saul, however, said, "There shall be no man put to death for my sake, for this victory is the Lord's doing."

Samuel then called for a convocation, declared an official assemblage, directed a worship service to the Lord, and crowned Saul

[1] Nahash the Ammonite
[2] Jabesh-gilead
[3] Also the fear of losing oxen
[4] Vietnam type of election

With all the great crowd present and the representatives from all the tribes assembled Samuel decided to make a declaration and he spoke to the entire nation saying, "I am getting old and my days are numbered. I want you to stand here as witnesses for me before God and before the new king. Have I ever stolen an ox? Have I ever defrauded anyone? Have I ever taken a bribe or given false information? If I have ever done such to anyone let him step forward and I will repay him."

The people said, "You have never done any of those things."

"You then," said Samuel, "and the new king are my witnesses to God."

"Let me remind, though," continued Samuel, "that it is the Lord who is the deliverer. It is the Lord God of Israel who instructed Moses and Aaron, who punished Israel when the people strayed from the worship of the true God, and then the people repented and the Lord raised up leaders to save the people in God's name. Yet you very people here insisted on an earthly king, when the Lord was willing to be your king.

Now you have a king. The Lord has agreed to the arrangement. Be careful though, for you must serve God and obey his voice and adhere to his commandments, you and your king both or the hand of the Lord will turn against you as surely as he did against any of the previous generations that deserted him."

Samuel let this soak in a bit and then he said, "As a sign that the Lord means business and that he deals in the affairs of man as a living God, I will now call upon God to declare his power in your presence and bring a mighty storm, which will reveal the displeasure of God at your decisions and warn you of his power."

The Lord then sent a mighty storm with roaring thunder and the people were terrified. The people then cried to Samuel and said, "Pray for us, for we know now we have sinned."

Samuel said, "Take it easy. Calm down. You have sinned, yet if you will surrender your lives to God and serve him the Lord will not forsake you. You must turn aside, however, from your greedy pursuit of profit. As for me, I will continue to pray for you and I will continue to teach you the difference between right and wrong as long as I live; so stand in awe of the Lord, serve him with all your heart, be grateful for his goodness to you and all is well, but if you continue to do wickedly you've had it!"

After Saul had been king for about three years he decided that it was time to give some of the army a workout and to become a bit active so he selected three thousand men, took two thousand under his command and one thousand under the command of his son,

Jonathan. The idea was to march against the Fascists who were beginning to stir up a little border trouble again.

Jonathan took his thousand men and attacked a small fort held by the Fascists and won a great victory. Saul had this news spread all over Israel; so that the people felt proud of their victorious nation. Then the Fascists became alarmed over this and gathered an army of 30,000 or more and came in force to the outskirts of Yorktown[1] where the people of Israel could see their numbers. Meanwhile Saul was at Province[2], waiting for Samuel and a little advice.

Samuel did not appear in seven days; so Saul began to worship God on his own, then Samuel came.

Saul said, "I was afraid to wait for you to conduct the services, for fear that the Fascists would get here before you did and God would not be on our side."

"You messed things up, Saul," said Samuel. "You should have not started this in the first place with that silly raid on Fort Sumter."[3]

"In fact", Samuel continued, "the Lord will no doubt want to replace you before long." After saying this Samuel went away mad.

Now Saul had with him about 600 men, for most of the Hebrews had sought hiding places in caves, and on the hills, and many had crossed the Jordan.

Another problem among the Hebrews was that for years the Fascists had been doing all the weapon making and there was no blacksmith in Israel to forge swords. The Fascists had control then of most of the weapons and they divided themselves into three large companies and planned to make raids on cities and subdue the Hebrews and take away captives and spoils. The situation looked very bad.

Chap.
14

Now Jonathan decided that he could take what men he could find and slip up on another unwary fort of the Fascists and have another victory, and raise the morale of the dispirited Hebrews. Since he doubted if his father the king would approve, he went without permission. Jonathan decided to cross the river and attack a garrison that he knew would not be expecting any trouble.

Saul in the meantime was sitting under a tree with about 600 men, all that he had left, and they were bemoaning their fate and pondering the situation.

Jonathan proceeded with his plan and came to the narrow pass between the hills that led down to the garrison. At this point Jonathan said to his gun-bearer, "We will present ourselves suddenly in front of the garrison. It is possible that the Lord will work for us, for numbers make no difference to the Lord, and he can give us victory with a few men as easily as with many."

[1]Michmash   [2]Gilgal   [3]Geba

Jonathan then said, "We will first suddenly appear in front of the garrison and show ourselves. If they seeing us say to us 'stay where you are. Do not come a step nearer,' then we will get the heck out of there, but if they say 'come on into the garrison' we will know the Lord is going to deliver us and this will be the sign that we are to be victorious."

When Jonathan and his men appeared before the Fascists they said, "Look at the Hebrews, for they have crawled out of their caves for a look at the world."

Then the leader of the Fascists called out and said, "Come on into our garrison and we will show you a thing or two."

Jonathan then yelled "charge" and he and his gun bearer between them killed about twenty men who could not run well because of the plowed ground in front of the garrison. Then the Lord shook the earth with an earthquake, and the Fascists pushed the panic button and the sky was darkened and the Fascists began to kill each other by mistake and there was great bedlam and great slaughter.

Meanwhile, back at the ranch, Saul said, "Let's call the roll and see who we have left." After roll call it was learned that Jonathan and a few others were missing.

Saul then took his 600 men and went to the place of the noise and saw the panic and set himself and his men on the Fascists.

It also happened that a lot of the Hebrews had joined the Fascists a few weeks before, figuring that there was no chance to win and if you can't lick 'em join 'em. These people now, sensing the victory of Saul and his men, also turned against the Fascists, and one of history's most mixed up battles of all time took place.

To add to this another little human touch, the Hebrews who were still hiding in caves and in some of the ladies' restrooms all began to come forth and suddenly join in pursuing the hapless and terrified Fascists. The Lord had again delivered Israel.

There was no celebration, however, as Saul posted a notice saying that no one was to eat anything at all for a whole day, but to continue pursuing the Fascists without even a coffee break.[1] The people didn't like this order.

As a bunch of the men were chasing the Fascists through the woods they passed a place where honey was dripping from a honeycomb. None of the men touched it because of Saul's order, but Jonathan had been so busy all day with his sword that he had not heard the order or seen the bulletin board. Jonathan then took the end of the club he carried in his left hand and dipped it in the honey and ate some and felt better.

One of the soldiers then came to him and said, "That is a no-no. King Saul has pronounced a curse on eating today."

"Well, the king made a big blunder. I already feel stronger and

_____
[1] They did not know about protest marches.

ready to kill more Fascists while you men are fainting and hungry. We could all do better on a full stomach."

The people, however, continued their pursuing of the Fascists without food, as they feared to disobey the king. Finally, however, the people became so hungry they began to kill sheep and oxen and eat the meat raw, for they were perishing of hunger and there was no barbecue pit handy.

Saul was informed of this and took a stone and marked the place so he would remember to make a judgment on their error. Then Saul said, "Let everybody bring meat here and we will cook it and we will eat heartily and properly." Then Saul erected an altar on the spot, as an acknowledgment of the goodness of the Lord.

Saul then thought that it might be a good idea to attack another wing of the Fascist army during the night and so he went with the priest to ask the Lord about this, but there was no reply.

Saul then decided that there had been some instances of sin or disobedience, else the Lord would have replied.

Then Saul spoke to the people and said, "Who has sinned? Let him confess, and even if it be my beloved son Jonathan, the sinner must die."

There was no comment. Saul then said, "We will let God decide where the sin lies. Jonathan and I will be on one side and the people on the other. I will toss a coin, heads you people have sinned, tails, Jonathan or I have sinned." Saul tossed the coin and it came up tails.

Saul then said, "It is between me and my son; so I will toss again, heads I am the sinner, tails, it is Jonathan." The coin came up tails.

Saul then said, "Jonathan, what is it that you have done?"

"All I did was eat a little honey," said Jonathan, "as I didn't know about that silly rule you passed."

"I cannot go back on my word," said Saul, "you must be executed."

The people then put up a big howl. Their spokesman said, "Are you going to execute the man responsible for saving Israel? You must have blown your mind. We the people all agree that he is innocent of wrong and not one hair on his head will you disturb, for he has worked with the Lord our God today and brought us deliverance. Don't you dare touch him."

"All right", said Saul, "since you put it that way."

Saul continued to be king in Israel and was constantly leading selected and trained men against various gangs that would harass the borders of Israel.

The Fascists were still the main enemies who caused most of the trouble. Saul had acquired a family somehow in the middle of all the little wars and raids and he had two sons and two daughters, the youngest, a girl named Greta[1] was truly stunning.

[1]Michal

141

When Saul would see any strong looking, healthy appearing young man he immediately drafted him into his army for all the time that Saul lived there was war of some sort with the Fascists.

Samuel then came to Saul and said, "Now you remember that I am the one the Lord sent to make you king so I want you to listen to me for I have a word for you from God. The Lord still remembers the Capone gang[1] and all the trouble they caused. This type of gang reorganizes and acts violently and for evil and the Lord is ready to crack down on them again. You are to do it."

"In fact," continued Samuel, "the Lord wants you to go to their area headquarters and destroy, the Lord wants all their possessions destroyed, you are to kill the women, children, donkeys, sheep and cattle."

As a result Saul gathered together over 200,000 armed men and approached Oklahoma City[2] and pitched his camp outside the city limits. Then Saul sent word into Chicago for all the good people and the worshippers of the true God to leave the city as he was going to tear it down and destroy it. Saul also suggested that the Shriners[3] leave the city as they had always been kind to the Israelites.

As soon as those who wished had withdrawn, Saul marched on Chicago with his tremendous army, and destroyed the people with the sword, but the mayor[4] he saved alive. Saul and the people also kept for themselves the best of the cattle and sheep, and they pocketed the jewelry, as well as many of the sporting goods of Abercrombie and Fitch.

Then the word of the Lord came to Samuel imdicating that the Lord was unhappy with the king situation again for Saul had not carried out the instructions that Samuel had relayed to the king.

Samuel was grieved over the matter and prayed earnestly about it. In the morning Samuel arose early and went to call on Saul, but the palace people gave him the runaround, saying Saul had gone to golf at Carmel and that he was going down to Province[5] to fish.

Samuel took out after him and when he found him Saul immediately said to Samuel, "Blessings on thee. I have performed as you told me to do."

Now Samuel was no stoop by a long shot and he said, "Why is it that I hear the cattle mooing in the stockyards of Chicago?"

"The people spared them," said Saul, "to offer as a sacrifice to God and to bring to the church."

"A likely story," said Samuel.

"Now you listen to me, Saul, for the Lord has spoken to me," continued Samuel.

"Speak your piece, Samuel," said the king.

[1]The Amaleks   [2]City of Amalek   [3]Kenites
          [4]Agag   [5]Gilgal

"Do you remember that when you were a nobody even in your own sight, the Lord anointed you instant king of Israel? Now that same God told you to destroy Chicago and all that was in it and you didn't do it."

"Now, Samuel," said Saul, "I obeyed God. I have the mayor in jail. I destroyed the city, but the people are the ones who kept the spoil and they say its for the church."

"Now, Saul, do you think the Lord has as great a delight in burnt offering as in obedience? To obey is better than to sacrifice. You can't buy off the Lord with the Sunday morning offering. For rebellion is a sin, and stubborness is iniquity. Because you, therefore, have rejected the word of God, God is going to reject you as king."

Then Saul said to Samuel, "You are right. I have sinned. I have disobeyed the command of God for fear of the protest marchers among the people. Pardon my sin. Let me again worship with you before God."

Samuel said, "I will not return to you. You rejected the word of God and God rejects you."

As Samuel turned to leave, Saul reached out to hold him by his cloak and the cloak tore and Samuel said, "This is a sign that the Lord is going to take away your kingdom and give it to another fellow, who is better than you are. Remember, God makes no mistakes, so he will not repent in your case."

"I have sinned, Samuel. I truly repent. At least let me worship God with you and stand with me before the altar in the presence of the people."

Samuel agreed and together in the presence of the people they worshipped God.

Then Samuel said, "Bring to me the mayor of Chicago."

The mayor came and approached Samuel very humbly saying, "Surely we've had enough bitterness, let us bury the hatchet and be friends."

"Your gang activities and your meaness and your contracts on people's lives have made many mothers childless, and so shall your mother be," said Samuel. Samuel then picked up a machete knife and cut the mayor into several districts.

Then Samuel went to Richmond[1] to be near the seminary there and Saul returned to Mount Vernon[2], and Samuel came no more to visit Saul. Nevertheless, Samuel grieved over this as he was greatly fond of Saul. The Lord, who never likes for his servants to be unhappy, regretted that Saul had ever been made king, as God knew all along how this would work into trouble for Israel and for Samuel.

Chap.
16

Then the Lord spoke to Samuel and said, "How long will you mourn for Saul? You need to do something beside sitting around and

[1]Ramah   [2]Gibeah

143

grieving about your playmate. Take the anointing oil and go to Bethlehem and visit Jesse, for I will let you select a new king and a new interest from among the sons of Jesse."

"How can I go, Lord?" said Samuel, "for if my good friend Saul hears of this, it will be called treason and I'll be killed."

"Come, come, Samuel, you know I am with you. Take your liturgical equipment for a service and appear before Jesse and then I'll tell you what to do, and I will reveal to you the one to be anointed."

Samuel did as the Lord said. When Samuel came into the city the town council members were troubled, for Samuel had a reputation for being tough on mayors and the like.

"Do you come peaceably?" they asked.

"Yes, I come peaceably. I come to conduct a service. All of you prepare yourselves to attend and I want to be sure that Jesse and his sons are present."

When the occasion came about, Samuel began to interview the sons of Jesse. The first one was Cary[1] and Samuel thought surely this handsome and talented man was the one, but the Lord said, "Not Cary."

Then the Lord said to Samuel, "Do not judge by his looks, or his weight, or his heighth, for the Lord looks to the inside of a man, to his heart, while man judges by outward appearances."

Then came Henry[2], and the Lord said, "Next". Then came Glenn[3], John, George and on until all seven sons had been interviewed, and all rejected as the new king.

Samuel said to Jesse, "Is that the works?"

"Yes," said Jesse, "except for a teen-ager that I left looking out for the sheep."

"Send for him," said Samuel.

When he came Samuel observed that he was sunburned and handsome and intelligent looking, even for a teen-ager.

The Lord moved within Samuel and Samuel said, "This is the one."

The boy's name was David and he was anointed that day and the spirit of the Lord began to grow within him from that hour.

Samuel went back to Richmond, and Jesse and his sons and the town council all went back to their normal life.[4]

Now the spirit of the Lord left Saul the king and he was depressed and no one could cheer him.

One of the servants suggested that what Saul needed was a little soul music that would make him feel better.

Saul said, "I'll try anything. Bring me a man who can play well and who will lift my spirits."

[1]Eliab   [2]Abinadad   [3]Shammah
[4]They probably thought Samuel was senile and a bit off his rocker.

One of the servants said, "There is a young man in Bethlehem who plays a guitar and sings folk songs. He is a handsome lad and the people gather every Saturday night to hear him play."

"Go get him," said Saul.

As a result messengers were sent to Jesse and he was told to let them bring his son David to the king as a folk singer. David came and appeared before Saul and Saul was pleased with him and put him on the payroll at once.

Saul sent a message to Jesse saying that David pleased him and he was keeping him at Mount Vernon.

When Saul became depressed David took his guitar and sang soul music to him and brightened his spirits.

Chap.
17

The Fascists began to activate themselves again for they were always seeking to overcome people and take in new territory. As a result they gathered their army together on Beverly Hill[1] and Israel gathered their army together on an opposite hill, with a valley between the two armies.

There appeared one morning in the valley a Fascist named Goliath, who was truly a giant, about 6 foot 5 weighing around 280, and he was the biggest, strongest man anyone had ever seen in that day. Goliath also had arrayed himself with a big football helmet, shoulder pads, and complete armor, plus carrying a mighty sword. To top it all, he carried a spear that most men could not even lift.

Goliath then shouted a proposal to the army of Israel saying, "Why should we have a big battle and get a lot of people killed, not to mention all the expense, when we could settle the whole matter with two men? You send out your best fighting man and I will fight him. If your man wins, all the Fascists will be your servants and we'll be the satellite nation. I defy you this day and challenge any man. I can lick anybody in the place."

When Saul and all the Israelites heard these words and saw the giant, they were terrified.

Now some of David's brothers were in the army of Israel, but David was back at the ranch tending to the sheep.

Goliath came forth with his same thundering little speech every morning for forty days, and it was wearing on the nerves of the men of Israel as well as Saul.[2]

Jesse, David's father, talked to David at supper one night and said, "Tomorrow I want you to go to the Beverly Hills area and find out what is going on, how your brothers are doing, and what gives with the war. Your mother will send some chocolate chip cookies and some homemade bread."

David arose early in the morning and went to the Beverly Hills area and saw that the armies were preparing for battle. When David

[1]Shochoh   [2]Particularly on Saul who was the biggest man Israel had

145

had reached the camp and delivered the box from home, he saw the giant Goliath come forth and he heard him issue the challenge as usual. David also observed that all the men around the camp were afraid.

David then said, "What reward has the king offered to the man who will defeat this big slob that defies Israel?"

"The king will bestow on him great riches, shall give him the king's best looking daughter for a wife, and make the man's family tax exempt."

David's oldest brother didn't like David's asking questions and embarrassing the soldiers and he said, "Why don't you go home and tend to the sheep? You're just down here to see the battle and make fun of us."

"What is eating all of you?" said David. "Is there not here a worthy cause?"

Now this conversation was passed along the grapevine to Saul and so he sent for David.

David then spoke to Saul and said, "You can tell the army boys not to be so up tight. I will go and fight the big Fascist."

"You don't have a chance," said Saul, "for you are young and inexperienced, and Goliath is a veteran and twice your size."

Then David said, "Well, when I was keeping my father's sheep there came a lion and a bear and each one raided our flock; so I went after them and killed them, both the lion and the bear. As far as I am concerned, this big gorilla is just like one of them."

"On top of that," said David, "I am confident that the Lord who delivered me from the paw of the lion and the paw of the bear, will certainly deliver me from the heathen with the big mouth."

Saul then ordered that his own personal armor be brought and put upon David. The outfit was so big and heavy that David couldn't move or even see out of it; so he took off the armor.

David decided to go with his own familiar weapons; so he took his shepherd's staff and his sling, and went then to the brook and selected five smooth stones and he went forth to meet the big Fascist.

The Fascist and his shield carrier stepped forth to meet David. When Goliath saw David he scoffed and became enraged saying, "It is an insult. Am I a puppy dog that you send a young boy to fetch?" Then Goliath began to curse something awful.[1]

"If you will step a little nearer, boy," said Goliath, "I will cut you in pieces and feed you to the birds."

David then said calmly, "You come to me with a spear, and a sword, and a shield, but I come to you in the name of the Lord God of hosts, and this day the Lord will deliver you into my hands, and I will remove your head and leave it on the ground for the jackals in order that all men may know that there is a God in Israel.

[1]Most of you can fill in your own words

146

Furthermore, this whole assemblage shall know that the Lord saves not with the sword and the spear, for the decisions of battles are the Lord's, and he will deliver you today into our hands."

At this point, Goliath began to advance on David; so David took a stone and put it in his sling and began to twirl it around his head and when Goliath was in easy range David snapped the sling free and sent the stone with deadly accuracy right between the eyes of the Fascist and the stone sunk into his forehead and it knocked him out cold.

Since Goliath had an extremely hard head, he was only cool cocked; so David took Goliath's sword and cut off his head while he was out cold, and this ended the engagement.

When the Fascists saw this, they were terrified and ran and the men of Israel came to life and chased them to secure servants or kill those who would not surrender.

David took the head of Goliath to a taxidermist in Jerusalem and then kept Goliath's armour as another souvenir.

When Saul saw David go against the giant he asked his aide saying, "Whose boy is that?"

"I really don't know," said Bouncer.[1]

As a result, when David returned Saul asked him saying, "Who is your father?"

"He is Jesse, a loyal supporter of yours from Bethlehem."

Now Jonathan had been around while all of this was going on and he became devoted to David, and David enjoyed Jonathan and the two became great and inseparable friends.

Jonathan and David exchanged gifts and made a pact of friendship with each other, and became blood brothers.[2]

David stayed with Saul and behaved wisely. Saul made him a captain in the army and David became very popular with the people as well as with the soldiers.

After the big victory over the Fascists, it was decided to have a big parade in celebration. The women came out in great numbers for the parade[3] and they sang, and danced, and rattled a lot of various noisemakers. The women had also come up with a folk song that they began to sing loudly, the main words of which were, "Saul has slain his thousands, but David has slain tens of thousands."[4]

Now this song went over like a lead balloon with Saul and he began to fret about David. Saul reasoned that David had everything but the kingdom as it was.

As a result, Saul got into one of his depressive spells and so David came with his guitar and played soft music to comfort him.

Apparently David played the wrong song, for Saul picked up a javelin and threw at David twice. David decided he wasn't wanted at

[1]Abner   [2]Indian style   [3]The men were all in the parade
[4]Women still go for the younger men. Too bad, but true.

the time, but Saul was afraid of David for the Lord was with David and was not with Saul.

Saul then promoted David to Colonel and sent him to operate in a different area, and David continued to behave wisely and the Lord was with him.

The people loved David, for he was around them a great deal, and he dealt wisely and fairly with the people.

Saul then said to David, "My oldest daughter [1] I will give you as a wife if you will go forth again and fight the Fascists for me and the Lord."

Now Saul's reasoning was that David was so brave that he would get himself killed.

David said to Saul, however, "Who am I to be the son-in-law of the king. I come from an insignificant family."[2]

In the meantime, an aide to Saul known as Sly Knox, [3] talked Saul into letting him marry Phyllis.[4]

In the meantime, Greta,[5] had fallen for David and the word of this pleased Saul, because he knew his youngest daughter was cute, but also a trouble maker, and Saul had a devious plan to boot.

As a result, Saul sent word to David that he would be honored to have him as his son-in-law, that Saul now was fond of David.

When the servants brought this word David again said, "I am a poor man and I have no dowry or gift to bring such a prize as the king's daughter."

The servants of Saul reported this and Saul sent them back to David saying that the king did not need a dowry of money, but so David would feel that he was bringing something, let him go and bring back an inch of skin off the private parts of 100 Fascists[6]. This pleased David greatly, as he was young and a bit on the warrior side of things.

As a result, David assembled a part of the men under his command and then went out looking for Fascists. Since the operation could be performed more easily on a dead Fascist than a live one, David and his men killed 200 Fascists and brought a double measure of skin to Saul.

Saul realized for sure then that the Lord was with David and that Greta truly loved David, and Saul became all the more afraid of David and his influence.

The Fascists instituted a revenge raid because of what had happened to the 200 of their number and David took his men and handled this situation wisely and merely added to his great prestige.

Saul became increasingly disturbed about the growing popularity

[1]Not the good looking one   [2]David had seen the eldest daughter
[3]Adriel   [4]Merab, the eldest daughter   [5]Michal
[6]Tricky, tricky-Saul thought this would get David killed for sure.

of David and so he spoke to Jonathan and all the soldiers around the palace telling them that David had to be killed.

Jonathan did not go for this and he secretly told David that there was a contract out on him and the hit men were going to look for him the next day and Jonathan suggested that David make himself hard to find.

Jonathan also told David that he would try to change his father's mind.

Jonathan spoke to his father the king and said, "Why pick on David? He's never done anything to you but good things. Didn't David put his life on the line against the Fascists, and through David the Lord delivered Israel. Why should you sin and have an innocent man killed?"

Saul listened to this reasonable approach from Jonathan and cancelled the contract to kill David. Jonathan then brought David into Saul's presence and they were friendly as in earlier times.

The Fascists shortly started a war again and Saul sent David to handle the situation and David had great success and returned home again as a conqueror.

Naturally, Saul turned sour again, and so when David started playing the guitar for Saul, Saul picked up a javelin and threw it at him[1]; so David ducked and left the area.

Saul then sent a few of his killers to watch David's house and to kill him when he came out the next morning. Greta, David's wife, who kept her ear to the ground all the time, told David of this, and suggested that he slip out during the night; so she tied some sheets together and let David out the second story window in the night and he escaped.

Greta then fixed a dummy in the bed and when the messengers from Saul came in the morning and asked for David she said that he was sick in bed.

When the messengers reported this, Saul said that they should go and bring him bed and all and then Saul himself could kill David.

When the messengers came and got the bed they soon realized that there was only a dummy in the bed.

Saul then brought Greta to task and asked her why she helped David escape when David was an enemy of her father.

Greta said, "I had to help him as he threatened to kill me if I didn't." This got Greta off the hook, though it didn't help David.

Word came later to Saul that David had been seen around Mo-Ranch[2] and so he sent a squad of killers to find him there and kill him. When the killers arrived Samuel was conducting a revival meeting and the killers attended looking for David, but became converted and joined the church. Saul sent three different groups on this errand and all of them were converted.

Finally Saul decided to go himself and when he got as far as Black

---

[1] And it wasn't even an electric guitar   [2] Ramah

Mountain[1] he asked saying, "Where are David and Samuel?"

The filling station attendant said, "They are at the Assembly Inn in Mo-Ranch."[2]

As Saul approached the spirit of the Lord again fell upon him and he began to testify as a witness for God. This amazed the people and they wondered if Saul was turning into a prophet.

Saul's conversion was pretty temporary, however, and only furnished time for David to get away. David went to Jonathan and said, "What gives with all this jazz of killing me? What have I done?"

"I don't know," said Jonathan, "but the old man always consults me on everything, great or small, and I don't think he is trying to kill you."

"You're wrong there, buddy," said David. "I think your father knows of our close friendship and he has not told you what he is doing as he doesn't want to upset you. I'm not kidding, for I'm real close to getting killed."

"Tell me what to do," said Jonathan, "and I'll help anyway I can."

"Well," said David, "tomorrow is the new moon and that's my regular time to play for Saul at dinner. Let me hide in the field outside the palace for 3 days and let's see if Saul misses me playing. If Saul asks for me, tell him I had to go home to Bethlehem to put a rose on my mother's grave. If he accepts this excuse and gives his blessing that's fine, but if he gets furious then I'll know he is still after me. If I am in the wrong, Jon, and have done something worthy of death, then you kill me, but don't turn me in to the king."

"Don't you worry. I'll tell you exactly how things are."

"How will I be able to get the information?" asked David.

Jonathan said, "Let's go out near where you will be hiding and mark a place. After I have sounded out my father and determined his mood then I will send word to you to come to the palace or to flee, as the case may be."

The two young men then made another arrangement between them, obligating themselves to always look out for each other and for each other's family, with the Lord as a witness to the agreement.

Jonathan then told David, "I will send word on the third day by signal. I will come to the field as if to practice with my bow and arrow. I will shoot three arrows and in the direction of the rock we marked, and if I yell to the boy retrieving that the arrows are on this side, then come with me to the palace, but if I say the arrows are away from you, flee, and the Lord always be a witness and a common cause between you and me."

David hid in the field when the new moon came and Saul sat down to dinner. David's accustomed place was empty, but there was no

[1]Sechu   [2]Naioth in Ramah

mention made of it.

On the second day, however, Saul said to Jonathan, "Where is the son of Jesse, for he wasn't here yesterday and is not here today?"

Jonathan said, "David asked permission of me to go to Bethlehem to put a rose on his mother's grave."

Saul then blew his top at Jonathan, and bellowed, "You son of a mean and rebellious woman, don't I know that you are a close friend of David? I tell you this, as long as David lives, you shall not be settled and you will not inherit the kingdom. Now go and find him and bring him here to me, for I want to execute him."

Jonathan then said, "What has he done to deserve death?"

Then Saul tossed a javelin at Jonathan,[1] which left him under the impression that all was not well at home.

Jonathan was greatly disturbed over his father's actions and words and he grieved greatly over the matter.

The next day Jonathan went out to the field with his boy retriever as if to practice with the bow and arrow.

As the lad started out in the field Jonathan shot 3 arrows well beyond him and called to him saying, "The arrows are well beyond you. Hurry, get them, and run back here." The boy did as he was told.

Jonathan then gave his bow and arrows to the boy and said, "Take them back to the house."

As soon as the boy was gone, David came out of hiding and he and Jonathan had a reunion, with tears.[2] Then the two shook hands and wished each other well. Jonathan returned to the city while David fled to the hills.

Chap.
21

David was without food and he had no weapons with him; so he went to the church in Jerusalem and asked the minister for some bread. The minister knew something was wrong and he could not understand why this prominent man was by himself, and without food, and was asking for supplies.

The priest said that it so happened at that moment that there was no bread available for travelers and that all that was on hand was the communion bread. David then talked the minister into giving him five loaves of bread.

Then David said, "Are there any weapons around somewhere in the basement or a closet?"

"The only weapon in the place is the sword of Goliath, which you brought to the church as a souvenir."

"That is fine," said David, "give it to me as it is a real good weapon and I need one badly."

David then fled from Jerusalem for he knew that the soldiers of the king would be searching for him.

[1]Saul was not too good with the javelin [2]Men used to cry in those days

David figured he might be safe in another county so he went to an area controlled by Milton,[1] who thought of himself as a king.

The associates of Milton told him that they thought the stranger who had arrived was David, the great warrior about whom the number one song was centered, entitled, "Saul has killed his thousands, but David his tens of thousands."

As a result, there developed suspicion about David and what he was doing in Milton's country; so Milton had a tail put on him.

David discovered this and decided that he would pretend to be nutty; so he started writing crazy messages in the rest rooms, carving on trees, and drooling at the mouth.

Milton then decided that David had lost his marbles and he began to gripe at his aides for letting David hang around the area.

As a result, David decided to depart before they put the hounds on him and he fled to Carlsbad Caverns[2] and began to make himself at home there.

As word of this began to spread in the area every man that was too deep in debt, or was having trouble with his wives, or was in some distress, began to come to the cave to join David, until he had a band of 400 men, all discontented.[3]

David then went privately to the Governor of Mississippi[4] and asked him to take care of his father and mother, as he was afraid Saul might use them for vengeance. David said that he would not forget his kindness.

One day a prophet of the Lord came by Carlsbad and told David that the Lord thought David should go to the area where the tribe of Judah lived. David did this, and arrived in the area known as the Black Forest[5] with his strange band of men.

Saul began to hear through the grapevine that David had been seen in a place or two and Saul was also having one of his depressive and self-pity moods.

Saul then sat under a tree with a large number of his soldiers around him. Saul was holding his inaccurate javelin in his hand, and Saul said, "Why do all of you favor David? Can he give you vineyards, or bestow government property on you, can he promote you and get salary raises for you? Yet none of you seem to sympathize with me or feel sorry for me. You never even told me about the agreement that Jonathan had with David. I am greatly disappointed in all of you."

"You are wrong, King Saul," said Fast Buck Otto,[6] "for I was just about to tell you something that I learned. It was just relayed to me that David went to the priest in Jerusalem, Father Peel,[7] and the priest gave him bread and the sword of Goliath."

[1]Achish   [2]Adullam   [3]A real leadership challenge
[4]Moab   [5]Hareth   [6]Doeg   [7]Ahimelech

"Send for Peel at once," said Saul, "and get his family along with him, and assistants."

When Peel arrived Saul said to him, "Why have you plotted against me, to feed and arm my enemy David, and you've probably arranged an ambush."

Then Peel said, "You aren't thinking very clearly. David is the most loyal of all your subjects. As far as I know, David is your son-in-law, free to come and go in the king's house, how in the world could I think that he was your enemy? I am absolutely innocent."

"I don't believe a word you say, and you and your family shall be executed."

The king then turned to some of the soldiers standing near him and said to them, "Kill Peel and the assistant ministers as well as Peel's family."

The soldiers, however, would not kill a priest of the Lord. Then Saul turned to Fast Buck Otto and asked him to kill them. As a result Fast Buck killed the priests that were present and then went into town and killed everyone he found with a reversed collar.

One of the local ministers managed to get out of town and went to the Black Forest and told David all that had happened.

David said, "I was afraid of something like this, because ole Fast Buck was at the church when Peel supplied me with food and Goliath's sword. Well, at least you might as well join me, as you'll be missed in Jerusalem and Saul will put you on the same wanted list on which I am."

Chap.
23

Word then came to David that a band of Fascists had been raiding the barns and warehouses around Junction.[1] David then prayed to the Lord and asked if he should take his more or less dirty dozen and go and fight the Fascists and save Junction. The Lord encouraged David to go.

When David announced his idea to his band of discontents, however, they were not happy as they reasoned that they were in enough danger living in Judah in fear of their own people without getting in trouble with the Fascists.

David prayed again, but the Lord encouraged David to make the effort and promised victory to David.

David persuaded his men to go with him and they fought the Fascists gang and defeated them, and in the process captured a lot of cattle, as well as saving the people of Junction.

Word of all of this came to Saul and he also learned that David and his men had moved into Junction and were living in the town. As a result, Saul was elated, for he figured that he could take a large army and surround the town and then demand that the people of Junction turn over David and his men to the king, or else Saul would wipe out

[1] Keilah

the whole community.

David, of course, heard of this through his wiretapping connections[1] and he sent for the priest and the two of them worshipped God and prayed together for advice. The Lord revealed to David that his information was accurate and also that the Junction people would turn against David and his men to save their hides.[2]

David then called together his band of men which had now increased to 600[3] and suggested that everybody leave town as fast as he could and it was an everyman for himself escape project.

David took to the hills and hid himself in the Blue Ridge Mountains[4] while Saul searched for him every day.

Jonathan was with the search party, which actually was almost an army but scattered about in patrol groups. Jonathan located David and encouraged him. Jonathan told David that he would help keep Saul from finding him and that one day he knew that David would be king, and Jonathan his chief assistant. They shook on this.

Then some of the Hatfields[5] who thought David had some Coy blood in him, came to Saul and told Saul where David was hiding. They suggested that Saul come with them and Saul thanked them heartily.

Saul then said, "Go and get a scouting report on him. Find out how he gets his food, who visits him, and then come and tell me and I'll take over from there."

David, needless to say, got word of all of this and he began to shift his hiding places. David had assembled again a band of discontents and this made hiding even more difficult. In fact, it became impossible, and finally Saul and his men had David and his men trapped on a hill.

At this very moment a messenger came to Saul saying that the Fascists had decided to take advantage of Saul's big chase deal and they had invaded the homeland and Saul, therefore, had to rush his army home at once.

David and his men, therefore, escaped, and they moved away to the area of Fort Knox,[6] a better stronghold.

Chap.
24

After Saul had handled the matter of the Fascists he took 3 thousand selected warriors and started out again for David, having already learned that he had taken refuge in Fort Knox.

It so happened that in camping and in choosing cubby holes and caves for spending the night, that Saul went into the very cave that David was in, though David was well hidden in the back with a few of his men. After Saul went to sleep, David slipped up to him and cut a part of his robe and returned to his men, telling them that he could

---

[1]Not as sophisticated as ours today.   [2]Think a little before criticizing Junction for this.   [3]Inflation and victory had helped.   [4]Ziph   [5]Ziphites
[6]Engedi

not kill his own king, who was the Lord's anointed, and he also restrained his men from doing this.[1]

The next morning Saul arose and left the cave and when he was a couple of hundred yards away David called to him and said, "Good morning, Saul, my king." David then bowed down to the king.

Then David said to Saul, "How did anyone convince you that I sought to ever hurt or harm you? Look, here is proof of my feeling toward you. While you were asleep my men thought I should kill you, but I assured them that I would not raise my hand against the Lord's anointed. Take a good look. Here is part of your robe which I cut off. I could have killed easily. There is no evil intent or malice in me toward you. The Lord can judge between you and me, but I will not raise my sword against you. What have you, the great king of Israel, come to seek? Are you looking for a dead dog or a flea? That's all the importance that I have. May the Lord judge and plead my cause before you."

Then Saul said, "Is this truly you, my son David?" Saul then wept.

"David," finally Saul said, "you are more righteous than I am. You have proven to me that you plan no harm, for if a man finds his enemy at a disadvantage, certainly he will not let him go. May God reward you for what you have done today. I also know now that you will succeed me eventually as king and the Kingdom of Israel will be established firmly under you; so promise me now that you will not eliminate my family, but that you will retain them in the kingdom."

David then took an oath to act accordingly. Saul then returned to his home and David and his men went back to Fort Knox.

Samuel died and they buried him in Mo-Ranch.[2] David moved his camp from Fort Knox and pitched his tent in the area near Yellowstone Park.[3] There was a big rancher in the area who owned land in Wyoming[4] and Utah[5] and his name was Nabal and his wife's name was Sharon[6]. It was generally known that Sharon was a wise and beautiful woman and that Nabal was a wicked and embittered man, completely self-centered.

Now word came to David that Nabal, who was exceedingly rich, had just finished shearing his sheep and he was now richer than ever, with cash in the bank.

As a result, David sent ten of his young followers to call on Nabal, to give to Nabal David's greetings, and present Nabal with a brochure showing how much help David needed for his army and to seek a contribution, being very courteous and polite with the whole presentation.

When this was done and the men called on Nabal he said to them, "Who is David? There are often fellows on the loose, why should I

[1]This is true greatness   [2]Ramah   [3]Paran   [4]Maon
         [5]Carmel   [6]Abigail

take what is mine and give it to this nobody. Go tell the man that sent you that I'm not in the least interested."

The young men returned and reported the conversation to David. Needless to say David was indignant; so he ordered his men to strap on their weapons, every man with a sword, and David put on his sword, and with 400 men David headed for Nabal's ranch, with destructive intent.

One of the young servants of Nabal then went to Sharon and reported to her that the young men from David's camp had been courteous and friendly, and had not stolen so much as one sheep, but that Nabal had given them a crude rejection and the servant was fairly certain that David would come for vengeance. The servant apologized for bothering Sharon but he said that Nabal was such a son of the devil that he couldn't talk with him.

Sharon then hit the kitchen running and began to bake two hundred loaves of bread[1] and she got together fruit, and wine, and plenty of meat. She did not tell Nabal what she was doing, but she told her servants to take all the goodies and head down the ranch road and that she would follow as soon as she got a shampoo and set. When she had caught up with her servants, for she was on a donkey, she met David and his men.

David, in the meantime, had regretted that he had kept his men from stealing or pillaging the ranch of Nabal, and so he had come now to teach the ungrateful wretch a lesson. In fact, David said that it was his intention to kill everybody on the ranch who urinated while standing.[2]

When Sharon saw David she jumped down from the donkey and bowed down to him and spoke to him saying, "Pardon me for being so bold as to speak to you. Please do not let this man Nabal upset you. Actually, he is a sad sack, with a bad attitude. If I had seen the young men you sent there would have been an entirely different answer given. The Lord has encouraged you not to shed blood unnecessarily and so spare Nabal. Accept the presents which I have brought to your young men.

I know you are a great man and I know you will prosper for you fight the battles of the Lord, and you have a wonderful reputation.

The Lord will continue to bless you and he will curse your enemies, and they will disappear as if shot from a sling shot, and then you will be king in Israel.

It would be a shame for a man of your greatness and your future to spoil his record by avenging himself against an arthritic old sour puss. Also when you become king, remember me, and here is my phone number."[3]

"Thank the Lord for sending you to speak to me," said David, "for this is good advice and you have kept me from shedding blood

---

[1]She had the biggest kitchen in the county.   [2]Probably meant all the men
[3]Words to that effect.

uselessly, and from vengeance. In fact if it were not for you, by tomorrow morning there would not be left on the ranch anyone who urinates while standing."[1]

David then accepted the gifts and told Sharon to return to her house in peace.

That night Nabal was having a big feast celebrating the selling of his wool and he finally passed out from over drinking; so Sharon did not tell him about David.

In the morning, however, Sharon told Nabal at breakfast how she had visited David and bowed down to him and talked him out of cleaning out the ranch. Nabal was so furious that he had a stroke, became paralyzed, and died in ten days.

When David heard that Nabal had died of a stroke he said, "Hurrah! The Lord was just seeing that Nabal got what was coming to him."

As a result David wrote a note to the widow Sharon and in the hand delivered note of sympathy he asked if she would consent to be his wife.

The messengers who came to Sharon with this note were well received and she washed their feet. Then she selected five handmaidens to go with her and she followed the messengers back to David and became his wife.

David had two other wives already, but he was one short of the three considered normal because Saul had made Greta leave David and marry another fellow.

Chap.
26

As time went by Saul had further periods of depression and the Hatfields came to him again and said that David and his men were in their area and that Saul should come and kill him as Saul would never have peace of mind as long as David was alive.

Saul then gathered 3,000 men and went to the Blue Ridge Mountains to look again for David. David's spies reported all of this to David, who was beginning to tire of this way of life.

David, who was a skilled woodsman by now, came near to the place where Saul was camped and saw where Saul and his bodyguard, Bouncer,[2] were stretched out, apart from the main camp. That evening the Lord caused a deep sleep to fall upon the two of them[3] and David then turned to J. Carson[4] and Flip Wil[5] and said, "Who will go down with me to visit Saul's camp?"

"I'll go," said Flip.

"I'll stay here and keep the fire going," said J. Carson.

As a result David and Flip silently slipped into Saul's camp and stood over Saul who had his untrusty javelin stuck in the ground by his side, and Bouncer was dead asleep on the other side of Saul.

[1]David liked this expression. I doubt if Sheila did.   [2]Abner
[3]With a boost from too much wine?   [4]Ahimelech   [5]Abishai

"God has delivered your enemy into your hands, David," said Flip. "Let me stick him through with my spear. One sticking is all I need."

"No, Flip," said David, "do not destroy him, for he is the Lord's anointed. His day shall come and he will perish no doubt in battle some day against the Fascists."

David, however, took the spear that Saul had stuck in the ground by his side, and he also took his canteen from the knapsack which was loosely tied to his waist, and returned to the safety of the hill.

Next morning David stood forth on top of a nearby hill and called out in a loud voice, "Good morning, Bouncer. How are you doing today?"

"What voice is that? Who is calling to disturb the king?"

"Are you a brave and careful watchman, Bouncer? Why don't you guard the king more carefully? Last night a couple of my people came to destroy the king. The king could have been killed. You ought to be killed yourself, for neglect, for you have not protected the Lord's anointed."

At this point David raised Saul's spear and held up his canteen for all to see.

"Take a look, Bouncer. These were taken from the king last night, and it could have been his life."

Saul was listening and he recognized David's voice.

"Is that you, David?" asked Saul.

"Yes, it is me, my lord and king," replied David. "Hear me now, my king. Why do you pursue me? What have I done that is wrong? If the Lord has stirred you against me, then let us make a peace offering jointly to the Lord, but if it be men that have caused you to turn against me, let them be cursed of God. This is silly for a great king like you to seek one man, who is only as a flea, or for you to hunt a man as if he were a quail."

"I have sinned again," said Saul. "I will do you no more harm. I have played the fool. I am sorry."

"Thank you," said David. "Now send one of your young men over here to get your spear.[1] May the Lord render to every man justice. Just as I had the chance to kill you and refrained because you are the Lord's anointed; even as I have spared your life may the Lord also spare mine."

Then Saul said, "Blessings on you, David. I foresee a great future for you, and I know that in the long run you will prevail."

After this Saul returned to his home and David left again for the hills.

Chap.
27

After David had a little time to think and review his knowledge of psychology, he realized that Saul would no doubt become depressed

[1] I think he kept the canteen, as he didn't have one.

again and try again to find and kill David. As a result, David decided that he had better leave the area and lose himself among the Fascists in Austin where he could easily lose himself on the drag. David took with him his six hundred men and his two wives Sharon and Susie.[1]

The word came to Saul that David was in Austin and Saul thought this was a good place for him so he quit worrying about him.

David then approached the Governor at Austin and asked him if he might be willing to give David a town, that was nearby, and then David and his men would not be in the way and the Governor wouldn't have to worry about David's presence.

This pleased the Governor very much and so he gave David the town of Dripping Springs[2] and David stayed there for nearly two years.

The inactivity began to get to David and his men so they decided to go north and make a raid on an old enemy of Israel that had not been properly handled. As a result David and his men went to Tulsa[3] and Oklahoma City[4] and they slaughtered the men, women, and children and took all the cattle and the loot they could carry, and returned by way of Austin.

The Governor of Austin said to David, "Where have you been? I heard that you had gone forth to war."

"We went south to fight against some of the Hebrews that have been giving me so much trouble."

This was told[5] by David so the Governor, who was a Fascist, would not know that David had attacked some of the Governor's allies. This is why he killed everybody; so there would be no one to report the matter. David stuck to this policy all the time. This fooled the Governor and made him think that David was totally estranged from his own people and would never be a threat to the Fascists again.[6]

Chap.
28

It was not long after this that the Fascists decided to get their armies together and invade Israel.[7] As a result, the Governor at Austin told David of this and said that he knew that David and his 600 men would join the Fascists in the war against Israel.

"Of course you know what I will do," said David.[8]

The Governor then said to David, "I expect you to be my chief protector."

Now Samuel was dead, and more or less in his honor, Saul had passed a law against fortune tellers, witches, mediums, or people using ESP.

When Saul, however, was told of the massing of the troops of Fascists, he became depressed and afraid, and his prayers to the Lord

[1]Ahinoam. I think he left one back in the hills.   [2]Ziklag   [3]Geshurites
[4]Amalekites   [5]not true, of course   [6]A nice place to stop and discuss foreign policy.   [7]There was no TV, football, or much else to do.
[8]The forked tongue touch

did not seem to get off the ground. Saul longed for Samuel, but Samuel was dead.

Then Saul said to one of his servants, "Locate me a fortune teller or a medium that I may go and get some inside information."

One of the servants said, "Well, there is one I've heard about, the witch of Endor, who is doing black market business as a soothsayer."

As a result, Saul disguised himself and with two servants went to the woman at night and he said to her, "Bring to me a person from the spirit world. I know exactly to whom I wish to speak."

"Unfortunately," said the witch, "Saul the king has passed a law against this. How do I know but what you are an undercover agent who is laying a trap for me, to catch me, and have me executed?"[1]

"I take an oath that nothing will happen to you, and there shall be no punishment," said Saul.

"Who do you want me to contact?" asked the woman.

"Get me in touch with Samuel," said Saul.

Now when the woman understood that it was the dead Samuel that was wanted, she said, "You have deceived. You are Saul, the king. He is the only one who would seek Samuel." At this point the witch gave a pitiful shriek.

The king said to her, "Be not afraid. Tell me what you have perceived."

"I see various forms and one of them is an old man, and he is covered with the robe of a prophet."

Saul then decided that the witch was in touch with Samuel and he bowed his head to the ground.

Then a voice said, "Why have you disturbed me, Saul?"

"Because of the Fascists," said Saul, "and because God has deserted me, and there are no more prophets.[2] I have called on you to tell me what to do."

"Why call on me, if the Lord has left you, and I am with God?"

Saul remembered the very words of Samuel who had said when he was alive, "The Lord hath rent the kingdom out of your hands and given it to a neighbor, even to David, because you did not obey the voice of the Lord."

"Therefore hath the Lord done this thing to you," said the voice of Samuel, "and moreover the Lord will turn Israel over to the Fascists, and tomorrow you and your sons will join me in the next world."

Then Saul fainted. For one thing, he had not eaten all day, nor all night.

Then the good witch came to Saul and said, "I have obeyed your voice and trusted you with my life, and I have listened to your request, now let me feed you and give you strength, and get you out of here."

[1]You would think a Grade A witch would know.

[2]Saul had killed most of them

160

Saul, however, refused to eat, but the woman and the servants forced food into him, and finally he was able to sit up on the side of the bed. The woman then went to the kitchen and fixed some barbecued ribs, and a good meal and fed the men properly, and they left strengthened.

Chap.
29

Now as the Fascist army began to assemble and the thousands of soldiers passed along to the gathering place, David took his men and got behind the Governor and his men.

When the leaders of the Fascists met to plan their strategy, one of them asked about David and said, "What in the world are those Hebrews doing with our army?"

"These men are David and his men, and they have been with me a long time and I have found no fault with them."

The Fascists leaders were angry about this, however, and said, "Send this fellow back. We don't want him in back of us. We don't trust the Hebrews and he may decide to help Saul. David is a powerful man, and our enemy, for there was even a folk song about him saying 'Saul has killed his thousands, but David, his tens of thousands.' Those were Fascists that he killed."

Then the Governor sent for David and said, "You have been good to me and I trust you completely, but the other Fascists leaders don't agree, so I think the best for all concerned is for you to return to Dripping Springs and we will fight Israel without you."

"What have I done wrong? I am disappointed. I don't see why I can't be allowed to help."[1]

"I know you are right, David," said the Governor, "but the princes of the Fascists have out voted me and they say definitely that you shall not enter the battle with them. My suggestion is that first thing in the morning you and your men get up and go." This they did.

Chap.
30

When David and his men returned to Dripping Springs they found the place had been burned to the ground by one of the Fascist outfit, a group known as the Sooners,[2] that the mayor had been killed, the women taken captives, and all the cattle and valuables stolen. The wives and children of David and all of his men had been taken captive and all that David and his men could do that day was weep.

In fact, the people were so upset that they considered stoning David to death for having gone off to join the Fascists and leaving the homestead defenseless.

David then went into the church with the priest and stood before God with his problem, asking God if it were wise to pursue the

[1] Apparently David was going to sabotage the Fascists from the rear

[2] Amalekites branch

Sooners and attempt to recapture their families.

The Lord encouraged David to pursue and promised that the trip would succeed.

David and his six hundred men pursued the Sooners and finally came to the Red River.[1] About 200 of the men were too pooped to cross the river, so David continued the pursuit with only 400 men.

In their pursuit they found a wetback[2] walking in a field and the men brought him to David, and fed him, and gave him something to drink.

David said to him, "Who are you?"

"I am a wetback," said the man, "and I have been working as a slave to one of the Sooners, but I became sick and they left me behind. In fact, I was with them when they burned Dripping Springs."

"Can you tell me where I can find this bunch of Sooners?" asked David.

"If you promise not to kill me or to deliver me back to the Sooners, I'll put the finger on them."

As a result David, of course, gave his promise and the wetback led David and his men to the place where the Sooners were camped. When David and his men saw them, the Sooners were spread out over the valley, eating, drinking, and dancing, celebrating their good luck. David and his men interrupted their evening drinking and eating, and caught them completely unprepared and stayed after them all through the next day so that only 400 escaped, and these were young men who fled on camels.

David recovered the cattle that had not been eaten and also his two wives. In fact, David took control of everything that the Sooners had and declared immediate possession of the flocks, herds, and material things.

David then began to return to Dripping Springs, and when he came to the Red River the 200 men who had stayed behind came out to salute David.

Some of the men with David then said, "Since these fellows were not in the fight, we don't think they should get any of the spoils, except their wives and children which we bring back to them."

"No," said David, "we will not operate in this fashion. It is important to always have men left behind to guard our tents and equipment. Also we must remember that it is the Lord that gives the victory; so we will divide properly the profits with those that remained and guarded the equipment as well as with those who did the fighting." This then became a policy in Israel from that day.

Upon returning to Dripping Springs, David took some of the excess profit and he sent messengers to the various tribes in Judah and throughout Israel making valuable gifts to each in David's name

[1]Besor   [2]In this case an Egyptian

and as a notification of his victory.[1]

In the meantime, the Fascist army moved against Israel and the army of Israel was defeated and fled. The Fascist followed with great determination, particularly wishing to kill Saul and his sons who fought valiantly.

Jonathan and his brothers Bill[2] and Pete[3] were both killed in the battle. About this time one of the archers wounded Saul with an arrow and he could not continue to fight. Saul then turned to his armorbearer, who was by his side, and said, "Kill me with your sword. I do not want to be killed by the heathen Fascists and I know my end is close at hand."

The armorbearer said, "I cannot kill my king."

So Saul took his own sword and stuck the hilt in the ground and fell on his sword, killing himself. When the armorbearer saw what Saul had done, he did the same thing to himself.[4]

As soon as word of this defeat spread, the Hebrews across the Jordan, and the ones occupying the cities of Israel all fled to the various places in the wilderness and the remote areas. The Fascists moved in and took over Israel.

The Fascists found the bodies of Saul and his sons, and they beheaded them, and they took the head of Saul and sent it around the various cities on display and they took the armour of Saul and put it in the Smithsonian Institute.[5] Now the bodies of Saul and his sons had been hung on the wall of the Astrodome,[6] but these bodies were stolen in the night and taken to be burned and buried by friends.

---

[1] It is hard to realize that he had no PR man

[2] Abinadab

[3] Malchishua

[4] This is maybe taking loyalty too far

[5] Ashtaroth

[6] Bethshan

After David had been back at Dripping Springs for about two days a man came into town with his clothes all torn, dirty, and exhausted, and he found David and bowed down to him.

David asked, "Where have you been? What gives with you?"

"I have just escaped from the camp of Israel," replied the man.

"How did the battle go?" asked David.

"The people of Israel have fled and Saul and Jonathan have been slain," reported the man.

"How do you know this?" asked David.

"As I happened to pass by the area," said the fellow, "I saw Saul leaning on his own spear and the chariots and horsemen were coming down upon him. Then Saul begged me to kill him, so I did as he asked, for I could see that he could not live in his present condition anyway. While I was there, I took the head piece of the king from his head and the arm band marker of the king, and I have brought them to you."

Then David tore his clothes in anguish as did those others standing around and they mourned the passing of their king and his son, and for the whole house of Israel and its troubles.

David then sent for the man who had brought the news and asked him to identify himself.

"I am a Sooner," said the man.

"Why were you not afraid to smite the Lord's anointed, the king of Israel? No heathen has this right."

David therefore ordered that one of the soldiers should kill the Sooner who claimed to have killed Saul, for David said that the man had convicted himself by his own testimony.[1]

Then David composed a folk song of praise for Saul and Jonathan, and this song was to be recorded and sung thoughout Israel.

The Song

The beauty and glory of Israel is gone.
The great and mighty have fallen.
Mention it not among the heathen.
Let there be no rejoicing among them,
Better let the mountains have no dew,
Or the soft rain cease to fall
For the shield of the mighty Saul is gone.
The brave Jonathan is no more,
He never retreated in the face of the enemy;

[1]David obviously didn't believe that Saul would ask a heathen to kill him.

Oh! Saul and Jonathan were great in life,
It is fitting that they died together,
For they were swifter than eagles,
And stronger than lions,
Weep, girls, weep for Saul
For Saul clothed you in scarlet
And he trimmed your dresses with gold.
The mighty have fallen in battle.
Oh! Jonathan, Jonathan, how sad I am,
Even though you had a warrior's death,
How joyful and great was our friendship,
More enduring was our love,
A love more binding than other loves,
How strong a friendship we had,
How are the mighty fallen!
How sad this day for me and Israel!

Chap.
2

After everything had settled down a bit and the mourning period was ended, then David prayed to the Lord for guidance, and God encouraged David to return to Judah and to investigate the possibilities of some restoration.

As a result, David with his two wives and all his men and all their possessions were assembled and they moved into the area of Judah and settled in a town called Rochester[1]. The men of Judah came there and anointed David as king of the tribe of Judah. The men also told David about the fellows from the University of Louisville[2] who had come and stolen the bodies of Saul and his sons from the Fascist and had given them proper burial.

David then sent messengers to the University and extended his thanks and his blessings to those that had done this fine thing at great risk. David said also in the message that he would remember this and that their kindness would some day be amply repaid.

Bouncer, however, wanted to initiate the restoration through the line of Saul as he knew how he stood with David, so he took an older son of Saul who had not been in the Fascist battle and made him king over an area containing about five small towns and consisting of part of one tribe, but he felt it was a start. Shorty,[3] the king, lasted only two years.

During this time an interesting incident took place. Bouncer took a few of his young soldiers to a water hole and by prearrangement met Tuffy,[4] who was David's aide and who came with some of David's men.

Bouncer said to Tuffy, "Why don't we let our young men engage

[1] Hebron   [3] Ishbosheth
[2] Jabeshgilead   [4] Joab

165

in a contest, soccer or something, and we can watch."

"Great idea," said Tuffy.

As a result, twelve men from each side went together on the side of the pool supposedly for a contest, but it immediately broke out into a fight. Apparently they did not come to play as each man grabbed his opponent's head and stuck his sword in him and they were all killed. Then the rest of the soldiers joined the fight and the soldiers of Tuffy, David's men, defeated the soldiers of Bouncer.

Incidentally, they named the place Bloody Pool,[1] and placed there a historical marker.

One of Tuffy's brothers was named Lightfoot Harry,[2] for he could run like a deer, and he began to chase Bouncer.

Bouncer, while running, yelled over his shoulder, "Are you Lightfoot Harry?"

"You better believe it, man," called out Lightfoot.

"How about chasing one of the younger men who are running? I am about pooped out and I don't want to kill you. I can whip you, but I don't want to have Tuffy after me."

Lightfoot would not listen to him and he caught Bouncer, but as he reached for him Bouncer thrust a spear through him and killed him.

This made a bunch more people mad, and a group from the tribe of Benjamin met on a hill and organized a posse under Tuffy.

Bouncer then called out to Tuffy and said, "Let's call this thing quits before more people get hurt. Are we not all Hebrews? Why should we start a civil war that will just lead to more and more trouble?"

"You spoke just in time," said Tuffy, "for in the morning we were going to pour down on you."

As a result, Tuffy had the bugler blow recall and everybody went his own way in peace. Tuffy was satisfied to be able to report to David that they had lost only 19 men while they had killed 360 of Bouncer's.[3]

Chap.
3

This by no means settled everything for the supporters of David as the followers of king Saul's son were constantly on the warpath with raiding parties and the like. The men of David, however, seemed to increase in number and their success began to grow as the followers of the line of Saul became weaker and weaker.

David, in the meantime, had added four wives to his string, more in keeping with his prosperity, and the total of six wives brought him six sons in a fairly short span of time. The third son was one born to Trudy,[4] one of the new wives, and the boy was named Absalom, though his playmates called him Abby.

[1]Helkathhazzurim

[2]Asahel

[3]Bouncer had a good reason for peace talk

[4]Maacah

Now Bouncer was asserting himself pretty strongly in assembling men to serve for Shorty and Bouncer made himself General over the forces of the son of Saul, and developed a real sense of self-importance.

Bouncer had decided to take for himself the former mistress of King Saul, a girl named Mame,[1] and King Shorty didn't like this.

"What are you doing fooling around with my dead father's mistress?" Shorty asked Bouncer one day.

"Don't talk to me that way. If it weren't for me you wouldn't be king. In fact, I control the army, and I could easily turn you over to David, and here you are squalling because I'm having a little pleasure on the side. If you aren't careful with me I'll turn the whole house of Saul over to David."

This hushed up Shorty real fast.

Bouncer then sent a message to David and said, "Let's make a deal. I will join with you to take over Israel."

"Not until you have the king return to me my first wife, the daughter of Saul, my true love, Greta."

Bouncer relayed the request of David to Shorty, who was scared anyway, and so he sent for Greta and packed her off in a hurry to David. Now Greta's husband was greatly upset and followed her down the road weeping and wailing until Bouncer had to order him home.[2]

Then Bouncer began to pass a message along to the elders of Israel saying that he knew that they had long wanted David for their king[3] and it was about time that this came to pass for it was common knowledge that the Lord had promised to save Israel by the hand of David, from the Fascist as well as other enemies.

After Bouncer had spread the word pretty well among the tribes he went to see David personally, taking with him only 20 men. David received the group graciously and had a big banquet in their honor.

Bouncer then told David that he would start gathering all the people of Israel together and get all the tribes to consent to accept David as king. As a result, David let Bouncer and his men depart in peace.

A couple of days later Tuffy returned to David's camp after a successful raid on a Fascist ranch, and Tuffy learned that Bouncer had been in David's camp.

"What did you do, David?" asked Tuffy. "How could you let that snake in the grass Bouncer come here and leave unharmed. You know that Bouncer is up to no good and that he is working some trick play to spring."

Tuffy, who was still properly sore at Bouncer for having killed his younger brother Lightfoot, sent messengers to Bouncer telling him to

[1]Rizpah [3]Bouncer was cagy

[2]Greta must have been something else for real

return for a brief conference.

When Bouncer arrived at the entrance of Raleigh, where the headquarters of David was, Tuffy met him at the gate and said, "Step aside over here, Bouncer, and let me give you a little inside information before you go to see David again."

Bouncer then stepped aside behind the corner of the wall and the inside information that Tuffy had for him was a sword inside the fifth rib, which killed Bouncer on the spot.

When word of this came to David he did not seem to be in the least disturbed, but he did say, "As a matter of record, let it be known that this was not my doing, nor that of my kingdom, but a personal thing between Tuffy and Bouncer. I think also that Tuffy and his house should be blamed for this unsatisfactory settlement of an old feud."

David then called a meeting of the leaders of the people and said, "It is proper that we mourn for Bouncer and give him a decent burial, for he was a warrior, the protector of King Saul. It is great that he died as a warrior, not as one with his hands tied, or in chains."

David then said, "Let there be mourning in my house. I will not eat all day long for I will weep over the death of Bouncer. There has fallen today a prince and a great man in Israel."

All of this favorably impressed the people, and it became known far and wide that David was in no way responsible for the death of Bouncer.

Chap.
4

Now when Shorty heard that Bouncer was dead he knew the jig was up and he trembled. Lots of people in Israel became nervous, for they had been supporting Shorty's regime.

When Jonathan and Saul had been killed, the five year old son of Jonathan accompanied by his nurse fled to the hills and in running the child fell and became permanently crippled. The name of the boy was Sonny[1] and he remained hidden in the hills with his nurse.

Now Shorty had two young men who were captains in his army, one was named Mert[2] and one was called Hoot.[3] These two figured the kingdom under Shorty was a goner so they decided to get in good with David. During siesta time, therefore, they went into the house of Shorty and found him taking an afternoon nap and they killed him and cut off his head and slipped away without being seen.

In a couple of days they arrived at the headquarters of David in Raleigh and presented him with the head of Shorty, saying, "Here is the head of your enemy, and you are now avenged of all that Saul did to you."

[1]Mephibosheth   [2]Rechab

[3]Baanah

David then said, "Will you birds ever learn? When the man reported to me that Saul was dead the messenger thought he brought good tidings, but I had him killed for saying that he had put Saul to death. The nut thought I would reward him. I am not a man of blood and vengeance; so I had the messenger killed.[1]

"How much worse it is for wicked men like you to have killed a righteous weakling in his bed in his own house. Surely you do not belong on this earth."

David then commanded his soldiers to kill Mert and Hoot, to cut off their hands and feet, and hang the remains from a tree, but he ordered a decent burial for the head of Shorty.

Chap.
5

Then came all the tribes of Israel to David and told him how they had known all along that he would be their ruler, and they spoke of their close kinship and reminded him that they were all Hebrews, and then they anointed him king of Israel.[2]

David and his soldiers then went to Jerusalem which was at the time controlled by the Apache Indians[3] and David wanted to know if these people wanted to be taken under the new kingdom.

The Apache reply was to the effect that the lame and the blind among the Apaches could hold off all David's army without help from any of the warriors.

David was greatly insulted and he told his men to surround the city and crawl in under the walls through the gutters and the tunnels and to fight fiercely and make the Apaches eat their smart remarks. David's men took the city, and it became known as the city of David.

David continued to grow in greatness and he increased his possessions and the power of the Lord was with him.

As a tribute as well as good public relations, the king of Tyre sent a crew of carpenters and masons, along with a lot of wood and stone, and built David a fine house, with many rooms. David counted the rooms and realized that he did not have enough wives to put in all the spaces in the girls dormitory, so he recruited some of the best looking and most attractive girls in the area. It was not long before David had eleven more children[4].

Now the Fascist heard that David had been made king of Israel, and the Fascist as usual began to get organized and decided to march against David from Valley-Low.[5]

David, as his custom was, prayed to the Lord for guidance and decided that the Lord wished him to move against the Fascists and that the Lord would give Israel the victory.

David met the Fascists at a place called Custer's First Stand and

[1] Good place for discussion and dialogue

[2] David was always getting anointed. I think he liked it.

[3] Jebusites

[4] Since daughters were often not counted, there may have been more than listed.

[5] Rephaim

David and his men beat them so thoroughly that the Fascists fled in all directions like water spilling from a broken dam. David then changed the name of the place to Broken Dam.[1] The Fascists fled so rapidly that they left their flags and insignia, and David burned these.

The Fascist reorganized again, however, and again set up camp near Valley-Low. David prayed again for guidance and from his meditation came forth the plan to slip up on the Fascist by having his men move cautiously using mulberry branches and trees as cover. The ruse worked beautifully and David had another victory over the Fascists.[2]

David, feeling that the Fascist matter was pretty well handled, assembled an impressive army of 30,000 men and set forth to march to Montreat and bring back to the city of David the ark of the covenant of the Lord.

Upon arriving at Montreat, the ark of the covenant was taken from the Assembly Inn and placed on a cart to be drawn by oxen. The trip back was really a big parade with the men playing all kinds of musical instruments, and various bands from the small towns joining the parade. One of the drivers of the cart was a fellow by the name of Jinx[3] and when nearing one of the resting places the cart hit a bump as it was being driven into the barn for the night; so Jinx reached forth his hand and touched the ark of the covenant to steady it, and he fell over dead, for the Lord had decreed that no hand but that of a priest conducting service should ever touch the ark.[4]

This incident scared David and he was afraid to bring the ark to his house or to his city, for David feared the Lord. As a result the ark was left in the house of a man named Moody.[5] The Lord therefore blessed the house of Moody greatly and the family became well-to-do and prominent in business as well as in the Lord's work.

David learned of this; so he decided that maybe the ark of the covenant should be in the city of David after all. As a result, David sent for the ark and it was brought into the city of David, and there was a proper sacrifice made at the gate, and David led the parade down the street. The parade was a wild one, with the men singing and dancing and playing all kinds of instruments. David led the parade and he danced himself into a frenzy, even doing the watusi.

It so happened that Greta, David's first wife and his favorite, looked out the window and saw David doing his thing, and she was furious.

The ark of the covenant was then brought into the tabernacle and

[1]Baalperazim

[2]Shakespeare picked up this item for his Burnham wood account

[3]Uzzah

[4]It was always loaded on the cart by pole lifters

[5]Obededom

proper offerings were made to the Lord. Then cake, cookies, and coffee was served to all the people and there was great joy and thanksgiving.

When David came home, however, Greta lowered the boom on him saying, "You made a jackass of yourself in the parade. Doing those crazy dances and throwing up your skirts to attract the attention of all the girls watching the parade. Shame, shame!"

"You are wrong, Greta," said David, "for what I was doing was part of the worship service. What is more, I am ruler of the people, chosen by God, and I'll probably do worse things than this. As for the girls, I hope I did impress them, for I go for girls pretty strongly."

Greta then refused to allow David to touch her for the rest of her life.[1]

Things settled down in the city and all was quiet on the western front and David was having little to do but look for something to do. David sent for Nathan, the prophet of the Lord, and said to him, "I live in a big fine house and yet I notice that the ark of the covenant of the Lord is just in a little place shut off with curtains."

"As far as I'm concerned, David, if you want to do something about it, have at it," replied Nathan.

That night, however, the word of the Lord came to Nathan suggesting that he go and talk to David and tell him that the Lord did not want David to build a temple.

Nathan called on David and said, "The Lord says that the temple bit can wait. The ark of the covenant has remained without its own house for many years, in fact ever since it was built in the wilderness under Moses. There has never been any request from God for a temple for the ark.

"Tell David also, the Lord said to me, that I brought him from being a little runny nose sheepherder to be the king of Israel, that I have protected him and delivered him from all his enemies. Remind David that I will establish my people in my way in my own time. The Lord also has promised to see that the line of David is continued, and his son shall build a proper temple in the fulness of time. The Lord also will provide through the line of David a kingdom that shall be forever and not subject to defeat."[2]

Then David prayed to the Lord himself and said, "Who am I to be so greatly blessed? I am deeply touched. I know that thou art great, O Lord, that there is none like thee, nor is there any other God. What more could a nation ask than to have the Lord as their God, and to worship him?

[1] I think she was the first Greta to say "I want to be alone."

[2] Christ came through the line of David

171

As for the word about the line of David and the eternal kingdom, accept my gratitude. I know you are the true God, and the one Lord of all. Continue to bless this house of mine and may it be blessed forever, even as you have decreed."

There developed a slack year or two in Israel so David decided to go and give his army a workout and to build up the treasury and extend his kingdom; so he started by attacking Naples[1] where one of the Fascist outfits were stationed. David took Naples without any trouble and then he decided to move against some of the places in Mississippi.

David captured several hundred of the men and made them all lie on the ground face down. Then David ordered the soldiers to kill two and skip one all the way down the line as he wanted to save a hundred or so as servants.[2]

David then went into Tennessee[3] and defeated the forces of Jimmy, mayor of Memphis, and he extended his territory this way to the Mississippi River. In this raid David captured one thousand chariots, 700 horsemen, and 20,000 footmen. David was afraid that the chariots might be used against him sometime so he had all the chariot horses' tendons cut so they would be lame, and he gave them to poor people for their farms.

The Syrians from Damascus then came to the aid of the mayor of Memphis and David and his men killed 22,000 of them before the rest decided to return home and tend to their own business. David then began to build forts in all parts of the land and in every place that he conquered, he left small bands of his men to rule these forts and to keep the peace.

The spoils of these little wars were great, and David brought great riches in brass and silver back to Jerusalem.

Now when Tito[4] heard that David had defeated his old enemy from Memphis he sent his son Joey[5] to visit David, to thank him, and to give him some very expensive presents of silver, and gold, and brass. David dedicated all of these spoils and gifts to the Lord.

David's fame spread greatly after defeating the Syrians and he returned a great hero.[6]

David reigned over Israel, with justice and fairness to all, and he made Tuffy commander in chief of the army under David.

David still often thought of his friend Jonathan and he still grieved over his death and so he asked one of his servants if there was anyone left in Saul's family that David could help for Jonathan's sake.

---

[1]Methegammah   [2]David thought this easier than saying I want one-third of the men saved.   [3]Hadadezer   [4]Toi   [5]Joram
[6]But still no Greta reception

A man who had worked for Saul was located and he came to David and David asked him if there were any descendants of Saul left alive.

"Yes," replied the man. "Jonathan left a son who was crippled in an accident when he was a child."

"Where is he?" asked David.

"He is living in a little town in the hills called Woodsville."[1]

As a result David sent for Jonathan's son and when he arrived he fell on his face in front of David.

"Are you Sonny, the son of Jonathan?" asked David.

"I am," said Sonny.

"Do not be afraid, Sonny, for I have no thoughts but kind thoughts for you because of your father. I plan to restore to you the land that was your grandfather's and I expect you to live in a guest house here with me and to eat with me continually."

"I am greatly honored, for actually I am only as a dead dog, being crippled and no longer of any use," said Sonny.

Now J.P.,[2] the man who reported about Sonny, was a man with fifteen sons and twenty servants and David put him in charge of the old Saul place and told him to run the place and bring the profit to Sonny, but that Sonny would live on the palace grounds. J.P. was to get well paid, of course, for his work.

As a result, Sonny and his wife and young son moved into the guest cottage and Sonny was a regular guest at the table of King David, though he was still lame in both legs.[3]

Chap.
10

Not too long after this, word came to David that the mayor of Cleveland[4] had died and this his son Hubert[5] had taken his place. David remembered that the mayor had been kind to him one time and he thought of him as a friend; so he decided to send some of his young warriors to Cleveland to put some roses on the grave of his friend and show goodwill to Hubert.

Some of the city councilmen, however, were very leary of this and they told Hubert, who seemed to be the gullible type, that David was probably using this as an excuse to spy on Cleveland and to lay plans to capture it.[6]

As a result, Hubert ordered that half of each man's beard that David sent be shaved off and that they all be put in mini-skirts and sent home. The warriors were mortified beyond description.

When David heard of this he went to meet the men, and reassured them about themselves, and then told them to go to Chicago[7] until their beards grew again to full size.

David let it be known that when he faced in the direction of

[1]Lodebar [2]Ziba [3]It was unusual to help the handicapped in those days
[4]Ammon [5]Hanun [6]Suspicion is still an international troublemaker.
[7]Jericho

Cleveland he smelled a bad odor, and the people of Cleveland learned of his dissatisfaciton. As a result, Hubert made a deal with the Syrians to join them in battle against Israel.

David then sent Tuffy and all the array of mighty men that he had in the army, and when they arrived in the area, Tuffy saw that the Syrians were gathered on one side and the men of Cleveland on the other. As a result, Tuffy split his army, and took the best warriors from the army and put them with him, and the less experienced men he put under Abbie[1], his younger brother.

Then Tuffy said, "I will attack the Syrians and you attack the men of Cleveland. If I'm having too much trouble with the Syrians then you come and help me, and if you can't handle the men of Hubert, then I'll come help you."

When Tuffy and his crack troops stormed into the Syrians, the Syrians came right soon to the conclusion that the fight wasn't worth the money; so they began to flee. When the men of Cleveland saw that the Syrians were fleeing, they decided the war was not such a good idea after all, and they fled.

Then Tuffy returned to Jerusalem and dismissed the army for the time being.

The Syrians decided to do a little more recruiting and to try again with a larger army, and a man named Rumel[2] stirred up the people and moved with great confidence and great speed against Israel.

When David learned of this, he ordered the army to reassemble and then did a little extra recruiting also and David crossed the Jordan and met the Syrians at Bunker Hill.[3]

David and his men defeated the Syrian army again and the Israelites killed 700 chariot loads of Syrians and 40,000 cavalry men,[4] and also killed Howe,[5] one of the prominent generals.

As a result, the Syrians decided to make peace with David and they also decided that they would no longer try to help Cleveland.

Chap.
11

About a year had elapsed and it was time again for the winter games, which meant sending troops to worry the Fascist, locating any new Dalton gangs, and fighting the Mafia, if they could be located. David decided to sit this season out, and he remained in Jerusalem, but Tuffy directed the field operations in various sections of the country.

One day after his afternoon nap, David was walking on his rooftop in the sun as he often did, and he looked over the fence and saw an exceedingly beautiful woman taking a bath in her backyard.[6]

At supper that night, David asked one of his aides, "Who is the lady who lives next door?"

"If you are talking about the neighbor we think you mean, her

[1]Abishai [2]Hadarezer [3]Helam [4]Counting in those days was not always accurate [5]Shobach [6]I think she knew what she was doing

name is Gina[1]," said one of the men.

"Incidentally," said one of the fellows, "she is married to an army man and he is out on maneuvers."

As a result David sent for her and she came over and spent the night with him, and returned home in the morning.

A few trips later and she remarked to David that she was pregnant, and that her baby would be the child of the king.

David then decided to send for her husband, Corps Happy,[2] and so the good captain Corps Happy came to the palace from the front line.

David said to him, "How are things at the front? How's Tuffy? How are the raids going?"

Corps Happy gave a good report.

David then said, "You'd better go home and wash your feet and get a good nights rest before returning to the battle lines."

David gave him a big box lunch to take with him. Corps Happy, however, did not go home, but slept on the floor in the king's palace. David was told of this the next morning so he sent for Corps Happy and said, "Why didn't you go home last night, especially after such a long journey?"

Corps Happy then said, "The ark of the covenant and my comrades in Israel and Judah are sleeping on the ground in tents, and some of them, even Tuffy, are sleeping in open fields, how then when my friends are having it so tough can I go to my house and eat and drink and lie down with my wife?"[3]

"Well, if you feel that way about it, stay around the palace today and tomorrow go back to the troops."

In the morning David wrote a letter to Tuffy, sealed it, and gave it to Corps Happy to deliver. In the letter, he told Tuffy to let Corps Happy lead the next charge against the Fascists, and then let the fellows around him back off and leave Corps to fight the Fascists by himself.[4]

Tuffy did his job well and he put Corps Happy in a place where he would charge the strongest point of the Fascist garrison. In this unnecessary attack a number of the soldiers of David were slain, and in the group was, as planned, Corps Happy.

Then Tuffy sent a messenger to David and told him of the attack on the strong garrison of the Fascists. Tuffy also told the messenger that David would probably criticize his strategy, and complain about getting so close to a strong point to attack, and he might even mention the case of the girl dropping the stone on Patton's [5] head. After he has complained a bit, then you say to the king, "your trusted warrior, Corps Happy, was also killed in the action."

The messenger came to David and said, "We had a rough time the other day. We pursued some of the Fascists and we came too close to

---

[1]Bathsheba   [2]Uriah   [3]Another good place for a heated discussion
[4]This has to be the dirtiest trick of the week   [5]Abimelech

the walls of the city, but Tuffy had told us to do this. As a result some of the archers began to get the ones in the front, and some of the king's soldiers are dead, and so is Captain Corps Happy."

David then told the messenger to return to Tuffy and to tell him not to be discouraged, but take his time and approach the city with more caution and in time conquer it.

When Gina heard of the death of her husband, she went into mourning. When the accepted mourning period was through, however, she was brought to the palace and Gina became David's wife and gave birth to a son.

The Lord, however, was greatly displeased with the thing that David had done.

Chap.
12

The Lord then sent Nathan, the prophet, to David and he spoke to David saying, "There were two men in the city and one was rich and one was poor. The rich man had plenty of sheep and cattle and the poor man had only one little ewe lamb, and it was part of his family, eating with them, and was greatly beloved by the poor man.

The rich man had an occasion when he needed to possess a ewe and he decided that instead of taking one from his many, he went and took the only one the poor man had."

The story stirred David's sense of justice and he said to Nathan, "That is awful. As the Lord lives, so help me, I'll find that rich man and have him executed, and he shall have to restore four lambs to one for what he has done."

Then Nathan said to David, "You are the man."

Nathan then proceeded to remind David that the Lord God of Israel had anointed him king and made him safe from Saul, and delivered to him great riches and many wives, as well as the whole house of Israel. The Lord would have done even more if it had been desired. Why then would David despise the commandment of the Lord, and do such an evil thing as have Corps Happy killed?

Nathan further said, "The Lord says that for this sin the sword shall be part of your house. The Lord will raise up evil out of your own house and he will see to it that some of your wives are unfaithful, and it will become public knowledge, for the same thing that you tried to do secretly the Lord will have done to you publicly."

"I have sinned against God," said David.

"The Lord will forgive you, but you will still be punished by the death of one of your sons; so you will know how God feels when one of his sons rebels against him."

As a result, the Lord caused the child that was born to Gina to be very sickly, and David and his servants prayed and fasted hoping to save the child's life. David was very distraught and on the seventh day the child died.

The servants and friends of David were afraid to tell him when the child died, for they felt that the news might cause David to have a stroke. David saw them whispering, however, and he knew then that the child was dead.

David then asked, "Is the child dead?"

"Yes," the servant replied.

Then David arose and took a bath and put on his robes and went to the church and there he worshipped God. After this David returned to his own house and began to eat again.

One of his friends then said to him, "What gives? While the child was alive you would not eat or sleep, and now that the child is dead you seem to be all right. We don't understand."

"Well, while the child was alive, there was some hope that I could implore God to save the child's life, but now the matter is done, and the child is now with the Lord."

David did the best he could to comfort his wife, Gina, for it was her firstborn that had died. David continued to keep Gina close to him and she became pregnant again and delivered another son, and they named him Solomon, and the Lord was delighted and blessed the new baby.

Tuffy continued the siege of Venice,[1] the city of waters, and he saw that success was close at hand, so at the suggestion of his PR man he sent for David and told him to come with reinforcements and get in on the big victory.

As a result, David and additional troops joined Tuffy and they captured Venice, and David took the crown from the head of the mayor of Venice and put it on his own head, and there were great valuables taken along with the city.

Although David spared the lives of most of the people of Venice, he made them yardmen and maintenance workers at low salaries.[2] Since this seemed to be a good idea, and since he had his army already all together, David did the same thing to two or three smaller cities on the way home to Jerusalem.

Chap.
13

With all the wives that David had who bore him children, the property of David held several houses and there were many half brothers and half sisters running around the palace. Absalom, David's favorite son, had a beautiful sister named Tamar and one of her half brothers, a fellow named Aubrey,[3] fell in love with her.

Since Tamar was his half sister Aubrey didn't know exactly what to do, though he had a friend who was ready with some poor advice. The friend was a high ranking army man named Flint[4] and he outlined a scheme for Aubrey.

Flint explained to Aubrey that if he could get Tamar alone and get her to go to bed with him, then Aubrey could tell King David

[1]Rabbah [2]Well before minimum wage programs [3]Amnon [4]Jonadab

177

about it and David would let them get married.

Aubrey followed the plan devised by the cunning Flint. Aubrey played sick, and when David inquired of him, he said that he thought he would get well if his half sister Tamar would come and nurse him and feed him in bed.

As a result, David sent for Tamar and she came and cooked some chocolate chip cookies and fixed some meatballs and came to feed Aubrey. Aubrey then asked all the rest of the help to leave and he propositioned Tamar. Tamar said it was not the proper thing to do and she would not get in the bed with Aubrey; so he raped her.

When the deed was done, Tamar said, "The only thing to do to keep me from shame is for you to tell the king and he will then let us get married."

Aubrey, however, was apparently no longer interested in Tamar and merely sent her home. Now Tamar was Absalom's full sister, and when he learned of what had happened and saw his sister Tamar weeping and in shame, he was mad as a hornet, but he kept his anger to himself.

David, however, was angry over the matter and probably cut Aubrey's allowance in half.

About two years after this Absalom sent word from his ranch that it was shearing time and he wanted the king, his father, and all the sons of David to come help with the shearing. David wouldn't go, but the rest of those invited, including Aubrey, went to the shearing, as Absalom had insisted that his father send Aubrey.

Absalom then instructed his soldiers, who were also ranch hands, to watch Aubrey, and when in the evening Aubrey was fairly full of wine, then to kill him, which they did. The other sons of David decided that they might also get similar treatment and so they fled on camels or mules or whatever they could find.

The grapevine reports that came to David were that all the king's sons had been killed by Absalom. David then went into mourning.

Flint, however, came to David and told him that only Aubrey had been killed and that this was in exchange for the way he had treated Absalom's sister.

Absalom knew that the king and many of his soldiers would be upset over this murder and so Absalom left the country. Shortly after this the king's sons began to straggle back to the palace and there was a big reunion, with much weeping.[1]

Absalom stayed away for 3 years and David his father was sad over this, as Absalom was his favorite son.

Chap.
14

Now Tuffy could see that David was sad and he knew that he longed to have Absalom back home; so Tuffy decided to use an indirect approach.

[1] Weeping for men was still in style.

Tuffy paid an actress to dress herself as a widow in mourning and come to David with a plea. The woman was admitted to the presence of the king and she told David a big story about her husband being dead and her two sons having a fight in a field and one killed the other. Then the people in town thought the other son should be executed for murder, but this would leave her without husband or sons, and she wanted the king to intercede in her behalf.

David immediately agreed to intercede and said that he would see that she and her remaining son were protected. David also said that there was no point in useless killing and vengeance.

Then the actress said, "Can I have permission to speak an additional word without being punished?"

"Permission granted," said David.

"Why don't you practice what you preach? Is there any reason why you should not let Absalom return here? The people need Absalom and a lot of folks are out of work with him gone. Use the same godly wisdom in dealing with your own son, and the same sense of justice as you have decreed for me."

"All right," said David. "Now I want to ask you a question, for this whole session seems to be a staged affair. Did Tuffy put you up to this?"

"The king is as wise as an angel of God, and surely nothing can be hidden from you. Yes, it was Tuffy."

Then David sent for Tuffy and told him to go and get Absalom and return him to his property, but not to bring him to the palace.

As a result, Tuffy made the trip to get Absalom and Absalom returned to his own ranch, but he did not get to visit his father the king.

Absalom was the most handsome man in all Israel and he was very popular and quite a playboy. Absalom went to the barber shop once a year and had two pounds of hair cut off his head.[1]

Now Absalom had been back home for two years and he still had not seen his father; so he sent a message to Tuffy asking Tuffy to visit him. Tuffy wouldn't come. Absalom wrote him again and Tuffy still wouldn't come.

It so happened that Tuffy's ranch and farm land joined Absalom, so Absalom had some of his cowpokes go when the wind was coming from the proper direction and set fire to Tuffy's fields.

Then Tuffy came to see Absalom and said, "What in the thunderation do you mean by setting fire to my field?"

Absalom said, "Well, I sent for you twice and you wouldn't come, so I thought this would bring you. I want you to arrange for me to see my father the king for I've been here two years and have not been invited to visit him. If my father thinks I'm a bad boy that should be punished, then let him judge me to my face and have me killed."[2]

[1] I have no idea why this is in the Scripture

[2] Absalom knew that his father loved him very much.

As a result Tuffy arranged for David to receive Absalom. When Absalom came, he bowed on the ground to his father and David embraced him and restored him to favor in the kingdom.

Although David was getting old, Absalom decided he did not want to wait the extra years before he could make a bid for the kingdom, and so he began to plot in devious ways a revolution to overthrow his father's government.

One thing he did was to get 50 excellent horsemen, and a strong running escort, to go with him all around the city, and he attracted great attention and much admiration.

Also everytime people from another tribe would come to David with a complaint, Absalom would talk with them and tell them that if he were king he would be of more help. He also bribed strangers and travelers to spread the word throughout Israel and to put bumper stickers on their chariots saying "Absalom for King."

Absalom then came to David and asked permission to take a trip north toward the borders of Syria, saying that he felt called of God to make this trip. David consented, and Absalom went with some two hundred men, the men posing as civilians although actually they were the soldiers of Absalom.

Absalom also enticed Welby,[1] David's advisor, to leave David and join Absalom. The conspiracy against David was strong and many people began to gravitate to Absalom, for they thought that he was a winner.

Word came to David finally that the people of Israel had turned pretty completely against him and had gone over to Absalom's side.

David then took his servants and a fair number of his wives and family and fled from Jerusalem. Many people from the city joined David in his flight and went with him over the hill and across the river.

There came then the mayor of Atlanta to David and said that he and his men appreciated all that David had done and they wished to join him in his time of trouble.

David advised them to go back to Atlanta and stay out of his troubles as the future looked dim. The men from Atlanta, however, said that trouble was no stranger to them and they would stick with David, which they did.

The ark of the covenant was also brought on the trip and it was under the care of Sheen.[2] David told Sheen to take the ark back to Jerusalem and said that if the Lord blessed him that he would return in triumph, and if not, then David said that he would accept the Lord's will for his life.

David then said further to Sheen, "You are a prophet, are you not, and a holy man with vision? Return with your two sons Ned[3] and

[1]Ahithophel   [2]Zadok   [3]Ahimaaz

Fred[1]", and they did.

In the meantime, David had already learned that Welby had defected and when David said his prayers that night he asked the Lord to confuse Welby's mind so that his advice to Absalom would be poor.

As David was climbing a small hill where he went to meditate and pray, he encountered an old friend, Rollow[2] from Arkansas[3], and he found his friend depressed over the political situation.

"Actually, my friend," said David, "joining me here is no help, but if you will go to Jerusalem and join Absalom, then I will have a source of information to offset the presence of Welby next to Absalom. If you have any information at any time just pass it along to Sheen at the church and he will get Ned or Fred to bring word to me."

Rollow did as he was asked and went into the city where Absalom was, for Absalom was taking over Jerusalem.

Chap.
16

After this meeting David moved over the top of the hill and saw there J.P., the right hand man of Sonny, the son of Jonathan.

"What are you doing here?" asked David.

"Sonny sent me with bread and wine for you and all the people with you."

"Where is Absalom?" asked David.

"He is in Jerusalem," said J.P., "and he expects to take over your kingdom today."

"You and those with you are all that are left out of the supporters of Saul, I guess." said David.

"Yes," said J.P., "and I hope we will find favor in your sight."

About this time, one of the food bearers from the supporters of Saul blew his top and came out in front of everybody cursing David, calling him a bloody killer, denouncing him for letting Saul fall to the Fascists. The cursing man also said that the rebellion of Absalom was the punishment of God.

Then Al, a younger brother of Tuffy, stepped forth and said, "Why should this dead dog curse our king? Let me cut off his head."

"Let him alone and let him curse. If the Lord has told him to curse me, we shouldn't stop him, and if not, it doesn't matter. It is the revolt of my son which disturbs me, not the cursing of this nut. In fact, it may be that this cursing will suffice, and the Lord will then bless me again."

This encouraged the cursing fellow a great deal, and as he walked along the hillside he continued to yell curses and to throw stones at the army.[4]

In the meantime, Absalom came to Jerusalem with Welby and

[1]J. Abiathar [2]Hushai [3]Archite [4]Some of his descendants are still living.

181

with all the host of Absalom and there Rollow joined the group. As Rollow came to Absalom he said, "God save the king, God save the king."

"Is this the way you treat your friend, my father. Why are you not with him?"

Then Rollow replied, "I go with the crowd. All the men of Israel have chosen you, so I am simply doing the same. What's more, should I not serve the son of my friend as I have served my friend? As I have been adviser to your father, so shall I be to you."

Then at dinner that night Absalom said to Welby, "Advise me what to do."

"What I think you should do," said Welby, "is go to your father's house in Jerusalem and publicly make free with his mistresses or wives that are left. Then all Israel will know that you have defied your father."

As a result of this advice, the men of Absalom put a tent on top of the roof of David's house and the public watched as Absalom would take one of his father's mistresses into the tent. Now Welby gave his advice as if it had come from God.

Chap.
17

The next day Welby came and said to Absalom, "I have some more advice. Let me select 12,000 of the best soldiers, and let me cross the Jordan and pursue David, who we know is old and weary. The small number of people with him will flee and I will kill only King David, and bring back all the rest of the people to join you, and the nation will be yours."

This sounded like a real good idea to Absalom and the local big shots sitting around him.

Absalom then said that he would like to hear what advice Rollow had and what he thought of the plan.

When Rollow came they told him of the suggestion made by Welby and then asked his opinion.

"I think it is a foolish plan," said Rollow. "You forget that your father is a warrior and he has a lot of strong and valiant men with him. Also David is as mad as a bear deprived of her cubs. As a result, you will encounter some real opposition and there will be much shedding of blood, while David will remain hidden in a cave or some safe place, as his loyal servants will protect him this way. Then the word will begin to spread around Israel that the followers of Absalom are blood spillers, and you won't have captured David either. My advice is that you gather together as great an army as you can and that you go forth in front of the city on the plains leading up to Jerusalem and challenge David and his army to come to you. You can lead this army, and then if you are victorious it will be understood, for it is proper to win a kingdom in regular battle. Then you can chase down all the men of David.

Your force will be so impressive that if David flees into a city, you can tie a rope around the city and drag the whole thing into the river Jordan."[1]

Absalom and all the big shots agreed that the advice of Rollow was vastly superior to that of Welby.

Then Rollow passed the word on the whole conversation to Sheen who passed the word to Fred and Ned, who did not try to slip out until it was dark. Even at that they were seen by a young fellow who passed the word to Absalom. Realizing that they might be caught, the two went to a friend's place near the edge of the city and the wife lowered the two into the well, then covered the well with a cloth and spread corn and shucks over the cloth as if she had been drying her corn.

When the search on the house to house plan developed, there came two to the place where Fred and Ned were hidden, but they could not find them. The lady said she thought she had seen them crossing the creek back of the house.

After the searchers left, the lady retrieved Fred and Ned from the well and they escaped to the camp of David and told him to get across the river and then decide what to do.

Now Welby was so upset over having his advice rejected, and since advisors had no advisors, Welby went out and hanged himself.

Absalom had, of course, fired Tuffy as chief of staff and Tuffy had slipped over to David's side.

Friendly people in the wilderness brought food and supplies to David and many valiant men and great warriors began to gather to fight for David, for he had built a great record of success and many people were loyal to him and had received great kindness for him.

David then organized his army.[2] He divided the army into three main sections, putting Tuffy in command of one section, dependable Al in command of another, and the third section was the group from Atlanta under the command of McDill.[3] David then said that he would also go into battle, in spite of his age and sore feet, as well as a touch of arthritis. The people would not agree to this, and they insisted that he remain on the wall of a small fortress and wait there for news of the battle.

David, the King, stood by the gate and blessed the people and their army, and they all heard him instruct the three generals to spare the life of Absalom.

The battle was engaged near the Vienna[4] woods and the three armies of David had trapped the army of Israel under Absalom in the woods, and the army of Absalom was badly beaten and more of his men were lost in the woods, running into trees, fleeing helter-skelter.

Absalom was riding a mule full speed[5] and Absalom's head became caught on a limb in the fork of the branches, and he was

---

[1] A wee bit oratorical at this point.   [2] David was truly a military genius.
[3] Ittai   [4] Ephraim   [5] This was a scared mule

hanging there kicking and asking for help. One of the soldiers of David saw the accident and came and reported it to Tuffy.

"Why didn't you kill him?" bellowed Tuffy. "I'd given you $500 for that."

Then the man said, "I would not have killed him for a million, for I heard the king say that he wanted Absalom's life spared. King David eventually learns everything that goes on, and it would have cost me my life to kill Absalom."

"O.K.," said Tuffy, who immediately went to the place where the soldier said Absalom was hanging and pierced his body with three short arrows, and then several other fellows who were there took an unnecessary hack or two at Absalom with their swords.

Then Tuffy had the bugler blow recall and he did not want to kill anymore Israelites, figuring that they would be needed in a couple of years probably to fight the Fascists again.

Tuffy and his squad of aides took the body of Absalom and buried it in the woods and covered it with a huge pile of stones.[1] Later the head stone, which Absalom had made for himself, was secured from his home and placed on the grave.

Then said Ned to Tuffy, "Let me go and tell David of the victory."

"Not today, Ned, for the king's son is dead and there will be no mail today," said Tuffy.

Then Tuffy turned to Owens and told him to go. After Owens left Ned then talked Tuffy into letting him go also.[2]

Ned took the shortcut which he knew and he arrived before Owens, and the watchman saw him coming and said to David, "A runner comes."

"If he is alone there is news. Just so it isn't the whole army running."

Then the watchman said, "There is another runner coming."

"He also brings news," decided the king.

"The first runner looks like Ned to me."

"He is a good man, so he brings good news," said David.

Ned arrived, panting, and said, "All is well. Blessed be the Lord God who has delivered our king and smitten the men that rose up against him."

"Is Absalom safe?" asked David.

"I don't know," said Ned, "there was a great tumult and much excitement over something, but I don't know what it was."

Then Owens arrived and began saying, "Good news, my king. The Lord has avenged us today of those in rebellion."

Again the king said, "Is Absalom safe?"

"He and others of your enemies are dead."

Then David went up to his room over the gate of the city and as he climbed the stairs he was heard in anguish saying, "O, my son,

[1] They didn't want an autopsy   [2] There's something here I don't quite get.

Absalom, my son, my son, Absalom, would to God that I had died instead of you! O, Absalom, my son, my son."

Word came to Tuffy and began to spread all through the city and among all the people of Israel that the king was in mourning for his son.

Instead of celebrating a great victory the people walked softly in the city. Then Tuffy came to David and complained that the king was embarassing his army and his friends because he was sad in victory and did not appreciate that his servants and his friends had saved his kingdom. Tuffy even suggested that David acted as if he wished Absalom had lived and all the friends and soldiers of David had died.

Then David arose and sat in his regular place of judgement and justice near the gate of the city.

Now following the battle every rebel in support of Absalom had fled to his own home and there was worry and strife through all the land.

David then sent for Sheen as well as Ned and Fred and suggested that they pass the word to the various leaders in all the areas of Israel and tell them that the king had forgiven their rebellion, that he considered all of them Israelites, and that he would greatly appreciate being invited to be their king again and to reunite the tribes of Israel.[1]

"Particularly get the word to General Carter[2] who was the chief of staff for Absalom, and tell him I will bring him back on equal rank with Tuffy," said David.

As this word spread, the peoples' hearts melted for David and they sent servants and gifts, asking him to return as their king.

J.P. came with his various vehicles to help David. The crazy nut who had cursed David also came and he fell at David's feet and apologized, saying that he was first of all the true sons of Joseph to come to David and he sought David's blessing.[3]

Al stepped forward then and suggested for the second time that he be allowed to cut off the guy's head, reminding the king that it was the man who cursed him. David, however, said that there would be no blood shed on the day of peace, for on this day David again became the king of Israel.

Then there came to meet him Sonny, the son of Jonathan, who had not washed his clothes since all the trouble began as a means of showing his sympathy to David.[4]

Sonny apologized to David for not coming to meet him in the wilderness, but he had no transportation and being lame he could not walk.

[1] And get anointed again. [2] Amasa [3] He still sounds crazy
[4] The first Hippie to make Scripture

David was understanding and restored the land to J.P., and Sonny which they both had owned prior to the revolution. Sonny said he was so happy over David's return that he wouldn't mind if J.P. took all the land.

There was a grand old man of the times named Holmes, who was one of the oldest men in the country, and he came to see that David was safely transported across the Jordan.

David then said, "Come with me to Jerusalem and eat with me in the palace."

"I'm sorry," said Holmes, "but I doubt if I have that much time left to live. I can't taste what I eat, or tell what I'm drinking, I'm too deaf to hear singing, so I'd just be in the way. I'll go with you a short distance, then I'll turn back and die in my own city, in my own house. I would appreciate it, however, if you would take my grandson, Scott[1], with you and let him have the advantage of growing up in the king's palace."

David was glad to do this.

When the entourage, consisting of the men of Judah, approached Jerusalem escorting David, the men of Israel were jealous and asked why they were not included in the big parade.

The men of Judah explained that they were already near to the place where David was and that no offense was meant. There was much discussion over the matter and loud talk, but the men of Judah out talked the men of Israel.

Chap.
20

There came upon the scene at this time a devilish fellow by the name of Adolph[2] who was fanatically ambitious and he made a big noise, and gathered a throng on the courthouse lawn and said, "Why do you Israelites let the men of Judah select the king? Why don't we have our own king? I suggest that all the faithful Israelites return home and leave King David with the tribe of Judah, and then Israel can become organized under me."

As a result, the men of Israel pulled out, but the men of Judah stayed with David.

In the meantime, David had been told about the scandal involving the ten semi-wives that he left at the palace and whom Absalom had publicly confiscated; so he built a small dormitory for them and imprisoned them in it for the rest of their lives.

The king then said to General Carter, "Go gather together an army of men of Judah and be back in three days."

General Carter didn't return in three days and David became properly suspicious.

David then remarked to Al, "Adolph will do us more harm than Absalom, for I'm sure General Carter has joined him. Pursue after them before Adolph and Al have time to get organized and capture a

[1]Chimham   [2]Sheba

186

bunch of cities and fortify them."

Al assembled the army and Tuffy, chief of staff, led the mighty men in hot pursuit of Adolph and General Carter.

It was not long before the army caught up with General Carter, who in leaving had stolen Tuffy's coat and sword, with all the fancy and high ranking insignia.

Tuffy noticed this, and when he walked up to greet General Carter he said, "How goes it?" As if in friendly gesture he grabbed Carter by the beard,[1] and then took the sword he had in his hand and thrust it through the general. General Carter fell dead in the road, and Tuffy suggested that the pursuit of Adolph be resumed. With Tuffy and Al leading the way, the march continued.

So many of the people and soldiers stopped to look at the dead general in the road that finally one man dragged the body over in the bushes.

The word was passed everywhere as the march continued that all the people loyal to Tuffy and to David should join the march and help chase down Adolph and destroy his army.

The army of Judah finally caught up with Adolph and he was in the city of Nashville;[2] so Tuffy had the men build trenches and lay seige to the city. It so happened that there was a very influential woman living in Nashville and she was very wise.

The woman stood on the wall of the city and called out, "Tell Tuffy to come near enough for me to speak to him."

As Tuffy approached the woman called out, "Are you Tuffy?"

"I am he," said Tuffy.

"I've got something to say," said the lady.

"Say it," said Tuffy.

"I am one of the peaceful and loyal persons in Israel. You and I are both Hebrews, and yet you want to destroy a city and kill a bunch of people, including mothers like me. Why do you want to swallow up part of the Lord's kingdom?"

"I don't want to swallow up part of the Lord's kingdom. The trouble is that a man named Adolph has defied the king and wants to start a revolution. Deliver him to me and I'll leave the city alone," said Tuffy.

"All right," said the nice lady, "you just stay there a few minutes and I will throw his head over the wall to you."

The wise lady then turned to the people of Nashville and said that there was no point in a big bloody and losing battle, as the head of Adolph was all that was wanted.

In a few minutes one of the men brought the lady the head of Adolph and she threw it to Tuffy. Tuffy then had the bugler blow recall, and the army departed from around the city. On returning to Jerusalem David gave Tuffy a medal and a raise in pay and made a few other promotions in the army.

[1]This was a similar custom to our handshake   [2]Abel

The next item on the agenda in Israel was a three year drought, which meant a famine in the land. David, as his custom was in time of trouble, called on the Lord and the Lord explained that it was because of the useless bloodshed that Saul had managed to put on the Commanche Indians.[1]

David then sent for the chiefs among the Commanches and apologized for Saul and asked what he could do to make up for the trouble that had been caused them.

"We do not want silver or gold and we don't want you to kill any of the men of Israel as a balance."

"All right," said David, "what do you want?"

"Saul was the man that plotted against us and drove us from our watering places and hunting grounds, so we suggest that you turn over to us seven of his descendants[2] and we will hang them in a special sunrise service."

David said, "I will deliver them to you."

David did not permit Sonny to be one of them. David did arrange for five of them to be sons of Greta, Saul's daughter, but none that were David's sons, only the sons of another husband. The mother of the other two sent to the Commanches was Mame, who had been a mistress of Saul as well as Bouncer. Word came to David that Mame had gone into mourning and was also staying by the dead bodies of her sons, protecting them night and day from the vultures.

David then decided to locate the bones of Saul and of Jonathan and to put them in a proper and dignified burial ground with proper ceremony. This was done. After that it began to rain and the Lord again blessed the land of Israel.

It had been several years since the Fascists had caused any trouble and apparently David missed them for he took a company of soldiers and went into their area and fought against one of their smaller garrisons. David was getting too old for this type of thing and he fainted during the fight.

One of the Fascist, Big Roy,[3] saw this and came near to kill David. Big Roy was a giant of a man, and a high draft choice, but Al arrived in time to attack the big man and to kill him, saving David's life.

The company attacked three other garrisons and in each case one of the men of David's army killed one of the giants that was with the Fascists. The most impressive of these giants was one who had 6 fingers on each hand and 6 toes on each foot, and he could count to 24. A nephew of David's was credited with this kill.

Then David, realizing that his life was nearly spent and that the

[1]Gebeonites   [2]Saul had about 35, legitimate and otherwise   [3]Ishbibenob

Lord had placed him in great circumstances, in conjunction with a couple of local writers, composed his funeral service, in the form of a song.

The Song of David

The Lord is my rock, my fortress, my deliverer
I trust completely in God, who is my rock,
He is the shield and the horn of my salvation
He is my high tower, my refuge, my saviour.
I call on the Lord and he saves me from my enemies,
When the waves of death seemed near,
And the flood of ungodly men were on me
I called on the Lord, and he heard, and delivered me
The earth shook and trembled
Because God was shaking my enemies
The sight was one of smoke and fire rising
Coming up out of the earth.
Darkness he sent, and wind on wings
Thunder and lighting came from God
The lighting was like arrows on the enemy
The sea raged, the earth opened up,
From all of this he delivered me.
He delivered me from powerful enemies,
Enemies too powerful and numerous for me
The Lord saved me, for he approved of me.
The Lord rewarded me according to my goodness
For I kept the ways of the Lord[1]
I never departed from any of his commandments[2]
The Lord always shows mercy to the merciful,
He helps the afflicted and frowns on the snobs,
The Lord is my lamp, and he makes my path bright
Because of God's help I have defeated a troop,
I have even been able to jump over a wall
The Lord's way is perfect
The Lord is a strong support to those that trust him
For there is only the one God, and the one Rock
God is my strength and my power
God has made me swift as a deer,
He has trained me as a warrior, I am strong,
The shield of God's salvation protects me
My feet are steady because I trust God
I have pursued my enemies to their death
I've watched them lying at my feet
Anyone who rose against me was defeated

[1]With a few exceptions not for funeral service comment   [2]I think the local PR men added this

The necks of my enemies were under my feet,
I was able to spread them like dust on the street
The Lord has also delivered me from my own people
Even strangers saw the power, and submitted to me
The Lord liveth, happy am I in my Rock
It is the Lord that does all things
Therefore I give thanks to the Lord,
I will even sing God's praises to the heathen
For he is a tower of strength,
A tower of salvation for his king
The Lord is merciful to David and his family,
Forever, and forever, Amen.

Chap.
23

After this song was composed David spoke to the people and explained that he was moved by the spirit of the Lord in his song and in his speaking.

David said, "The Lord has said that anyone who rules over men must be just and he must fear God. If the ruler does this he will be as the light from the rising sun, and he shall be welcomed as the sight of tender grass with the sun shining on it after a rain."

David went on to say that the Lord had made an everlasting covenant with him and his people, and always the people of God must know that the sons of the devil are as thorns and must be dealt with carefully, though eventually the wicked shall be burned.

David then called out the honor roll of mighty warriors and he told of some great feats that they reputedly had accomplished. David even said that York[1] had killed 800 men at one time with one spear, and he gave him, of course, a medal.

This occasion was quite impressive when David had the medal ceremony, naming and awarding outstanding warriors. In telling about 3 of the men David recalled the night that he had longed for a drink of water from the well in Bethlehem, but Bethlehem was in the hands of the Fascists. On this occasion, three mighty men crawled over the wall of Bethlehem and pulled a mission impossible, returning with a cup of water from the well in the city.

David was so impressed by this action that it was well remembered how he took the water and said that he, David, was not worthy of such loyalty and courage, that only God should receive such a tribute, and he poured the water on the ground as an act of worship.

Al was one of these men and it made such a tremendous impression on him that Al killed 300 Fascists over the next few years in his zeal to please King David.

One of the warriors was decorated for killing an Egyptian, who

[1]Adino

had a long spear. The man of David attacked the Egyptian, took the spear away, and killed him with his own spear.

Another warrior jumped down into a snow pit and killed a lion that was trapped and hungry, and then came out and killed two men from Mississippi who had come to see what was happening.

The names, tribes, and lineage of these men are listed in II Samuel 23:24-39.

The people of Israel began to stray from following the Lord and the Lord was displeased and David was also displeased. David decided that he would punish them with a plan of his own, which was to put them to work; so he ordered a census.

Tuffy raised sand about the order saying that it didn't make any difference how many people there were as long as there were plenty of them. In fact Tuffy went so far as to indicate that all David wanted to do was to brag about the number. The captains tried to talk David out of the census also, but David wouldn't budge; so out went the teams throughout all Israel and counted Hebrews for nine months, all the way from Maine to California.

The report showed that there were 800,000 men able to draw a sword in Israel and 500,000 in Judah.

David then regretted what he had done for he felt that he had punished the people his way and had not gone to the Lord with the matter. David then prayed for forgiveness and asked for guidance.

The next day David's private prophet Billy Sun[1] came to him and told him that the Lord had provided three choices of punishment for the people.

The first was seven years of famine, the second was 3 months of fleeing from enemies, and the third was three days of pestilence. David was told that he could make the choice.

David said, "It is better to fall into the hands of God than in the hands of man, so we'll take the short one, the three days of pestilence."

As a result a plague fell upon the people and some 70,000 died before the Lord stopped the plague by using an angel to intercede.

David told the angel, "I have sinned, but why should so many of the people be punished?"

God then sent word to David to build an altar and to worship. As a result David bought a barn and converted it into a church and there he conducted a worship service and prayed in the presence of the Lord God of Israel, and the plague was stopped.

[1]Gad

191

David became old and had very little life left in him and so he was cold all the time. Blankets didn't seem to do any good and as a result one of the palace groups suggested that there be secured a beautiful teen-age girl who had a yen to serve her fellow man and she could wait on David some during the day and lie close to him at night and make like a hot water bottle.[1]

As a result there was staged a Miss Teen-Age Israeli contest and a girl named Susie Q[2] won the contest and was brought to the palace. The girl performed her services well and she kept the king warm, though David did not trifle with her at all.

There then arose an ambitious young man named Nap[3] who decided to see if he could take over the kingdom. The first thing he did was to get an escort of fifty men and a few chariots and began to make a show around town. Nap was a younger brother of Absalom and was a pretty nice fellow. When David did not criticize him for his activities, Nap decided everything was going his way. Tuffy and Al then both began to help Nap, as they knew David was near the end of his days.

Nathan, the prophet, the other priests, and many of the mighty men of war were still determined to be loyal to David until his death.

Nap then had a big outdoor bar-b-que and invited a lot of important people and he planned to announce his intentions of being king, but he did not invite Nathan, or Solomon, or any of the mighty warriors loyal to David.

Nathan then spoke to Gina, the mother of Solomon, and asked her if she knew what was going on, and if King David knew what was happening.

Nathan then said, "Let me tell you how to save your life and the life of your son Solomon. Go to David and remind him that he took an oath saying that he would see to it that Solomon became the king after David's death. Then while you are still talking with King David, I'll come and support all that you say."

As a result Gina went to the king, who was very old, and Susie Q was nursing him. Gina bowed to the king, and David said, "What do you want?"

"I want to remind you that you took an oath saying that Solomon would reign as king in your place and yet Nap is establishing himself. In fact, he is having a big bar-b-que as an announcement party, and he didn't invite Solomon. Tuffy and Al have joined Nap and so have most of your other sons. All Israel wants to know what you plan to do, for your silence has left the impression that you support Nap."

[1]No heating pads then. [2]Abishag [3]Adonijah

While Gina was still talking in walked Nathan, the prophet, and he said, "Is it true that you have approved of Nap as your successor? There is a big outdoor picnic being staged and all indications are that you don't mind. Tuffy and Al are saying 'God save the King' to Nap. Now Solomon, myself, and the local priests have not been invited. Have you approved this matter without consulting us? Who have you chosen to sit on your throne?"

Now Gina had left the room by this time and David sent for her and said in her presence, "As the Lord liveth, even as I took oath before, I do so again, saying that Solomon shall be the king in my place. I will tend to the matter today."

Then Gina bowed low to David and did him reverence and said to him, "May the king live forever."

David then said, "Call Sheen, and Nathan."

When Sheen and Nathan were present together David said, "Take my stoutest warriors as escort, put Solomon on my mule, and go to Montreat, and there let Nathan and Sheen anoint Solomon as king, and then blow loudly the trumpet and proclaim 'God save King Solomon'. Then follow him back here and immediately put him on my throne as king, for I have appointed him ruler over Israel and Judah."

Then Cosby,[1] one of the high ranking priests, said "Amen. The Lord God of the king says Amen also. As the Lord has been with David so will the Lord be with Solomon and the Lord will make the throne of Solomon even greater than the throne of David."

As a result, Nathan, Sheen, Cosby, and a group of warriors went with Solomon to Westminister Abbey and Sheen took the horn of oil from the tabernacle and anointed Solomon. Then was the trumpet blown in front of the tabernacle and the group shouted, "God save King Solomon."

This started a wave of celebrating and a huge crowd gathered and began to make a great noise blowing on various types of horns and instruments. There was so much noise that Nap and his guests heard it all while they were eating and Tuffy, who had heard the sound of the trumpet, said, "What goes on that causes all this noise?"

While everyone was wondering there came into the meeting a young priest named Jon[2] and Nap said to him, "You are a good man, tell us what good thing is happening."

Jon said, "Our lord King David has just made Solomon the king. There has been a complete and proper ceremony, and Solomon rode to the tabernacle on David's mule, and Sheen has anointed Solomon with oil, and Nathan was in the ceremony, and now the people of the city are rejoicing, and that is what the noise is that you hear. Furthermore, Solomon is already sitting on the throne, and the mighty warriors of David have visited him, and approved his action and they are determined to make Solomon an even greater king than

[1]Benaiah [2]Jonathan

193

David. King David has already given his thanks to God for enabling him to see the new king on his throne."

This broke up the picnic, as all the guests were afraid and each person went quietly to his own house.

Nap was also afraid and he went to the church and kneeled in front of the altar. The news of this came to Solomon and he said to tell Nap that he had nothing to fear as long as he was a good man, but if he was wicked he would be killed.

So Solomon sent for Nap and Nap bowed down in front of Solomon and acknowledged his kingship and so he was allowed to go home.

Chap.
2

David came to Solomon and said, "I am shortly going to die, for I will go as the way of the earth is, but I charge you to be strong, and be a real man, be sure that you keep the charge of the Lord your God, and walk in his commandments and follow his judgements and his testimonies as they are recorded in the constitution,[1] in order that you may prosper and that the Lord may continue his promise to me when the Lord said 'if your children watch their step, and walk before me in truth with all their heart, with all their soul, there shall not be a failure on the throne of Israel.'

"As for a few practical matters," continued David, "let me remind you that Tuffy has been a bloody man. You know what he did to Bouncer, and the two captains, what he did to General Carter, how he often shed blood in time of peace, and what a violent man he was. Deal with him according to your own wisdom, but don't let him die in peace.

Show kindness, however, to the people of Atlanta, for they helped me when I needed help, as did J.P. and his crowd. Invite them to be at peace in the palace.

You have also the problem of Foul Mouth,[2] the fellow who cursed me mightily and whose life I continually spared, for I promised not to kill him, but he should not go unpunished. I will leave the decision to you, but don't let him die a natural death."

Then David died and was buried in the city of David. Solomon was upon the throne and the kingdom was as well consolidated as it had ever been.

Nap then called on Gina and asked to see her. Gina said, "Do you come in peace?"

"Yes," replied Nap, "I come in peace."

"What do you want?" asked Gina.

"I want you to go to your son Solomon and ask him to give me Susie Q for my wife. I know that the king will say yes to anything his mother requests."

As a result, Gina went to Solomon and Solomon invited her to

[1]Deuteromic Code [2]Shimei

sit on his right hand and then he said to her, "Mother, what is it that you want?"

"Will you promise to say yes?" asked Gina.

"Tell me what you want and I'll grant it to you," said Solomon.

"I want you to give Susie Q, your father's bed warmer, to Nap for a wife," said Gina.[1]

"You must be kidding, Mother. Why don't you ask me to give the kingdom to Nap, since he is my older brother? What about Tuffy, do you want something for him, or Fred, the priest who joined Nap?"

Then King Solomon said, "So help me God, Nap has revealed his treason. As the Lord liveth and has put me on the throne of Israel, and established my house, I promise that Nap won't live through the day."

King Solomon then sent word to Cosby, his temple hatchet man, to kill Nap and it was done that very day.

The king then sent word to Fred, the priest, telling him to escape to his fields for Solomon was sparing his life for his work in bringing the ark of the covenant to Jerusalem. Then there was banished from the ministry the last of the descendants of Eli.

Word of all this reached Tuffy, who was getting a little old and creeky boned, and he was afraid for his life and so he went to the tabernacle and knelt in front of the altar.

The news of this came to Solomon and he sent word to his head hit man Cosby to have Tuffy killed.

Cosby came to Solomon and said that he had invited Tuffy out of the church to fight him in the street, but he wouldn't come.

"Kill him where he is," said Solomon. "For he is a man that has often shed innocent blood, and has brought violence into peaceful times. Did he not kill Bouncer without permission? And what of General Carter, and the two young captains? The blood of all of these and more is on the head of Tuffy. Let him have it!"

As a result, Cosby went into the church and killed Tuffy in front of the altar, and then let the family take the body home for burial.

Cosby was then promoted to General and Sheen was given the top spot in the church organization.

The king then sent for Foul Mouth and said to him, "Build yourself a house in Jerusalem and stay in it. You are not to leave the immediate area as long as you live, and if you so much as cross the creek you will be executed."

"Thank you," said Foul Mouth, "that is a fair arrangement."

About three years later, two of the servants of Foul Mouth went AWOL and left the city limits, figuring that Foul Mouth would not dare chase them.

Foul Mouth, however, figured the king might not learn of his

[1]I've never felt that Gina thought much of this Susie Q business.

leaving or that he may have forgotten the arrangement, and so he pursued the servants, caught them, and brought them home.

Solomon learned of this and he sent for Foul Mouth.

"Didn't I make you swear before God that you wouldn't leave the area?" asked the king. "Didn't I tell you that you would be executed if you left town? Didn't you say that this was a fair arrangement? Furthermore, you know your record of wickedness and how among other things you cursed my father. Your chickens have come home to roost."

Solomon then told Cosby to see that Foul Mouth didn't live another day, and so he was killed after he left the palace area. Then the kingdom settled down for a few weeks.

Chap.
3

Solomon's first plan in connection with protection for his people was to develop friendly relations with Egypt, which he did by bringing a daughter of the Pharoah to Jerusalem as one of his wives, and he kept her as testimony of his good faith during the entire time of his building a huge palace and the greatest temple ever constructed.

Solomon loved God and obeyed his commandments and he worshipped God in the high places in his kingdom and made sacrifices on various hills that had been designated holy places.

The Lord, on one of these trips of worship, appeared to Solomon in a dream and asked him to name the thing he would prefer to possess above all other things.

Solomon spoke to the Lord in prayer and meditation and he said "You showed great mercy in dealing with my father David who walked before you in truth and uprightness, and you gave him a son to sit upon his throne and I am that son. I seem to myself to be as a little child in charge of a kingdom, almost as if I do not know when to come and when to go.

Yet I am in the midst of a people that are too numerous to number, and so I would ask for an understanding heart that I may be able to judge the people justly and to discern between that which is good and that which is bad."

This presentation pleased the Lord, and God said to Solomon, "Because you have asked for what you did, and did not ask for riches or for long life or for the death of your enemies, but have asked for understanding, be certain that I shall give you such a wise and understanding heart that there had never been one like you and there will never again be one your equal in this capacity. I will also give you great riches, though you did not ask for such, and you will have honors, so that there will be no king like you as long as you live.

What is more, if you will walk in my ways and keep my commandments and my statutes, then I will also give you long life."

Solomon awoke and realized he had had this dream, and so he came to Jerusalem and entered the tabernacle and made an offering and praised God.

There came before the judgment seat of Solomon two women, neither of whom had official husbands.

One woman spoke to Solomon and said, "The two of us girls live together, and I had a baby son. Three days later this other girl had a baby son, and there were no other people in the house; so there are no witnesses.

Now this other girl's baby died in the night and while I was asleep she exchanged babies with me; so that in the morning I had the dead baby. I recognized immediately that the dead baby was not my child."

"That's not right, King Solomon. The living son is mine," said the second girl.

"You're wrong," said the first, and thus they continued back and forth.

The king then said, "Bring me a sword," and they did.

The king then said, "Take the sword and cut the baby in half, and give half to each woman."

Then the first girl said, "O, no, not that. Give the child to the other girl. I'd rather be deprived of my son than to have him killed."

The second woman, however, said, "I think dividing the child in half is a good arrangement, then it will be neither one of us who benefits."

Then Solomon said, "Give the child to the first woman. She is the real mother."

This account spread through all the countryside and the people developed a great respect for Solomon and his wisdom, for they perceived that the wisdom of God was in him.

Chap.
4

King Solomon began the first real organization of the kingdom of Israel. One thing that he did was to appoint rulers over various sections of the kingdom and to make them responsible directly to him. One of the neat things he did was to appoint 12 chefs for the palace, one for each month. The list of all the rulers and chefs are in I Kings 4:2-19.

Judah and Israel combined were really big by this time and there was much eating, drinking, and making merry under the wise rule of Solomon, for every man felt safe from any outside enemy.

The possessions of Solomon were quite impressive. There were so many people connected with the palace itself that 30 beef cows were killed daily to feed them, not to mention deer of various kinds, including the fallow deer.

Solomon had a stable with 40,000 stalls for the chariot horses, and men everywhere worked for the government to provide for all of these additions. Solomon's wisdom, his great gift from God, enabled him to rule wisely and his reputation was in itself a great protection to the people.

At one time or another, Solomon uttered 3,000 proverbs and wrote over 1,000 songs and he was knowledgeable about trees, animals, and fish. Kings and important people from all over the world came to visit Solomon to learn from him and to see the many tourist attractions that he added to the kingdom.

Chap.
5

Hiram, King of Tyre, who had been a friend of David's, sent greetings by messenger to Solomon, for Hiram was in the construction business.

Solomon sent word then to Hiram telling him that David, his father, had wanted to build a temple to the Lord, but that he had too much trouble with wars and internal enemies to do this, but that Solomon was ready to build.

Solomon said, "The Lord my God has given me rest from my enemies, and I plan to build a church in the name of the Lord my God, exactly as the Lord had told my father that I would. As a result, I want to place a gigantic order for timber, both cedar and other timbers."

Hiram rejoiced in this and blessed God for raising up such a wise son to David and Hiram agreed to fill the order. In fact, Hiram said that he would secure the cedars from Lebanon and float them down the Jordan to the nearest point of building. Hiram did the same thing with the fir trees which were needed.

Solomon paid Hiram a good price for this material and Hiram and Solomon made a permanent agreement of goodwill between them.

Then Solomon drafted 30,000 men of Israel as laborers rather than soldiers, and they went forth as wood choppers and transportation people, log rollers, and lineman, and Solomon appointed 3,300 foremen to supervise the work.

Then Solomon had great stones cut from the quarry and the stone quarriers and stone masons worked together, some of Hiram, some of Solomon, and they laid a foundation for the house of God.

Chap.
6

An intricate description of the building, with measurement details, material factors, and contruction plans. The summation — tremendous! It took eleven years to finish the building.

Chap.
7

In the meantime, Solomon was also building a new palace and this took thirteen years. Solomon built some other buildings also, furnishing one of the greatest employment plans ever devised.

The description of Solomon's house is concisely stated in I Kings 7:2-12. Solomon also built a special house on the grounds for Pharaoh's daughter, who was one of Solomon's wives.

Hiram then came from Tyre, for he was an artist in brass work and in decorating, and he worked on all the trimmings which are carefully described in I Kings 7:14-50.

After everything was finished, then Solomon brought into the temple the precious antiques of his father David. The silver things, and the gold things, and the artistic vessels and containers.

Chap.
8

Then Solomon assembled all the elders of Israel, and all the high ranking churchmen, and he had the ark of the covenant of the Lord brought to the temple and placed in the holy of holies. A worship service with proper sacrifices was conducted in the presence of the congregation. There was nothing in the ark of the covenant except the two tables of stone containing the ten commandments.

The glory and power of the Lord made a visible manifestation in the temple, and the priests even could not remain, for the cloud of God was thick in the temple.

Then Solomon spoke to the people saying, "The Lord said that he would dwell in privacy, and I have built for him a worthy place."

Then Solomon blessed the people and thanked them for their interest and help.[1]

Then Solomon spoke again saying, "Blessed be the Lord God of Israel who spoke through David, my father, and who has made good his promises. For the Lord called no city his own and no place his temple, although it was in the heart of my father, David, to build a house for the Lord, the Lord said to David 'It is enough that you desire to do this, nevertheless, it will not be you, but your son who builds the temple to the Lord.'

The Lord has performed his word and I have built the temple."

Then Solomon stood in front of the temple and spoke further saying, "There is no God like the Lord God of Israel, neither in heaven above or in the earth beneath. The Lord is the keeper of the promises, and he is merciful to those who follow in his commandments. The Lord has kept his promise to David, and may the Lord continue to do so, and keep the throne of Israel intact by providing righteous men, for sin brings destruction.

Yet how can man expect to contain God in a building, for his expanse is from heaven to heaven and to heavens, yet Lord, I pray that you will diligently watch this house day and night, and listen when the people pray facing this house, and forgive them when they sin.

Remember also, O Lord my God, to restore the people when they return after wandering from you, do not hold their sins against them for any length of time, and when they fully repent, please fully restore them.

When the people have sinned and are punished with a drought, and then they turn to this place and pray for help, hear their cry and

[1]Imagine getting a thank you from the IRS

give aid to their land, and forgive the people.

If there be pestilence, and disease, and mildew, or if enemies plunder and capture, hear then the prayers of those who face this place and seek your help.

Hear also, O Lord God, the prayer of the stranger who may come from a far country and face this place and pray in full belief. Answer the stranger's prayer so that all the people of the earth may know the one true God.

If the people of Israel go forth to battle and before the battle face this place and pray, hear their prayer, and support their cause.

If the people sin, and they probably will, and are captured and taken into strange lands, then if they repent and face this place and call upon the name of the Lord, hear their plea and support them.

Forgive thy people when they seek forgiveness, have compassion on them, for they are designated as the people of God. These people are chosen by the Lord to be delivered from Egypt and to have the special function of magnifying the glory of God. Let all of these things assist in making known that the Lord is God, everywhere, over every nation."

Then there were special services dedicating different parts of the temple and there were feasts, and all these things took eight days, and were all part of the dedication of the temple.

Chap.
9

Now it had taken Solomon many years to complete all his building programs. The Lord appeared to Solomon a second time and told him that God had heard his prayer and that the house that he built for the Lord would be blessed and that the heart of God would always be in his church. God then again remembered his covenant telling Solomon that if he would walk uprightly and not be diverted to strange gods, then the Lord would make the throne of the kingdom of Israel permanent,[1] but if Solomon or any of his descendants began to turn from God and seek off-beat idolatries, then the Lord said that he would cut Israel out of the land that was theirs, and the name of Israel itself would become the brunt of jokes.

When such a thing occurs people in the future who view the remains of the majesty of the temple shall be told that the calamity was because the people wandered from the Lord God of Israel, the keeper of the promises.

At the end of the building period of about 20 years Solomon paid the Hiram Building and Supply Co. for the materials and labor, and the price he paid was to give Hiram and Co. twenty whole cities in Galilee. Hiram, himself, came to view the cities and he was pleased with the price and desired to do more business with Solomon.

It was, of course, necessary for Solomon to raise taxes again for the payments as he needed to build replacement cities. Solomon

[1]Which I think he finally did in Christ.

began to tax all the people everywhere in every direction and he made bonded workers out of all people who were not Israelites, and made warriors out of all the able bodied men of Israel.

There were 550 men of Israel chosen to direct all the work camps, and all the reconstruction in the cities.

Pharaoh's daughter, the wife of Solomon, moved into her private home on the palace grounds.

Solomon went to church three times a year, as was required by the law of Moses.

Solomon then conceived the idea of developing a navy and a merchant marine, in order that gold and silver from faraway places could be brought to Solomon. Hiram Building and Supply Co. got the contract for building all the ships and Hiram supplied experienced seaman to sail with the men of Israel and train them.[1]

Chap.
10

Now the Queen of Sheba heard of the fame of Solomon, of his wisdom and his great tourist attractions, and so she decided to come and visit and see for herself.

As a result, the Queen of Sheba came to Jerusalem in an impressive fashion, with an escort of camels carrying rich spices, and much gold, and many diamonds.

Sheba met with Solomon and they had long conversations and she was tremendously impressed with his vast knowledge, and with the temple and the palace, and even with the fabulous foods which were served. She was also impressed with how well trained his staff was, how handsomely they dressed.

"It was a true report that I heard in my land about you," said Sheba to Solomon, "and I admit that I did not believe it. I was in error, for what I have seen is even more fantastic than had been told me. Your wisdom and your prosperity exceeds everything that I have heard. How fortunate are the people who know you and have the benefit of your wisdom. Blessed is the Lord your God for putting you on the throne to render judgements and to deal justly."

Then Sheba presented Solomon with many gifts, and chiefly were the gifts precious spices, for Solomon had everything else already.

Solomon then gave the Queen of Sheba all that she asked[2] and then Solomon added a big bonus from his own treasury.

About this same time Solomon had been told by Hiram of a special brand of tree known as an almug tree. Hiram said there were only a few in all the world and Solomon ordered everyone of them at a great price and he made beautiful posts, and there has never been another almug tree in the world.[3]

Solomon had an income of about 20 million a year direct,

[1]Hiram was an industrialist   [2]Which I bet was plenty   [3]I am suspicious of Hiram here. We still have some Hirams in the world, though no almug trees.

which did not include his cut on all the merchant marine, caravan taxes, and the protection game which he used on the Arab kings, as well as on all small-time rulers.

Solomon had such a gold problem that he made shields of gold, and targets of gold, and all of his cups, and plates were solid gold. To add to his splendour he had a throne made of solid ivory covered with gold and there were all kinds of figures of beasts around the throne.

Every three years the navy and the merchant marine came to port and brought Solomon gold, silver, ivory, apes,[1] and peacocks.

Kings and princes came from everywhere to visit Solomon, to seek his advice, enjoy his hospitality, and exchange gifts.

There was so much silver around that it became as worthless as stone and cedar boards became as worthless as sycamore planks. Linens were brought from Egypt and this also turned into a good business.

Then the foreign women began to get to Solomon. Not only Pharoah's daughter, but the rulers of many different places began to send their prettiest girls, and Solomon added to his household wives from India, Persia, Mississippi, some gypsies, and as Solomon became older [2] the foreign women mislead him and Solomon, for their sake, began to worship strange gods such as Ash[3] and Totem[4] and Solomon began to neglect his own church and the one true God. Solomon began to build private temples for his favorite wives, and the Lord became angry.

The Lord then said to Solomon "Because you have forsaken me, I will take the kingdom away from your descendants. I will not do it in your lifetime because of my promise to your father David, but I will keep one tribe only for your son, and the rest shall depart from your family."

Along with his neglect of God, Solomon also began to neglect his kingdom and there came into power in Egypt a refugee from the land of Canaan, who had heard of the death of David and Tuffy, and this man, named Tom Nester,[5] began to organize an army and to harass the southern portion of Solomon's kingdom. Tom had made friends with Pharoah by giving him his sister-in-law and he was therefore supported somewhat by the Egyptians.

The Lord also stirred into action a fellow named Reo Villa[6] who began to organize an army in the north, and he took command of Syria and he began to raid the northern outposts of Solomon's kingdom.

Then Jerry[7], the son of one of the palace servants, began to organize a little against Solomon, almost right under his nose.

[1]I still don't know why he wanted apes. Maybe because he didn't have any.
[2]Probably late forties [3]Ashtoreth [4]Milcom [5]Hadad [6]Rezon [7]Jeroboam

Now Jerry was a mighty warrior and an impressive person and so Solomon put him in charge of the tribe of Joseph, not knowing that he was a potential defector.

It happened one day that Jerry left Jerusalem on a short trip and he was stopped in a field by L. Evans,[1] a prophet of the Lord.

Now Jerry had on a new flowing cape, and the prophet took it and tore it into ten pieces and said "Thus says God, the Lord of Israel, for you are to take the ten pieces as a symbol that you will be given ten tribes of Israel over which you are to reign. One tribe will be left for a descendant of David, because of the faithfulness of David, and one shall be left to care for Jerusalem, which is my city. I am doing this, God has said, because Solomon is worshipping strange gods and neglecting his own church and his kingdom. I will not do this, God has said, in the lifetime of Solomon, but his days are numbered, for he has burned his candle at both ends for too long. You will take over ten tribes and the son of Solomon shall have one."

"As for you," continued the prophet, "God says that you will be king of Israel, and if you observe God's commands and walk in his truth, then God will build for you a name and a lineage as God did for David."

Word of this leaked out[2] and Solomon sought to kill Jerry, and put out a contract on him. As a result, Jerry fled to Egypt and remained there as a guest of Pharoah until Solomon died. Solomon ruled Israel for forty years and then he was buried in Jerusalem and his son Roger[3] assumed the throne of Israel.

Chap. 12

There was then a great assembly called at Baltimore[4] in order to make Roger king of Israel. In the meantime, the people had sent for Jerry and a great group of people joined Jerry in appearing before the new king and asking about his policy.

The spokesman for the people said, "Your father Solomon really hurt us with his taxes and we have decided that if you will lighten our tax load, we will all support you as king."

"Come back in three days and I'll give you my answer," said Roger.

Then Roger called to him a group of wise and experienced men and he asked these older men what they thought he should do with the request.

The men replied "Agree to cut the taxes. If you will let up a bit on these people they will be grateful and you will be a respected and beloved king over all the tribes."

Then Roger called to him a group of his young friends, who were inexperienced and also eager for their own benefits as friends of Roger. These young men advised Roger to reply sharply to the

[1] Ahijah   [2] Leak outs in church work are still common.   [3] Rehoboam   [4] Shechem

203

people and deny their request, and to raise their taxes, just for bringing the matter to his attention.

Three days later Jerry and the representatives of Israel appeared before King Roger for his answer.

Roger had decided to follow the poor advice of the youth group and he spoke sharply to the people as they had suggested saying "My father treated you lightly compared to what I plan to do. My little finger will seem as big to you as my father's leg. I will add to the yoke my father placed upon you and where he beat you with whips I'll do it with scorpions."

When the tribes of Israel saw that the king paid no attention to them, the people then said, "What have we to do with you? We are not in the tribe of Benjamin as David was, we don't have to recognize you as king, and you can go jump in the lake."

As a result every man of Israel returned to his home. The Israelites in the tribe of Judah and the small group of the tribe of Benjamin remained under Roger.

When Roger sent his tax collector to start work in Israel, the people stoned him to death. Roger then retreated to Jerusalem, for he feared for his own life.

As word spread regarding this, and as the news was out that Jerry was back from Egypt, the people of the ten tribes called Jerry into a big meeting and made him their king.

When Roger returned to Jerusalem he immediately began to recruit an army from the men of Judah and Benjamin to go and fight their fellow countrymen of the ten other tribes of Israel.

Then the word of the Lord came to Stewart,[1] a spokesman for God, and told him to go to Roger and to all the people of Judah and Benjamin and to tell them that the Lord was against their moving to fight the other tribes and that the Lord was commanding them to go home.

The people listened and they dissolved the army by each going to his own home.

Now Jerry was a plotting type and basically insecure, so he began to worry about the times that the members of the ten tribes under his rule would go to Jerusalem for their worship occasions.

It occured to Jerry that these people would come under the influence of Roger and might desert Jerry.

As a result, he decided to build two worship places of his own, that were readily accessible to his people. At each of these selected places Jerry had golden calves placed on display and he told the people that these calves delivered the Israelites from Egypt and that worship in these places would save the trip to Jerusalem and still count as church.

This was a great sin in the eyes of God, and Jerry made it worse by placing men not of the priestly line of Levi in charge, and

---

[1]Shemaiah

designating thereby his own priests.

Jerry worked out some sacrifices and an order of worship and led in the idolatry. It was an all-laymen church.

There came then a man of God out of Judah to one of the idol worshipping places, the one at Vegas,[1] and he spoke against the idol worship in the name of the Lord, and he prophesied saying, "From the line of David a child shall come to rule named Josiah and he will burn men on this altar. This shall be the sign, that the altar shall split in two and the ashes shall spill forth."

When Jerry heard these words he put forth his hand over the altar and ordered his men to seize the prophet.

When Jerry thrust his hand over the altar, his hand withered, and he could not move it, for it became paralyzed. Then the altar was split in two and the ashes poured forth as the Lord had decreed through his prophet.

Jerry then said to the man of God, "Pray for me. Ask the Lord to restore my hand."

The prophet interceded in prayer for Jerry, and the paralysis left his hand.

"Come home with me," said the king, "refresh yourself and I will also give you an honorarium."

"If you would offer me half of all you possess," said the prophet, "I will not go with you, for the Lord told me to eat no bread and drink no water, nor to vary from my path home, being careful to return by a different route."

Now there was an old prophet living in Vegas who heard of this and since his two sons had seen the road down which the real prophet had departed, he got on a donkey and went after him.

When he found the true man of God he spoke to him, as the prophet was sitting under an oak tree, and said "Are you the prophet that came from Judah?"

"I am," the prophet replied.

"How about coming home with me and having a meal?" asked the Vegas soothsayer.

"I cannot do it. I am under direct orders from God not to eat bread or drink water or turn aside until I have returned to my home church."

"Well," said the Vegas prophet, "it so happens that I am a prophet also, and an angel came to me just a short time ago and told me to tell you that your instructions were cancelled and you could return with me." Of course, the Vegas man lied.

As a consequence, the prophet of Judah returned to Vegas and ate bread and drank water and refreshed himself. The Vegas prophet knew that the Lord would not allow such disobediences and he

[1]Bethel

205

envisioned that the man from Judah would not have a safe trip back home.

After the meal was over, the prophet of Judah got on his donkey and as he was enroute home a lion attacked him and killed him and stood by his body.

Men on the road saw what happened and they saw the lion standing by the body and they reported this in Vegas.

When the Vegas prophet heard this, he thought surely it was the prophet from Judah who disobeyed the direct word of God.

Then the Vegas prophet got on his donkey and went to get the body. The lion was still there and ran off when the prophet came. The Vegas prophet took the body and brought it to Vegas and buried the man in the place he had fixed for himself saying, "Alas, my brother is dead. When I die just put me on top of my departed fellow prophet for surely he was a true prophet of the Lord and his words at the altar will be found to be accurate."[1]

None of this had any effect on Jerry as he continued his evil ways and his violations of worship, and the sin of all he did was disastrous to his whole family.

Shortly after this Tab,[2] the son of Jerry, who was but a small boy, became ill. Jerry then said to his wife, "Disguise yourself, so no one will know that you are the king's wife, and go to Montreat,[3] and visit there with the prophet L. Evans, who told me I was to become King, and ask him about our son and if he will get well, and take the proper fee and also a sacrifice for the altar."

Jerry's wife did as she was told and she came to L. Evans, who was now blind in his old age. The Lord, however, revealed to L. Evans that Jerry's wife was there to see him[4] and the Lord inspired Evans so that he knew what to say.

When L. Evans then heard the sound of the woman's feet approaching him, he said, "Come in, wife of Jerry. Why try to disguise yourself? I have bad news for you. Go tell Jerry that the Lord God of Israel exalted him and made him king over the people of Israel, and took the kingdom away from the house of David, and yet Jerry has not followed my commandments as David did, but has done evil in the sight of the Lord. The Lord, therefore, will bring evil against the house of Jerry, and will cut his son off from the line of the kingdom. The Lord will take away the remnants like a farmer cleaning his barnyard. The descendants of Jerry will die in the fields or in the streets of a city, and their bodies shall be left for the vultures and the jackals, and the dogs. When you leave here and return, your son shall die as you enter the city.

Because this young boy was blameless he shall be an exception, and Israel shall mourn his death, and he is to be given a proper

[1]This little account baffles me a bit [2]Abijah [3]Shiloh
[4]God sometimes used helpers to pass information, I think.

funeral.

Because of the sins of Jerry, and the sins of the people in following him in the worship of idols, the Lord shall scatter Israel and the Lord will depart from Israel."

Then Jerry's wife arose and returned and as she entered the child's room, the boy died, and all Israel mourned, and the boy was given a proper funeral.

Jerry reigned in war and wickedness for 22 years, and then he died.

In the meantime, Reo Villa was king in Judah and he also did wickedly and led the people in idol worship. The people began to buy and sell graven images, and to adopt the evil ways of the heathen neighbors who lived near them.

In the fifth year of the rule of Reo Villa, the king of Egypt, Clyde[1] came to Jerusalem with a troop of warriors and captured all the treasures of the temple, the gold shields, and the many valuables of David and of Solomon.

After this was done, Reo Villa had imitation shields and cheap ornaments made to replace the valuables stolen by Clyde.

There was also continuous strife between the people of Reo Villa and Jerry. Reo Villa died and was buried in the place of Kings, and his son reigned in his place. Huff,[2] the son of Reo Villa, did evil as his father did, and continued the wickedness of the kingdom and the strife with Jerry's people.

For the sake of his faithful servant David, however, the Lord allowed the reign to continue through Huff's son, Asa.

Now Asa was a fine man and he did that which was right in the eyes of the Lord and he launched moral campaigns, and fought crime, and tore down all the idols that had been erected by his father. Asa went so far as to remove his mother from having the status of queen because she had made an idol and placed it in the woods. Asa had the idol destroyed.

Asa also began to bring gifts of silver and valuables back into the Lord's house.

There was continued strife between Israel and Judah, and Baldy,[3] king of Israel set up his army on the border of Judah and stopped all traffic and all trade to the outside world in that direction.

Asa then took the treasures which he had accumulated and he sent them with messengers to Robinhood,[4] king of Syria, living in Damascus.

"Robinhood," the messengers said, "Asa would remind you of the treaty that has existed for many years between our nations. He is sending a valuable gift in gold and silver. He wants you to declare war on Baldy and smite Israel and relieve him of the pressure he is under."

[1]Shishak [2]Abijam [3]Baasha [4]Benhadad

Robinhood thought well of this, and he and his men went to Israel and destroyed many cities and gathered a great amount of spoil. When Baldy heard of this, he removed the great road block he was building in the form of a fort and he fled. Asa then took the materials from the fort and built a small town.

Asa was a good man and did many fine things, but in his old age his feet hurt terribly,[1] and he died and was buried in the place of kings with honor.

To get back a bit chronologically, Baldy had become king of Israel by getting a bunch of warriors together and fighting the wicked Theo,[2] who had taken his father Jerry's place as king. Baldy killed Theo and took his place. In fact, Baldy sought out every descendant of Jerry and had each one of them killed, as L. Evans had predicted.

Baldy, like Jerry and Theo, was also a bad boy.

The word of the Lord then came to a man named Jay[3] and the word was that the Lord was displeased with Baldy and he would do to Baldy's lineage what he had done to Jerry's.

While Asa was still king in Judah, Baldy died and his son Simbo[4] took his place. Now Simbo had a warrior named Zulu[5] who was in charge of half the chariots, and Zulu developed some big ambitions. As a result, when Zulu knew that Simbo was getting stoned at a friend's party, he entered and killed him, and declared himself king.

The first thing the new king did was to kill all the male descendants of Simbo, as well as all of his close friends and kinsmen. This is exactly what Jay said would finally happen.

Apparently Zulu did this killing very promptly, for he was king only 7 days.[6]

When word of Zulu's conspiracy and the murder of Simbo went around the country, the men of Israel didn't like it, and they appointed Rowan[7] to be head of the troops and to march against Zulu. When this occurred, Zulu became terrified and fled into the king's house, set fire to it, and burned himself up as well as the house.

Then the people were confused as they had no king, and half wanted to make Rowan king and half wanted a man named Martin.[8]

The people who favored Rowan finally won out and so they buried Martin.

Now Rowan was king for 12 years. The first six years he lived in the San Fernando Valley,[9] but then he decided to live on a hill. As a result, he bought a whole hill and built his palace on the hill and called the place Samaria.

[1]Phlebitis, no doubt [2]Nadab [3]Jehu [4]Elah [5]Zimri
[6]Hardly worth the trouble [7]Omri [8]Tibni [9]Tirzah

Now Rowan did everything evil that Jerry or Baldy or any of the others had done, and then he added some new twists of his own. Rowan also caused the people to sin and set an example of wickedness and he provoked the Lord to anger against Israel.

Then Ahab, the son of Rowan, took the throne after his father's death, and Ahab broke all the records for wickedness. The worst thing he did in the sight of the Lord was to marry Jezebel, a mean heathen woman, and to begin at once to worship Baal, who was the idol that Jezebel advocated. Ahab did more to provoke the Lord than any of the other kings.

During this time, however, the city of Jericho was rebuilt by a man named Zachry.[1]

The Lord raised in North Carolina[2] a great prophet named Elijah and he appeared before Ahab and told Ahab that there would be no more rain in all the land until Elijah asked God to send rain.

Then, following the inner voice of God, Elijah left the area and camped by a small spring fed stream, and there he was fed by the ravens who robbed area ranches and brought Elijah food.

Finally, the terrible drought in the land caused the spring to run dry and the inner prompting of the Lord told Elijah to go to Ashville, N.C.[3] and that there he would find a widow who would care for him during the remainder of the drought.

As Elijah approached Ashville he saw a woman gathering sticks and he said to her, "Bring me a cup of water."[4]

As she was going to get the water he called after her and said "and while you're up, bring me a sandwich also."

"So help me God, fellow," said the woman, "I don't have but one handful of flour left in the last barrel, and I'm gathering sticks to build a fire, bake one roll for my son and me, and lie down and die of starvation."

"Don't panic, now" said Elijah, "but bake me a roll and bring it to me, then you will find that there is still plenty left for you and your son, for the Lord God of Israel will see to it that you are never without flour and cooking oil as long as the drought lasts."

The widow woman did as Elijah said and as a result Elijah moved into her house and there was always food available for the woman, her son, and Elijah.

Some time after this the son became very ill and he fainted, and was not able to catch his breath.

"Why did I ever let a man of God into this house? You have come to punish me for my sin by taking the life of my son."[5]

"Hand me the child," said Elijah. Elijah took the boy to his room and gave him artificial respiration and he prayed to the Lord

[1]Hiel [2]Tishbite [3]Zarephath [4]It was polite to order women around in those days.
[5]Here you get to fill in your own sin.

209

for the child's life, and the Lord heard Elijah and breath came back into the boy and he revived.

Elijah brought the son to his mother and the woman said, "Truly now I know that you are a man of God, and the word of the Lord which you speak is true."

In the third year of the drought the word of the Lord came to Elijah and urged him to visit Ahab. There was, of course, a great famine now in the land.

In the meantime Ahab had called Dean Dusk,[1] his secretary of state, and told him to search one half of the land while Ahab searched another half to see if they could find anyplace to put their cattle and mules for grass and water.

Now Dean Dusk was a man who was upright and who respected God. In fact, when Jezebel had made a purge of the land in her style by having all the priests executed, Dean had helped 100 ministers to escape and he had been sneaking them food as they were hidden in a couple of big caves.

As Dean was searching his half of the land he met Elijah, and recognizing the prophet, he bowed to him, but to make certain he said, "Are you not Elijah?"

"I am. Now go tell Ahab that Elijah is here."

"What have I done to deserve such trouble? Ahab will kill me! Didn't you know that wanted posters are in every post office in the land on you, and every town has had to swear that you were not hiding in the town? Now you say, 'Tell Ahab Elijah is here.' Then as soon as I go to tell Ahab, the Spirit of the Lord will cause you to disappear again, and he'd kill me. Have a heart, Elijah. Haven't you heard of my hiding the preachers from Jezebel? Now you're pronouncing doom on one saying 'Tell Ahab Elijah is here."

"I am determined to appear before Ahab, as the Lord liveth; so get with it."

Dean then went to Ahab and told him that Elijah was here, and Ahab went to meet him.

When Ahab came to Elijah he said, "Are you the cause of all the trouble in Israel?"

"No, I am not," said Elijah, "but you and your household are. You have forsaken God and taken to the worship of Baal, and caused the people to worship Baal."

"Now listen to this," continued Elijah, "get word to all the people to come to the Yankee Stadium,[2] as many as can get in, and then assemble all the priests of Baal from everywhere, and we will have a great contest."

Elijah then began speaking to the people that he met telling them that the time for decision was come, either to follow the Lord

[1]Obadiah [2]Mt. Carmel

as God, or Baal. The people did not say anything as they were afraid.

"Apparently, I am by myself, yet Baal has 450 prophets. We will have a contest. Build an altar around second base in Yankee Stadium, and put sacrifices on the altar, and place the wood beneath, but set no fire to it. Then let the priests of Baal call upon Baal and I will call on the Lord God of Israel, and whichever sends fire to consume the altar, then let him be recognized as God."

All this was done, and beginning about nine in the morning all the way to noon the priests of Baal called on Baal for fire, the priests even began jumping up and down on the altar, but nothing happened.

Elijah was in the dugout and about noon he began to heckle the priests saying, "Cry louder. Maybe your god is talking to someone, maybe he's asleep, or he may be off golfing somewhere!"

The priests then called louder, and began to cut themselves with knives and let their blood spill on the infield grass, and still there was no response.

About three o'clock the priests were pooped out, and Elijah came out of the dugout and told the people to watch him closely as he rebuilt the altar which the priests had broken.

Then Elijah took twelve stones, representing the 12 tribes of Israel, and he built a new altar and he dug a trench around it, and he placed a sacrifice on the altar and he poured 4 barrels of water over the altar.[1] Then he had the helpers do this three times until the water had run down into the trenches.

Then Elijah called for silence and he raised his voice in prayer saying, "Lord God of Abraham, and of Isaac, and of Jacob, let it be known this day that you are the true God of Israel, that I am your servant and that I have done these things at your command. Hear me now, that these people may know that you are the Lord God, and that you are ready to receive the people again."

Then the fire of the Lord came flashing down and struck the altar and consumed it with fire.

When the people saw this they fell on their faces and said, "The Lord, he is God, the Lord is the true God."

Elijah then turned to the crowd and said, "All right, but don't let a single one of the 450 priests of Baal escape."

As a result, the people took the 450 priests and carried them down to the edge of the Hudson River[2] and killed them all. [3]

Elijah then spoke to Ahab and said, "Go somewhere and eat, for it is going to rain, can't you hear the thunder?"

Ahab went to eat, and Elijah climbed up to the top of the Press Box and bowed his head, and then he said to his servant, "Climb on the roof and tell me if you see rain."

"There is no cloud in sight," reported the servant. Elijah sent

[1]Some cynics have said this was kerosene [2]Kibron
[3]Losing really hurt in those days

211

him up seven times, and after the seventh trip the servant said, "I see a small cloud that looks no bigger than a man's hand."

Elijah then told the servant, "Go tell Ahab to get in his chariot and get out of here, for it is going to rain bull breetches."

In a few minutes the sky was black and the rain began to fall and Ahab raced in his chariot back to his palace at Jersey City.[1]

Elijah got a ride on a faster chariot and beat Ahab to Jersey City.

Ahab immediately went to Jezebel and spilled the whole story, and he put it on pretty thick about the killing of the 450 priests of Baal.[2]

As a result Jezebel sat down and wrote a letter to Elijah saying:
Dear Elijah:

May the gods do to me, and even worse, than you did to my priests if by this time tomorrow you are not as dead as my priests.

Love, Jezebel

Elijah, accompanied by his servant, fled in terror.[3] When Elijah got as far away as Denver he left his servant and went a full day's journey into the wilderness by himself.

Finally he came to a juniper tree and sat under it and greatly depressed he prayed saying, "Lord, take my life. I'm no improvement on the previous generation."[4]

Then Elijah fell asleep, as he had been running all day, and when he awoke he found that an angel of the Lord had brought him supper. Elijah looked at the meal and went back to sleep. The second time the angel stirred him and said, "Arise and eat. You're pooped from your journey."

Elijah then arose and ate and was strengthened. After staying in the wilderness for forty days, Elijah climbed a nearby mountain and took refuge in a cave.

The word of the Lord then came to Elijah saying, "What are you doing here?"

"Well," said Elijah, "I have always worked for the Lord and have been busy in the church for years, but the people would not listen, and they destroyed your ministers and broke your covenant, and they seek my life, for I am the only good man left."

"Step out of the cave," said the voice, and Elijah did.

The Lord then manifested himself and caused a mighty wind to blow, and then an earthquake, and finally a flash of fire, but the Lord was not in any of these natural happenings. Then as Elijah stood in the entrance of the cave there came a voice again saying, "What are you doing here, Elijah?"

"Just like I said before," said Elijah, "I have been a good minister but the people would not listen and now they seek my life,

[1]Jezreel [2]Jezebel cansidered [3]Not a bad idea [4]A terrible feeling for a young man

for I am the only good man left."

"You're way off, Elijah," said the voice, "for there are more than 7,000 in your own country who have never worshipped Baal. Now get on the road and get to where the action is. First go to the wilderness around Damascus and anoint Billy the Kid[1] as king of Syria and then anoint Jay king of Israel, and anoint Elisha as your successor. It will come about that the enemies that Billy the Kid doesn't handle, Jay will, and those that Jay doesn't get, Elisha will."

Elijah then departed and he found Elisha plowing in a field with 12 oxen and Elijah cast his cloak over him as a symbol of selection and appointment.

Elisha then followed Elijah and said, "Can I go and kiss my folks good-bye?"[2]

"Sure," said Elijah, "don't make such a big deal of this. Being a prophet is hard work."

Then Elisha returned, killed all the oxen, had a big dinner party for the friends and neighbors,[3] and then left to begin his apprenticeship under Elijah.

Chap.
20

Sometime after this Robinhood, king of Syria gathered an army together in his neighborhood and he signed up thirty-two kings to join him. As a result there was assembled a large but rather poorly organized army, and they went and laid seige to Samaria.

The King of Syria was impressed with his mighty numbers of chariots and men and so he sent a messenger to Ahab and told him that if he would pay a large fee in silver and gold, plus surrendering all his wives and children[4], then the Syrians would not attack his area.

Ahab sent word back to him that it was a deal. Then Robinhood decided that Ahab must be easy pickings so he sent another message saying that the price of protection had risen and that he was going to send his men to go through the palace and all the houses of the city and take anything they saw and wanted.

The king of Israel then called the city council together and said to them that he thought the king of Syria was a troublemaker.

The leaders of the city then told Ahab not to agree to the terms. As a result, Ahab sent word to Robinhood that he would still go with the first offer, but that the second one was out of order.

This brought another message from Robinhood by chariot express telling Ahab that the Syrians had the biggest army in history gathered, even more men than there were grains of dust in West Texas.[5]

Ahab then worked up a sharp reply suggesting that the time to

[1]Hazael [2]Elisha was ready to quit plowing right then.
[3]Farm work came to a screeching halt.
[4]I don't know why he wanted all the children. [5]Samaria

boast was after a battle not before it.

This last message came to Robinhood while he was doing some heavy drinking with his aides, and so he jumped up and yelled, "Let's go get them!"

There appeared then before Ahab a prophet of the Lord and he said, "The Lord says that he will deliver you from this Syrian horde and you shall know that the Lord is the one God."

"By whom shall we be delivered? Who shall lead the army?" asked Ahab.

"Select the young men from the area to lead the fight, and you are to be at the head of the army."

All Ahab could find was 220 young men, and there were 7,000 other people who were halfway willing to go along behind the young men.

It so happened that by noon Robinhood was pretty drunk in the big tent with the 32 kings, who were also drunk. Someone came and said that there were a small group of men approaching and Robinhood said that they should be invited to join the party.

The 220 young warriors began to kill the members of the drunken Syrian army and the 7,000 followers jumped in as the Syrians began to flee. Robinhood escaped on a horse, but there was great loss of life and materials on the part of the Syrians.

The prophet then came to Ahab again and suggested that he get organized for the next year for the Syrians would surely return mad.

Now the advisers to the king of Syria told him that the trouble was that the god of Israel was a god of the hills, and that next time Robinhood should fight Israel on the plains that were not under their god's control.

Another thing, the advisers said, is to get rid of the 32 kings as leaders, and put warriors instead of drinking politicians in charge of the army. Finally, they suggested that the king assemble an army as big as the one that he had before as it was better to have a big army than a little one.

Next year, sure enough, there came on the plains of Israel ole Robinhood with his tremendous army.

The children of Israel looked like a drop in the bucket compared to the vast size of the floods of Syrians.

Then the prophet came to Ahab and said, "The Lord is angry because the Syrians have said that he is Lord only of the hills, and so God will deliver the Syrians again into your hands, and you shall again know that the Lord is the one great God."

The two armies camped in sight of each other for over a week before the battle began.[1] The children of Israel fought soberly and well and killed 100,000 Syrians in one day.[2] A bunch more of the Syrians fled and all climbed up on a high wall and the wall fell with

[1] I think the Israelites were waiting for the Syrians to get good and drunk again.

[2] According to a press release from Ahab's place.

214

them and killed 27,000 more. Robinhood escaped along with a few friends,[1] and hid in a room in a nearby city.

The friends had a conference and agreed that Ahab had a reputation for mercy and that if they went to him and surrendered they might have their lives spared.

As a result, Robinhood and his group put on old clothes, tied bands around their heads, and tried to look dirty and humble, and then they presented themselves at Ahab's camp. Ahab was standing in his chariot and one of the men said, "I have a message from Robinhood."

"Is he still alive?" said Ahab. "We are brother kings together."

When they heard this brother Robinhood bit, they all shook themselves and Robinhood stepped forward and said, " I am Robinhood."

"Get up here in the chariot with me, brother Robinhood," said Ahab.

Then Robinhood said, "The cities which my old man captured from your old man I will restore to you. I will name a bunch of streets for you in Damascus.

"It's a deal," said Ahab, and he sent him home.

There was a certain man in the area who was descended from the prophets and he went to a neighbor and said, "In accordance with God's wishes, sock me in the jaw." The neighbor refused.[2]

The prophet then said to the neighbor, "Because you have refused to obey the word of the Lord, as soon as you leave me a lion will kill you."

Sure enough, that's exactly what happened.

Then the prophet found another man and he said to him, "Sock me one."

The man then knocked the stuffing out of the prophet and wounded him pretty badly.

The prophet then waited by the side of the road for the king, disguising himself as a wounded soldier. When the king came by he called out saying, "I was in the middle of the battle and a soldier brought me a prisoner and said for me to keep him, or it would be my life for the prisoners. Now I got busy in the battle and first thing I knew the prisoner was gone."

"You've condemned yourself," said Ahab.

Then the man took off his disguise and showed Ahab that he was a prophet, and then the prophet said, "The Lord says that because you let the man go, the king of Syria, whom the Lord delivered into your hands, it will be your life for his, and your people for his people."

Ahab returned home from his victory then feeling depressed and displeased.

---

[1] They left the fight a little early. [2] It does seem to be a nutty request.

It so happened that there was a rancher living on the outskirts of Jersey City just beyond the king's palace and he had a beautiful vineyard.

Ahab wanted the vineyard and so he went to the owner, a man named Naboth, and he said to him, "I want your vineyard. I will either give you a better vineyard for it or else I'll pay you what its worth in money."

"No, thank you, Ahab," said Naboth, "this vineyard was my father's and I want to keep it."

Ahab came home depressed and pouting, crawled up in bed, faced the wall, and wouldn't eat.

"What in the world is wrong with you?" asked Jezebel, his wife, "you must really hurt if you won't eat."

"The trouble is, Jezebel, that I tried to buy the vineyard from Naboth and I offered him money or another vineyard, and he still wouldn't sell," moaned Ahab.

"Aren't you the king? Come on, get up and eat like a big boy and I'll go get your little vineyard for you," cooed Jezebel.

As a result, the next day Jezebel wrote some letters and forged Ahab's name to them, put the king's seal on them, and sent them to the city council.

In the letter she suggested that the city have an appreciation dinner for Naboth and make a big affair. Of course, they complied.

Jezebel then bribed two crooks to attend the banquet and publicly accuse Naboth of blasphemy against God and treason against the king.

The banquet was scheduled and the crooks arose on the occasion and accused Naboth of blasphemy and treason. Since two witnesses were all that were required at a public gathering for conviction, the two crooks took Naboth outside the city and stoned him to death.[1]

The crooks reported to Jezebel that the mission was accomplished. As soon as the news reached Jezebel she said to Ahab, "Get up and go. Naboth is dead and you can possess his vineyard by just moving in and taking it."

Ahab then arose and started to the vineyard.

The word of the Lord came to Elijah and suggested that he go to Naboth's vineyard and encounter Ahab and prophesy his doom.

When Ahab saw Elijah, Ahab said, "My old enemy has found me."

"You better believe I have, " said Elijah. "I have found you because of the evil that you have done in the sight of the Lord. The Lord has decided to take away your posterity, and all your male heirs, and to clean you out like he did Jerry and Baldy, for you have provoked the Lord to anger."

[1]This revised the appreciation banquet.

"Also," continued Elijah, "the Lord is unhappy about Jezebel and the dogs of Jersey City shall clean the bones of Jezebel and none of your children will have a proper burial. All of this is because you have worked wickedness, and followed idols, and listened to Jezebel, and worshipped Baal."

When Ahab heard these words he went into a deep depression, and he fasted, and he walked quietly, and stood in awe of God.

Then the word of the Lord came to Elijah and said, "See how Ahab has humbled himself? Because he has humbled himself, I will not bring all this evil in his lifetime, but in his son's lifetime."

Chap.
22

There were three years of peace between Israel and Syria.[1] In the third year, Fatso,[2] king of Judah, came to visit the king of Israel. During the conversation, Ahab said, "Will you and your army join me in trying to recapture a city from the Syrians?"

"Consider us one outfit, my people and your people, my horses and your horses."

Then Fatso said, "Inquire about how the Lord feels about this plan."

As a result, the king of Israel gathered together 400 prophets and asked them saying, "Shall I go to conquer Buffalo[3] or not?"

The prophets all said, "Go, for the Lord will give you the victory."

"Is there not a prophet of the Lord that is not a member of this union, that we might ask him?" said Fatso.

"Yes," said the king of Israel, "There is an independent prophet named Fosdick,[4] but I don't like him because he always prophesies against me."

"You are imaging things," said Fatso, "let's hear what he has to say."

As a result a messenger went for Fosdick. Ahab and Fatso each sat on a throne, side by side, and they put on their kingly robes, and the various prophets came before them and did their thing.

One, a witch doctor type, made horns of iron and said, "Thus saith the Lord, with these horns shall you push the Syrians out of existence."

The big pep rally continued with all the various speakers saying, "Go, for you shall win!"

The messenger that came to get Fosdick told Fosdick that all the prophets had told the kings to go to battle and he suggested that Fosdick do likewise.

"I will say whatever the Lord wants me to say," said Fosdick.

Fosdick then came to the kings, and the king of Israel said to him, "Shall we go and try to capture Buffalo or not?"

[1]One of the longer peace times. [2]Jehoshaphat [3]Ramoth-gilead [4]Micaiah

217

"Go and prosper, for the Lord will deliver it to you," said Fosdick.

"Aren't you pulling my leg? Tell me the truth, Fosdick."

"The truth is that I see Israel scattered all over the hills as sheep without a shepherd. I see them each returning to his own home at the Lord's suggestion."

The king of Israel then turned to the king of Judah and said, "Didn't I tell you that he would prophesy evil for me?"

Fosdick then continued, "I saw the Lord sitting on his throne and all the assistants in heaven standing around, and the Lord said, "Who will persuade Ahab to go and attack Buffalo? One suggested one plan and another suggested another plan. Then one came forward and said, 'I will persuade Ahab to shuffle off to Buffalo.'

The Lord said, "How will you do this?"

'I will go as a lying spirit and enter the tongue of the prophets, telling them to say go, man go.'

Therefore, you see, the Lord has approved a lying tongue to lead you to destruction."[1]

Then the prophet with the iron horns came forward and slugged Fosdick. The smart elec witch doctor said, "What spirit was that that went from me to you?"

"You'll know one of these days," calmly said Fosdick, as he was getting back to his feet, "when you are hiding in terror."

Then the king of Israel said, "Take Fosdick and take him to jail, put him in solitary confinement on bread and water, until I return in peace."

"If you ever return in any fashion, then I have misunderstood God," said Fosdick, "and I want you people listening to remember this."

Then the two kings approached Buffalo. As they drew near, Ahab said to Fatso, "You dress as a king, but I'm going to disguise myself, because they will be looking for me for sure."

Now the king of Syria instructed his 32 leaders to look for the king of Israel, telling them that the death of Ahab was all that mattered.

Of course, when the chariot leaders saw Fatso dressed as the king they took after him in a bunch.

Fatso yelled, "I'm a sucker for sure," and he turned and headed for the hills. The chariot leaders soon saw that this was not Ahab, so they quit chasing Fatso.

One of the Syrian archers was behind a rock just shooting his arrows in the air[2] and one of the arrows happened to enter the chariot of Ahab and killed him. Some of the men brought his body to Jersey City and he was buried there. One man washed the chariot, and blood ran in the street and the dogs licked it, as the prophet had

[1]This ruined the pep rally   [2]Lots of soldiers operate this way in every war

said would happen.

Fatso was 35 years old when he began to reign and he ruled Judah for 25 years. Fatso worshipped God and he fought wickedness all his days, and cleaned out a lot of the evil in Judah.

Fatso went into ship building, and built a small fleet to go get gold from Africa, but all the ships sunk.

Then Thumbs[1], the son of Ahab, suggested that Fatso get some more ships and let Thumbs furnish half the sailors, but Fatso had had enough of Ahab's family.

Thumbs lasted only 2 years as king and he did evil in the sight of the Lord, and he followed in the muddy tracks of his father and mother, and like Jerry he caused his people to sin in worshipping Baal, and he provoked God to anger.

[1]Ahaziah

After the death of Ahab, Mississippi revolted and began to cause Thumbs, Ahab's successor a lot of trouble.

Thumbs had a household accident and fell through the lattice to the ground floor and suffered internal injuries.

As a result, Thumbs ordered a couple of messengers to go to Seattle[1] where they worshipped the god Gull[2] and to ask the god there if there was any chance of recovery.

The angel of the Lord then came to Elijah and told him to intercept the messengers, which he did. Elijah stopped the messengers and said to them, "Is it because God is not recognized in this country that you go elsewhere for a god? For this neglect, tell Thumbs that he will not recover from his fall."

The messengers turned back and came to Thumbs who asked, "Why are you back so soon? You could not possibly have made it to Seattle."

"We were intercepted by a man who told us to turn around and go and tell you that it was because there was no recognition of the true God in our country that you had to go elsewhere for help. Also the man told us that you were going to croak, right where you are."

"What kind of looking man was it that said this?" asked Thumbs.

"He was a hairy man," said one of the messengers, "and had a belt around his waist made of leather."

"It's Elijah," said Thumbs, "the fellow from North Carolina."

Thumbs then ordered a captain to take fifty men and go and get Elijah. When the captain and the fifty men approached Elijah they found him on a hilltop.

"Man of God," called out the captain, "the king wants to see you."

"If I am a man of God, then fire from heaven will come down and wipe you out," said Elijah. Immediately a ball of lightning hit in the crowd and cleaned them out.

The king then sent another captain with another fifty men and the same thing happened to them.

Then the king sent a third captain and fifty men[3], and this time the captain bowed down in the presence of Elijah and said, "O man of God, please spare my life and the lives of my men. We know what happened twice before and it seems silly to keep this thing going. Save us, please."

The angel of the Lord then said to Elijah, "Go on with them, for they will not harm you."

When the group arrived at the king's place Elijah spoke to

[1]Ekron   [2]Beelzebub   [3]All this reminds me of an attempt to take
a hill at Okinawa

Thumbs and said, "Is it because there is no God in Israel that you sent to Seattle? For your faithlessness you shall die in bed."

Shortly after this Tumbs died in bed from his fall. Since he had no son to take his throne, Spiro[1], his brother, became king.

The time arrived for Elijah to die and Elisha had been with him as an apprentice for about 2 years. The two men went to Norfolk[2] and Elijah told Elisha to remain there while he went to Vegas.[3]

"I will not let you go by yourself," said Elisha.

When they came to Vegas some of the congressmen there said to Elisha, "Isn't it true that your leader is about to be taken away by God?"

"It is true," said Elisha, "but just don't get in a stir about it."

Elijah then said to Elisha, "Stay here in Vegas while I go to Jericho."

"No," said Elisha, "I'm going with you anywhere you go."

When they arrived at Jericho the group of up-to-date leaders there said to Elisha, "Don't you know that your leader is about to die?"

"Yes," said Elisha.

Elijah then spoke to Elisha and said, "The Lord wants me to cross the Jordan here by Jericho, so you stay in the city."

"I'm going with you," said Elisha, and the two went toward the Jordan together.

Now fifty men stood on the wall of Jericho and watched the two men go to the banks of the Jordan.

When Elijah and Elisha reached the Jordan, Elijah took his mantle and hit the water with it, and the waters parted and the two crossed on dry ground.

As soon as they reached the other side, Elijah said, "My time has come. Ask me what you want from me before I am taken by God."

"I would like to be twice as capable as you are," said Elisha.

"That's a mighty big asking," said Elijah, "however, if you see the Lord take me, your request will be given, and if you don't, it won't."

As they were talking there came down from the sky a ball of fire in a whirlwind and blew them apart from each other and the whirlwind took Elijah up to the heavens, and Elisha saw it and he cried, "My father, my father, the chariot of Israel has taken you."

Then Elisha tore his own clothes to pieces as a sign of mourning, and he took the mantle which Elijah had left and went back and stood by the Jordan River.

Elisha then took the mantle of Elijah and struck the water saying, "Where is the Lord God of Elijah?" Then the waters parted

[1]Jehoram　[2]Gilgal　[3]Bethel

and Elisha crossed the Jordan on dry ground. The fifty men from Jericho witnessed this and they came to Elisha and acknowledged him as the chief of prophets.

The men said to Elisha, "There are fifty of us and we saw the whirlwind take Elijah and perhaps his body is in the hills, or smashed against the rocks, and we will go and try to find him and give him a proper burial."

"There is no point in it," said Elisha. The men kept insisting, however, and Elisha finally told them to go but that it was a hopeless task.

The fifty men went across the Jordan and searched for 3 days, but they could not find the body of Elijah.

When they returned to Elisha he said, "I told you so."[1]

"We have a problem, Elisha," said the men of the city, "for we have a nice and beautiful community but our water is bad that comes from the spring, and so our grass won't grow."

Elisha then took some salt and put it in the source of the spring and said, "Thus says God, that from now on this water will be pure, and the grass and diarrhea problem will no longer occur."

Elisha then left Jericho and returned to Vegas wearing for the first time the mantle of Elijah and appearing as a true prophet of the Lord.

As Elisha came near to Vegas some young hoodlums and kids came out and began yelling at him, saying, "Hi, there, you ole slick top, and here comes Baldy, ole hairless top."

Elisha then turned and pronounced a curse on them for their indignities, and in a few minutes two female bears came out of the woods and began to attack the youngsters and wounded forty-two of them before they could get back to the city.

Chap. 3

Now Spiro, the brother of Thumbs, and the son of Ahab and Jezebel did evil in the sight of the Lord during his reign as king of Israel. Spiro was not evil like his mother and father and did not worship Baal, but his morals were bad and he had little concern for his fellowman.

Now the governor of Mississippi had been paying a protection fee to Israel for a number of years in the form of sheep and wool. After Ahab died the Mississippi governor decided there wasn't much protection left and so he quit paying the fee. Thumbs was king too short of a time to get involved, but Spiro decided to try and collect.

As a result, Spiro sent a message to Fatso, king of Judah, and suggested that they join forces against the Mississippi group.

Fatso gave his usual agreeable reply, "Count me as being with you, my people with your people and my horses with your horses.

[1] As far as I can find this is the first time this phrase is used-not the last.

Which way shall we go?"

Spiro suggested that they go by way of Alabama[1] and get the governor of Alabama to join them so that there would be 3 rulers and 3 armies to one.

By prior arrangement, the 3 rulers and their armies met on the border of Mississippi and there was no water for their horses or for their cattle.

Spiro immediately panicked and said, "We're ruined. The Lord has decided to destroy us all at once."

"Not necessarily," said Fatso, "Isn't there a real prophet of the Lord to whom we can turn and ask for advice?"

"Yes," said one of the servants, "there is a prophet of the Lord named Elisha."

As a result, the three rulers called on Elisha. Elisha immediately jumped verbally on the king of Israel saying, "What have I to do with you, you godless one? Go to some of your strange gods if you want help."

"Not so fast, Elisha," said Spiro, "it appears to us that the Lord God himself is preparing to deliver us to the heathen, all three of our armies."

"All right," said Elisha, "but I am prophesying only because of Fatso, the king of Judah, who is a God fearing man."

Elisha then prepared himself to meditate and communicate with God, beginning first with some music. While the music was being played the spirit of the Lord came to Elisha and he understood what he should advise the kings.

"In the morning," said Elisha, "take all your men and let them dig trenches[2] and then though there will be no wind the trenches will be filled with water which will provide for you, your cattle and your horses. This type of thing is no trouble at all for the Lord to do, and he will also deliver the Mississippi group into your hands. When God does this, you are to destroy as many of the towns and cities as you can, cut down all the trees you see, and plug up all the water wells, and put stones in the fields so they can't be plowed."

In the morning, flood waters from Alabama came into the area and filled the trenches.

Now the governor of Mississippi had gathered together a small army and he led his army to the place where the three kings were camped. Just as the sun was rising the Mississippi group looked toward the enemy camp and the waters in the trenches appeared to them as blood on the land, for they did not know about the trenches and the water.

"Look at the blood!" said some of the men. "Surely the kings have quarreled among themselves and there is not much left of any of them. Let's go and gather the spoils."

When they arrived, however, they found 3 armies waiting for

---

[1]Edom   [2]What's an army without a trench?

them, and they were greatly surprised, disorganized, and soon badly defeated.

The men of Israel, Judah, and Alabama then did as the Lord had told them to do and they destroyed cities and towns, and ruined fields with stones, cut down good trees and plugged water wells. The sling-shot experts handled Biloxi.[1]

When the governor of Mississippi saw that things weren't going his way, he took 700 men and tried to break through the battle to kill the ruler of Alabama, but he could not.

The governor of Mississippi then took his own son and offered him as a burnt offering on an altar in front of everybody, and this disgusted the men of Israel so much that they quit fighting and went home.[2]

Chap.
4

A daughter-in-law of one of the local ministers came to Elisha and asked for help. The woman said, "My husband has had an untimely death and the creditors have come to me to claim my two sons in payment for what is owed."

"What do you have in your house?" asked Elisha.

"Not much of anything, just one small container of cooking oil."

"Go borrow as many empty jars and containers as you can," said Elisha, "then take them into your house with your two sons and shut the doors and begin to pour oil from your container and you will be able to fill all the vessels that you have borrowed."

The woman did as she was told and when she had filled all the vessels with oil she came back to Elisha and told him that she had plenty of oil now in the house.

"Go then," said Elisha, "and sell all that you need to pay your debts and keep the rest to live on until your sons are old enough to work and support you."

One day Elisha came to a small town called Midway[3] and there was living there a wonderful woman named Betsy. She was impressed with Elisha and she invited him to dinner. After that, everytime Elisha came through Midway he stopped and had dinner with Betsy and her husband.

One day Betsy said to her husband, "I have decided that the prophet whom we have often invited to dinner is truly a man of God and a very holy man. I think we should build him a small room on the wall and put a bed, a table, a stool, and a candlestick in it, and then he can stay here overnight anytime he comes this way.[4]

This was done and on a later occasion when Elisha was staying in the guest room he said to his assistant, a fellow named Billie So,

[1]Kirharaseth   [2]It had been a long day anyway.   [3]Shunem   [4]This was probably the first guest room ever built specifically for this purpose.

"Call Betsy, I want to talk with her."

In a few minutes, Betsy came and Elisha said to Billie So, "Tell Betsy that we appreciate this guest room and the nice meals, and that I want to know what we can do for her. Would she like for me to say a good word about her to the king or to the commander-in-chief of the army?"[1]

"I live with my own little group and have no interest in politics," said Betsy, and she left the room.

"What can be done for her?" Elisha asked Billie So.

"She has no son, and her husband is getting old," said Billie So.

"Call her back," said Elisha.

Then Betsy came again and stood in the door.

"In the proper time of about nine months, you shall have a son," said Elisha.

"You shouldn't lie to me, for you are supposed to be a man of God," said Betsy.

As Elisha had said, however, she became pregnant and in the normal time gave birth to a son.

When the boy was somewhat older, though still a child, he went to watch his father who was cutting grain in the field. In a few minutes the child said, "Daddy, my head is hurting something awful."

"Go to your mother at once," said the father.[2] Another boy, one of the workers, then carried the child to Betsy.

Betsy held the boy on her lap until he ceased to breathe. Then she took the child and placed him on Elisha's bed in the guest room and she called out back to her husband, "Send me one of the workers to saddle a donkey for I'm going for Elisha."

"Why do you want him today? It is not one of the regular times," said the husband.

"Just do as I say," said Betsy.

Betsy then kept telling the donkey driver to keep pouring it on the donkey as speed was important. She came to the man of God who was at Yankee Stadium preparing for services.

Elisha saw Betsy coming in the distance and said to Billie So, "Run and meet Betsy and ask her if all is well with her, and with the child."

She told Billie So that all was well, but she headed straight for Elisha and fell at his feet. Billie So tried to drag her away but Elisha said, "Leave her alone, for obviously something is wrong, though the Lord has not revealed any problem to me."[3]

"Did I ask you for a son? Didn't I tell you not to deceive me?" moaned Betsy.

"Here, Billie So, take my staff and don't turn aside to even speak to anybody until you have placed my staff on the child."

[1]The indirect approach   [2]Still standard first aid treatment
[3]Some odd thinkers say his ESP was broken.

"Elisha, I am going to stay with you. I doubt if the staff without you is any good."

Elisha then started to Midway with Betsy, but Billie So was already long gone, and he placed the staff of Elisha on the boy, but nothing happened.

Billie So met Elisha and Betsy and said, "The child has not moved."

When Elisha came to the house he found the child breathless and he entered the room, closed the door, prayed to the Lord, and then gave the boy oral resuscitation.[1] Breath began to return to the child and Elisha warmed the boy's body with his own body, and then the child sneezed seven times and opened his eyes.

Then Elisha called to Billie So, and said, "Call Betsy."

When Betsy came into the room Elisha said, "Take your son."

Betsy first bowed herself at Elisha's feet and then took her son and departed.

Elisha then came to the area around Kansas and there was a great drought in the land and there was nothing much to eat.

There was a men's conference scheduled and Elisha was to be the speaker but there was no food. Elisha then told the men to go out and gather what herbs they could and they would cook a big pot of soup. The men did, and they gathered various things for the soup, but one of the men, being partly ignorant, brought toadstools and put in the soup.

As the men began to taste the soup one of them cried out that the food was poison, and he said to Elisha, "There is death in the pot."

Then Elisha said, "Bring me some meal." When they did, he tossed it into the soup.

The soup became all right then and the men could eat, and so they could have their conference.

One of the men who came late to the conference was from Missouri City[2] and he brought some bread and fruit for the group and he said, "Serve it to the men."

The fellow in charge of the dining hall then said, "How can I put this small amount in front of 100 men?"

"Give it to the men," said the donor, "for the Lord has blessed it and there shall be enough, and some left over."

And that's just the way it was.

Chap.
5

General Naaman was head of the Syrian army and he was a man highly regarded by the king and he was also a very honorable man, and very courageous. In fact, the Lord had given success to Syria because of Naaman, but he contracted leprosy.

[1] The first account of this of which we know.   [2] Baalshalisha

There was a young teen-age slave girl of Israel working in the Naaman household and she said to Mrs. Naaman one day, "I wish General Naaman would get with the prophet of the Lord who lives in Samaria for he would heal him of his leprosy."

Mrs. Naaman had this word passed along to the king. The king then sent a messenger with a gift of money to the king of Israel saying that he was going to send General Naaman to Samaria to be healed of leprosy.

The king of Israel immediately began to climb the wall and groan saying, "Does the king of Syria think I am God to kill or to make alive? He knows that I cannot heal leprosy, and he is just looking for an excuse to raid my kingdom again and take off a bunch of slaves."

Elisha heard about this and he sent a message to the king of Israel saying, "Why are you so disturbed? Send the fellow to me and I'll show him that there is still a prophet in Israel."

As a result, the king of Syria sent Naaman with his horses and chariot and he arrived at a little place in Samaria where Elisha was staying.

When Naaman stopped in front of Elisha's place, Elisha sent word to him by Billie So that the great General was to go and take a real good bath in the Jordan river.

Naaman was really burned up about this message and said, "What kind of a nut is that prophet? Certainly he could have come and prayed over my hand, and done something. This 'take a bath' bit is crazy. I could have bathed at home where we have clear water, a sight better water than the old Jordan has." Then Naaman started away in a great rage.

One of the aides of Naaman, who wasn't ready for another 70 mile chariot ride, said, "General, if the prophet had asked you to do something very difficult we know you would have done it; so why not do something that he asks that is simple?"

This reasoning made sense to Naaman and he went to the Jordan and took a real good bath, and when he had finished bathing he was no longer a leper.

The General returned to the place where Elisha was, accompanied by his official escorts, and he said, "There is no God in all the earth except in Israel. Please, Elisha, accept a big fee for this great healing."

"As the Lord liveth," said Elisha, "I will accept no fee." Naaman urged the prophet to accept, but Elisha continued to refuse.

Then Naaman said, "As I return I will take two mule loads of earth from this place as a sign of my faith and I will never worship or sacrifice again to any God except to the Lord God of Israel. In fact, even when I am required to accompany the king when he worships at the altar of Rimmon, in my heart I will be bowing to the true God."

Elisha said, "Go in peace."[1]

Now Billie So was not too happy with this deal and he mumbled to himself, "My boss has let this Syrian General go without accepting a red cent; so I think I'll go chase him down and put the bite on him myself."

Billie So then chased after Naaman and when Naaman saw him and recognized him, he stepped down from the chariot and said, "Is anything wrong?"

"All is well," said Billie So, "but my boss sent me to catch you for two young men from Union Seminary just came by and they are looking for some scholarship help. A little silver and a couple of suits of clothes as a morale factor would be appreciated."

"Fine. In fact, I'll give you twice as much as you asked," said Naaman. Then he ordered two of his servants to take the gift back to town. Billie So then returned to his work as receptionist and aide to Elisha.

"Where have you been for the last couple of hours, Billie So?" asked Elisha.

"Nowhere in particular," lied Billie So.

"Don't you know that I felt it in my heart when you chased Naaman down. Is it right for you to act this way, to receive money, clothes, cattle, servants, vineyards and the like? You have been stealing secretly for a long time, and so the leprosy which I took from Naaman I will bestow on you."

Billie So turned white at these words, and he became a leper.

Chap.
6

Elisha had gathered a few students who wished to learn to become ministers and he had a small seminary in operation.

A committee of the students came to Elisha and suggested that living under his constant supervision was a little too much for them and they wanted to build a small dormitory about a half a mile away on the banks of the Jordan river.

"That is fine with me," said Elisha.[2]

"Will you go with us and help us with advice?" asked one of the students.

"Sure, I'll go along," replied Elisha.

When they arrived at the Jordan they began to cut down the wood but as the one with the axe was swinging on one tree the axe head flew off and fell into the Jordan river.

"Woe is me," said the student. "I borrowed that axe, and I'm in for it now."

Then Elisha asked, "Where did it fall?" The student then showed Elisha the exact point of the splash. Elisha then took his knife and cut a stick and tossed it on the spot and the axe head

[1]It is not certain if he used the finger sign or not.   [2]He was a little tired of supervising, too.

floated to the top.

"Now just pick it up," said Elisha and the student did.

The king of Syria decided that it was about time to initiate a few raids against the king of Israel and so he instructed his chief officers to set up a couple of secret camps and ambush the king of Israel and some of his men.

Elisha, informed mysteriously through God about these camps, told the king of Israel and warned him to stay clear of the areas, which he did.

The king of Syria was irked about his ambush not working and he asked his officers what was the trouble or where was the information leak.

"There is only one leak, O King," said one of the officers, "and that is Elisha the prophet, who apparently knows what you say even in your bedroom."

"That does it," said the king. "Find out exactly where this prophet bird is living and then bring him here."

"At present, sir, he is living in the little town of Dothan," volunteered one of the officers.

As a result, the king of Syria sent a troop of horses, chariots, and men and they came in the night and surrounded the town of Dothan.

The next morning, Elisha's new assistant, looked out the window and saw that the city was circled with soldiers. Terrified, the young man said to Elisha, "What shall we do?"

"Don't worry," said Elisha, "for we have more going for us than they do."

Then Elisha prayed to the Lord that his young assistant might see visions of many soldiers on his side, to comfort him, and then he asked the Lord to send a blinding dust to strike the eyes of the men surrounding the town. The Lord then smote the Syrians with blindness.

Then Elisha went out of the town to the blinded soldiers and said that he would lead them to the place they needed to go to find the man they sought, and so they blindly followed Elisha who led them into Samaria close to the headquarters of the army of the king of Israel.

When they arrived Elisha prayed to the Lord to relieve their blindness and their eyes began to clear and they saw where they were.

The king of Israel then said to Elisha, "Shall I kill all these Syrians while I have such a good chance?"

"No," said Elisha, "Would you kill prisoners? These men I led in here as captives. Feed them, be kind to them, and send them back to their master."

So the king prepared a big meal for the men and when they had finished eating and drinking they returned to Syria and were no longer interested in trying to pull anymore raids in Israel.

A year or so later, however, Robinhood gathered together a pretty big army and decided to lay siege to Samaria. The siege cut off all transportation and prices became unbelievable in the isolated town, dove leavings sold for $10.00 an ounce and the head of a dead donkey was worth $8.00.

As the king of Israel was walking on the wall of the city a woman cried to him saying, "Help us, O king, help us."

Then the king said, "If the Lord doesn't help, where can help be? The barns are empty and the wine is gone. What is your particular problem?"

"We are starving to death. My next door neighbor has suggested that we turn cannibal and eat my son today and hers tomorrow."

When the king heard this he was greatly distressed and stood on the wall and tore his clothes and mourned for his city.

Then the king said, "At least I can do something. I'll kill Elisha, because he has not secured help for us from God."

In the meantime Elisha was sitting in his house discussing matters with some of the older men when the king sent a messenger to summon him.

Elisha turned to the men and said, "This son of a murderer, the king, has sent a messenger to summon me to my death. When he comes don't let him in, and then in a few minutes the king will come himself and I'll deal directly with him."

The messenger came and then the king who said, "This trouble is of the Lord, why should I wait any longer to do something about it?"[1]

"Now hear what the Lord has to say about all this trouble," said Elisha. "By this time tomorrow inflation will be ended and the price of flour will be reasonable."

"Yeah," said an aide to the king, "I doubt if this could be if the Lord made windows in heaven and lowered the food down."

"You will see it with your own eyes," said Elisha, "but you will not get to enjoy it."

There were four lepers about to enter the gate of the city to beg and one of them said to the others, "How stupid can we get? This city is starving. If we go in here we will only die with the rest of the people."

"Well, we surely will die if we just sit here at the gate, too." said another.

"Why don't we go to the camp of the Syrians? If they feed us fine, if they kill us, we'll just die, which we are going to do anyway," suggested another.

[1]In those days if things didn't go right you killed the preacher.

230

As a result they went to the camp of Syrians to beg for food and they found no one home. The camp was completely deserted.

What happened was that the Lord had sent a storm, with roaring hail, and hearing it in the distance the Syrians thought that the noise was chariots and horsemen and a great army coming and they said to one another, "The king of Israel has gotten the Eyptians and a Green Beret[1] army and they have come to wipe us out, let's get home before we get killed."

As a result they fled in panic, even leaving their tents and many of their pack animals, and provisions.

The lepers finding this situation first ate and drank their fill and then began to take various articles that were left behind and hide them.

One of them soon said, however, "This is not a good thing to do. Today is a day of good news and we should not keep it to ourselves, but let us go to the city and tell the king of Israel."

As soon as they came to the entrance of the city they told the gate keeper what they had found, and he told two bell hops, and they sent word to the king.

The king immediately got out of bed, for it was night, and he took a dim view of the report saying, "It is a trick. The Syrians have just gone and hidden in nearby fields and when we come to their camp they'll ambush us, figuring they will then have the city all to themselves."

"Just in case it isn't a trick though," said one of the hungry servants, "why don't we send some fellows on the five horses that are left alive in the city."

"All right," said the king, "but we will only risk two horses and they can pull a chariot."

The two messengers in the chariot trailed the Syrians all the way to the Jordan and found many garments and weapons dropped along the way by the Syrians who fled in a panic from the roaring storm.

The messengers returned and told the king and the people poured out of the city and gathered great quantities of food and clothing and other spoils from the deserted Syrian camp. As soon as the people returned with ample provisions, inflation was ended and the price of flour returned to normal.

The king had appointed the man who was to kill Elisha to be in charge of the gate of the city and the people stomped him to death pouring into the city at night with all their free goods. [2] Just as Elisha had said, the man saw the price of flour drop, but he never got to enjoy it.

Chap.
8

Some months after this Elisha was at Midway and he told Betsy

[1]Hittites   [2]It never did pay to tamper with Elisha.

to take her son and leave the area for there was going to be a seven year drought and famine. Betsy did as Elisha suggested and moved her household into the Fascist country a long way from Midway.

At the end of the seven years drought, Betsy returned and went to the king and wanted her house and land back. Now Billie So had recovered from his leprosy[1] and he had been telling the king of all the mighty and wonderful acts of Elisha and that Betsy was very special to Elisha. As a consequence, the king restored to her the land and house that had been hers.

Elisha made a trip to Damascus and he was told there that Robinhood was sick. Robinhood was also told of the arrival in the area of Elisha.

The king then said to his top gun, Billy the Kid, that he should go visit Elisha, take him some presents, and ask him if Robinhood would get well.

Billy the Kid then drew expense money from the treasury of about $1500 and called on Elisha.

"I have come from the king," said Billy the Kid, "to ask if he will recover from his illness."

"Go tell him that he will get well," said Elisha, "however, privately the Lord has shown me that he will die, but don't tell him." Then Elisha became very sorrowful.

"What's wrong?" asked Billy the Kid.

"I am sad because I know all the evil that you will do in Israel. You will raid their towns and villages and set fires, you will kill the young men, and even children, and you'll violate and kill the women."

"Do you think I am some kind of a dog that would do such things?" asked the Kid.

Elisha then only said, "The Lord has revealed to me that you will be king of Syria."

Billy then returned to his king who said, "What did Elisha have to say?"

"He told me that you would recover," said Billy the Kid.

The next day Bill the Kid took a wet blanket and held it over the king's face and smothered him to death. Then Billy the Kid announced that he was the new king of Syria.

During this period several sections of the smaller tribes in Israel revolted because of the evil reign of Spiro in Judah and they were never reconciled.

Sprio's son, Thumbs, came into power, as has been previously mentioned, and he was wicked. Thumbs did, however, get with Jo Jo and went to war against Billy the Kid. Jo Jo was wounded and went to Jersey City for recovery. Thumbs visited Jo Jo in Jersey City when he was sick.

---

[1]I guess Elisha took pity on him.

Elisha sent for one of the seminary students and told him to get ready to travel. Then Elisha gave him a box of holy oil and told him to go to Buffalo and locate Jay.[1]

"When you find Jay," said Elisha, "he will no doubt be with some of his army group; so call him out and privately anoint him with the oil and tell him the Lord wants him to be king of Israel."

The young man found Jay eating with a bunch of army captains and he said, "I have a message for you, captain."

"For which one of us," asked Jay.

"For you," said the young man.

Captain Jay then arose and went into the room with the young man and the messenger from Elisha poured the oil on Jay's head and said, "The Lord God of Israel has chosen you to be king of Israel. You are to wipe out the house of Ahab as part of the penalty for what Jezebel did to the Lord's ministers. The Lord has said that he will make the house of Ahab as vacant as the house of Jerry and the dogs shall eat what is left of Jezebel in the streets of Jersey City."

As soon as he finished speaking, the messenger ran away as fast as he could go, for he was obeying Elisha and was not interested in being involved in a revolution.

When Jay returned to the table where the other captains were, one of them said, "Is everything all right? What kind of a nut was that who came in here?"

"You know who that was and what he had to say," said Jay.

"Cross my heart, man," said one of the captains, "we have no idea what that was all about."

"In short," said Jay, "the messenger anointed me king of Israel."

"Hurrah!" they shouted. Then they took a trumpet and sounded it in front of the restaurant and yelled, "Jay is king!"

Now Jo Jo[2] was king of Israel, but he had been wounded fighting Billy the Kid's outfit and was recuperating in Jersey City. Jay said then to his cohorts, "Seal the city here in Buffalo. Don't let anyone leave to go to Jersey City and report the revolution."

Jay then organized a small force and drove his own chariot in the lead and headed for Jersey City. Now Thumbs was in Jersey City visiting Jo Jo, and Thumbs was king of Judah at the time.

The watchman on the wall at Jersey City saw the Chariot group approaching and sent word to Jo Jo. Then Jo Jo suggested that messengers be sent to meet the group and ask if they came in peace.

The messenger came to Jay and said, "Are you come in peace?"

"You'd better join us, fellow," said Jay and the man did.

The watchman then reported to Jo Jo that the messenger didn't return.

[1]Jehu   [2]Joram

"Send another one," said Jo Jo.

The second messenger arrived and the same thing occurred.

The watchman then told Jo Jo that the second messenger did not return. The watchman said that the way the chariot took the corners on one wheel, he thought that the driver was Jay.

Jo Jo then limped out to his chariot and Thumbs got in his chariot and with their escorts they rode out to meet Jay.

When Jo Jo saw Jay he said, "Do you come in peace?"

"How can there be peace with a whore like your mother Jezebel running things?"[1]

Jo Jo decided that things looked bad, so he called to Thumbs and said, "There is treachery here!" Then Jo Jo turned his chariot around and started to leave, whereupon Jay shot him in the back and the arrow came out through the heart and that ended Jo Jo.

Then Jay told Plummer[2] to throw the body in an open field as the Lord had decreed this to be done in punishment for the way Naboth and some of the ministers had been treated.

When Thumbs saw all this, he also fled, but some of Jay's soldiers caught him going around behind a hot house and wounded him so that he died on the way to the hospital in the next town.

When Jay came storming into Jersey City Jezebel heard of it, and she put on her makeup and curled her hair and looked out the window from the second floor.

When Jay entered the city she called out, "Did Żulu who killed his boss have peace?"

Then Jay looked up and yelled forth, "Who is on my side? Anybody for me?"

Then two or three semi-fellows who were with Jezebel looked out the window also.

Jay called to them, "Throw her down." The three eunuchs then threw Jezebel out of the window and Jay ran over what was left of her with his chariot. As had been predicted, her blood was left for the dogs of Jersey City to lick.

After Jay had taken the city and had a good dinner he suggested that the remains of Jezebel be found and that she be given a decent burial because she was the daughter of a king.

Only the skull, feet, and hands were left and they reported this to Jay. Jay then remarked, "This is just as the prophet of the Lord said when he told us there wouldn't be enough left of Jezebel to recognize her."

Chap.
10

Now Ahab had about seventy male descendants left in Jersey City anyone of whom might become a king, so Jay sent a letter to the city fathers and suggested that they select the best from among the seventy and make him king.

[1]This was intended as an insult, though true.   [2]Bidkar

The city fathers thought about this and remembered that the two previous kings had simply brought trouble and so they wrote Jay and said that since he was the powerful ruler in the area they would rather serve under him than select a king from among Ahab's relatives.

Jay wrote back and thanked them and added a postscript saying that if they meant what they said he would become their ruler in exchange for the lives of the seventy relatives. The seventy were present when the letter was read and the city fathers immediately had the local police execute the seventy and they sent the 70 heads in baskets to Jay.[1]

When the heads arrived Jay had the baskets placed on either side of the entrance to the city and in the morning Jay went to the place and spoke to the people gathered there saying, "I admit that I killed my boss in order to become king, but I did not kill these 70 men. This represents the punishment of God which was promised to Ahab for his wickedness."

Then Jay departed for Samaria and was eating at Sheep's Inn where they served hamburgers when the associates of Thumbs, king of Judah, entered also to eat.

"Who are you?" asked Jay.

"We are associates of Thumbs and we are on the way to pay our respects to the king and queen."

Jay then instructed his soldiers to sieze the men, disarm them, and then take them out in the back and kill them in the sheep pit. There were 42 men killed this way.

As Jay was traveling that afternoon he ran across Little Red.[2]

"Hello, Red," said Jay, as he stopped his chariot. "Are you as much for me as I am for you?"

"You'd better believe it, sir," said Little Red.

"Then take my hand and get in the chariot with me," said Jay, and Little Red did as he was told, for he had no real choice.

When Jay arrived in Samaria and had finished killing everybody he could find that had supported Ahab, he made a speech in the court house square, "As you know, Ahab followed in the way of a little worship of Baal, and I expect to double all he did. Call to me then all the priests of Baal and everyone who is devoted to Baal, for I wish to make a public sacrifice."

Jay did this as a means of getting all the Baal crowd in one place.

Jay then announced a great assembly of all Baal worshippers and sent through all the land passing the word about the time and place.

The day of the assembly found the auditorium packed with worshippers, and each was given a name tag on which was written, 'We worship Baal.'

[1]Apparently there were no postal inspectors   [2]Jehonadab

Then Jay and Little Red went through the crowd and passed the word up and down the pews to make certain that there were only worshippers of Baal present.

Then Jay ordered his crack soldiers to get outside the auditorium and as soon as the service of worship started he ordered the soldiers to enter the auditorium and kill every worshipper. The soldiers did as they were told and they also took the images of Baal and burned them. In this manner, Jay destroyed the religion of Baal in the land.

Jay was no purist, however, and he did not bother to tear down some of the remote idols. The Lord, however, was pleased that at least he cleaned out the Baal worshippers, whether the method was right or not, he had carried out the Lord's plan for the house of Ahab. Jay did not walk carefully in God's commandments, but followed some of the violent and sinful tendancies of Jerry.

Because of this, the Lord did not support Israel entirely and Billy the Kid began to make successful raids again, particularly along the coast of Judah.

Jay died after a violent reign of 28 years and his son Little Jay[1] became king in his place.

Now when Reba, the mother of Thumbs, saw that her son was dead she was furious and ordered all the young descendants killed. Lucy, however, stole one of the young children and hid him with his nurse at the temple, for Lucy was the daughter of Jo Jo and had temple privileges as well as a place of her own. The young son of the king, named Bing,[2] was hidden in the temple for 6 years while Reba ruled the kingdom harshly.

Matt Dillon[3] was priest of the people at that time and in charge of the temple and the temple guards.

At the end of seven years of Reba's cruel reign, Matt Dillon called together the leaders of the people and the captains of the temple guards, put them under oath of secrecy and showed them the king's son, their rightful ruler. Dillon then explained to them the plan and issued to each man weapons from David's private collection in the temple.

From that time the young boy was under careful guard until each of the assembled leaders had time to recruit others and wait for the appointed day, which was to be the first sabbath when the people gathered to worship. On this occasion, Dillon brought Bing, a seven year old boy, before the people and announced that he was king, and he put the crown on him, and gave the proper affirmations, and anointed his head with oil. The people and all the leaders clapped their hands and shouted, "God save the King."

When Reba heard all the noise and the shouting she came to the

[1]Jehoahaz   [2]Joash   [3]Jehioada

temple and when she entered she was amazed to see the seven year old king, with guards around him and the people rejoicing; so she began to tear her clothes and yell, "treason, treason."

Matt Dillon, however, in his quiet way ordered one of the deputies to take her out of sight of the temple and execute her, as he did not want a killing in the temple. The men took her out by the barn and killed her.

Then Matt Dillon made a promise and an arrangement between the Lord, the king, and the people that they should be the Lord's people, and he also made an agreement of service between the young king and the people.

As a result, the people left the temple and went into the house of Baal and tore it down, destroyed the graven images, and killed the high priest of Baal, a man called Lazy Dan.[1]

Dillon then arranged for the young king to move to the palace and to be given all the rights of a king and so Bing began to reign at the age of seven.

Chap.
12

Bing reigned for 40 years and he did that which was right in the sight of the Lord according to the instructions of Matt Dillon.

Bing said to the priests one day that all the offerings and all the tax deductible gifts that were brought to the church and the priests should be used to repair all the church buildings in the area and restore all the sacred things.

At the end of 23 years Bing noticed that this had not been done and he called Matt Dillon and the other local leaders together and demanded that the churches be repaired. As a result, all future offerings went to carpenters and masons and the various houses of the Lord were repaired. The only offerings that were not used were the sin offerings, which were kept for the use of the priests.

There was no accounting made for all the church repairs as the superintendents were all honest and faithful men and no contracts or records were necessary.

Then Billy the Kid began to cause trouble again with his raids and he captured Gath and began to rob and pillage various villages and threatened to come to Jerusalem. As a result, Bing took all the gold he could find around the palace, and all that was left at the temple, and all the beautiful pieces of jewelry and valuables that were left in the kingdom and he sent them to Billy the Kid as protection, and Billy the Kid stayed away from Jerusalem.

Two disgruntled servants named Bonnie[2] and Clyde[3] went on a spree one day and killed Bing, and so his son, Greg,[4] became king.

Chap.
13

During part of the time that Bing was king of Judah there came

[1]Mattan   [2]Jozachar   [3]Jehozabad   [4]Amaziah

to the throne of Israel the son of Jay, a man named Jason and he did evil in the sight of the Lord and followed the sins of Jerry.

The anger of the Lord was again kindled against Israel and Billy the Kid and his son Robinhood the Second both made successful raids against Israel and caused much trouble. Finally Jason sought help from God and the Lord heard the cry and delivered them, but the people still did wickedly and their leaders were still not dedicated, God-fearing men.

Finally, Lester,[1] the son of Jason became king and he continued the evil ways of his father.

In the meantime, back in Judah, Elisha became ill and the good king Bing of Judah came to visit him and lamented over the illness of the mighty prophet.

"Open the window," said Elisha, "and shoot an arrow." Bing shot an arrow.

"That is the arrow of the Lord's deliverance from Syria," said Elisha.

"Take the remaining arrows," said Elisha, "and beat the ground with them." Bing did this three times.

"That's not enough," said Elisha, "for you shall now smite the Syrians only three times and you need to do it five or six times to really wipe them out."

Bing was impressed and moaned over Elisha and said, "O my great father, you who are the chariots and the horsemen of Israel, you are our great strength."

Then Elisha died.

The next year a band of raiders from Mississippi were in the area and one of their number died. About this time the group saw some of the natives coming over a hill and they threw the dead man aside and his body fell on the bones of Elisha, and the man came to life and stood on his feet.[2]

Billy the Kid died and Robinhood the Second, his son, took his place and three times Bing moved against him and three times Bing won victories, and recovered some of the places previously lost.

Chap.
14

While Greg was king of Judah he did that which was right in the sight of the Lord, not as well as his ancestor King David, but he did as well as Bing.

One thing that he did promptly was have Bonnie and Clyde executed for killing his father, but he did not have their children killed as the book of the law of Moses containing the commandments of God said that fathers should not be put to death because of their children nor children killed because of their father's mistakes.

Then Greg sent a message to Lester, king of Israel, and suggested a confrontation for Greg was fresh from a great victory

[1]Jehoash   [2]I think everybody fled the scene then.

238

over the Colts.[1]

Lester sent a message back in the form of a fable saying, "There was a thorn in Lebanon that went to a cedar in Lebanon and said give thy daughter to my son for a wife. A wild beast passed by and stomped on the thorn. That is what will happen to you. You are over-elated over your victory over the Colts, but you'd better stay at home and not come to meet me. You will fall and lose Judah also."

Greg would not listen to this reasoning and he took his army and confronted Lester and Greg was defeated and the men of Judah fled to their tents.

Lester then went to Jerusalem and tore down a large portion of the wall and took as spoil all the treasures of Jerusalem.

In time a conspiracy developed and a group found Greg and killed him and his son, Elmer,[2] who was 16 years old, was made king of Judah. Elmer did some restoration work for Judah.

In the meantime, Jeb,[3] one of the sons of Jason began to reign in Samaria. Jeb did evil in the sight of the Lord, but because of his promises to Abraham and to David, the Lord had pity on the children of Israel and their plight and he used Jeb to save them from complete destruction.

Chap.
15

Zeke,[4] son of Jeb, became king of Israel.

Greg's son Elmer became king of Judah at the age of 16 and he did that which was right in the sight of the Lord, although he failed to abolish the idolatry practiced by the people in the hill country. Because of this, the Lord caused Elmer to contract leprosy and he was forced to live in isolation during part of his reign. Because of this, Don, the son of Elmer did most of the active work for his father while his father lived in isolation.

Meanwhile, back in Israel, Zeke reigned for only six months, as he did evil in the sight of the Lord and a man named Ringo plotted against him and killed him in public and assumed the throne of Israel. Ringo lasted only one month as king because Link[5] came down from the north and killed Ringo and took the throne of Israel.

Link reigned for ten years and he killed the people of Long Island Sound[6] because they would not give him proper social recognition and during his reign he continued to do evil in the sight of the Lord.

Then Cagey,[7] a leader from Assyria, threatened to destroy Link and take over his operation so Link began to pay him protection money. Needless to say, he raised this money by taxing the people. Cagey took the pay and left Link alone.

[1]Edomites [2]Azariah [3]Jeroboam [4]Zachariah
[5]Menahem [6]Tiphsah [7]Pul

Then Greg Peck,[1] son of Link, became king and he also did evil in the sight of the Lord and Mitch[2], one of the more ambitious soldiers in the employ of Greg Peck plotted against Peck and killed him while on a pleasure trip to Samaria, and made himself king.

Mitch ruled for twenty years and continued the pattern of doing that which was evil in the sight of the Lord.

Finally, a man named Hooty[3] decided to become king so he killed Mitch and took the throne.

In the meantime Don was the king of Judah and he did that which was right in the sight of the Lord, except that he too failed to destroy the idols and burnt incense worshipping in the hill country. When Don died his son Ahaz became king.

Ahaz immediately adopted the wicked ways of most of his predecessors and even sacrificed his own son on an altar in accordance with a heathen practice that had been condemned by the Lord.

The king of Syria and the king of Israel declared war on Ahaz and besieged Jerusalem but they were not able to take the city itself. Ahaz considered his plight to be great, however, and he sent a message to Tiger[4], the Assyrian king, and offered him a big price to attack the forces besieging Jerusalem or to divert them by attacking their other bases.

Tiger liked the idea and he first captured Damascus and created enough other diversions to draw the armies away from Jerusalem.

Ahaz later visited Tiger in Damascus and while there he observed an altar that he thought was exceptionally beautiful. As a result, he instructed his home priest at Jerusalem, Marvin,[5] to make an exact copy of the altar for him in the temple at Jerusalem and to take the old altar and put it in a special place for the private use of Ahaz.

All of this was done as a further sign of the heathen and idolatrous inclinations of Ahaz. When Ahaz died he was buried in Jerusalem and his son Hez became king.

When Hooty began to reign as king of Israel he did evil in the sight of the Lord but he was not as bad as some of the previous kings.

One of the things Hooty did was to pay protection to Assyria, but on the side he conspired against the Assyrians with the king of Egypt. The king of Assyria learned of the matter and put Hooty in chains. Consequently, the Assyrians were encouraged to further conquests and besieged all of Samaria and finally captured the people

[1]Pekahiah   [2]Pekah   [3]Hoshea   [4]Tiglath-pileser   [5]Urijah

240

of Israel and took them as prisoners and scattered them in many strange and remote places.

This was actually God's punishment to the people for their continued failure to worship God and walk in his commandments. Although the children of Israel sometimes made a show of worshipping God, they secretly did many things displeasing to God and they continued the practice of placing idol markers and graven images on some of the hill tops for the worship of strange gods.

The Lord had often sent prophets and sometimes wise kings who instructed the people in the ways of the Lord, but the people did not listen, and they hardened their hearts and would not submit to the simple discipline of the one true God, Jehovah. The people repeatedly worshipped idols and joined the strangers in their heathen worship and they forsook God.

The people even went to the extreme of sacrificing their children on the altar of fire as a worship service and they did many things to cause the anger of the Lord to rise against them.

The tribe of Judah sinned also and followed the wickedness of Israel and the Lord rejected Israel and he delivered the people to the spoilers. As a result, Israel was carried away out of their own land into the vast areas of Assyria.

As a result, the king of Assyria brought men from strange and faraway places such as Lima,[1] Honolulu,[2] and Lisbon.[3] When these people came to dwell in Israel they did not know or fear the God of Israel and so God sent hungry lions to attack them and terrify them.

As a result, these people called on the king of Assyria to help them and the king was advised that the trouble was their ignorance of God, who ruled Israel. The king then sent a priest selected from the captives and he was dispatched as a missionary. The priest came and stayed in Aspen[4] and tried to teach the people about the God of Abraham, Isaac, and Jacob.

The various nationalties, however, began to devise gods of their own and to erect statutes and to place idols in various prominent places. Along with all the many weird gods they worshipped the people also tried at times to give some amount of token recognition to the Lord God of Israel, but they never ceased to continue their strange idolatries.

In spite of being amply reminded that the Lord God of Israel was the one God, and that there should be no other god served, and in spite of the clarity of the commandments of the Lord, and the assurance that faithfulness would be blessed and that unfaithfulness punished, the people, even though they stood in some awe of God, continued to worship idols and violate the commandments.

[1]Cuthah   [2]Ava   [3]Hamath   [4]Bethel

In the meantime, during the 3rd year of Hooty, as king of Israel, before he was captured, Hez became king of Judah. Hez was 25 years old when he became king and he was more of the type of his ancestor David, and he did that which was right in the eyes of the Lord.

Hez even had the idols destroyed, the hidden places in the groves removed, and he trusted completely in the Lord his God. As a result God was with him and he prospered him and as a result he did not pay protection money to Assyria. Hez was also successful in attacking the remnants of the Capone gang.

During this time the king of Assyria captured Israel but he did not attack Judah. Some ten years later, however, a new Assyrian king gathered together a tremendous army and the new king, whose name was Big Hun,[1] came down upon the country of Judah and began to take all the towns and villages. Hez did not want war and he offered to pay Big Hun to go home.

Big Hun said that for $1,500,000 he would go home. Hez tried to pay this with golden doors and various ornaments. In spite of the gifts, Big Hun brought his army and camped with his tremendous numbers in sight of Jerusalem and demanded a conference with Hez.

Hez sent a committee and stayed at home to hear the result. The committee consisted of Senator Fulbright,[2] Wilbur Mills,[3] and Harry Truman.[4] The spokesman for Big Hun made a bombastic type of speech to them, full of threats and sarcasm, saying, "Big Hun wants to know why you all are putting up such a brave front. You indicated that you have strength for war, but on what is this based?

We have been told that you are counting on help from Egypt. In the first place Pharoah is a double-crosser and he'll join the strongest side.

Maybe you trust in God? This is a big laugh. In fact, just for kicks, Big Hun has said that he will give you for free 2,000 horses if you have enough soldiers to ride them, just so we can have some sport.

As for the Lord, it might interest you to know that Big Hun says the Lord is the one that told him to come and capture Jerusalem."

"Look here, sir," said Fulbright, "can't you speak in latin so our people on the wall can't understand what you are saying? We can understand a little latin, and we don't want our people to hear all this big talk."

"Not a chance," shouted Rickles,[5] "what I have to say is for

[1]Sennacherib   [2]Eliakim   [3]Shebna   [4]Joah   [5]Rabshakeh

everybody. They are the ones that are going to starve to death in the city and die of thirst with the food and water supply eliminated."

Then Rickles stood on a little mound and shouted to the people on the wall of Jerusalem, "Don't let ole Hez fool you. He can't deliver you. Don't let him sell you on that ole line about God delivering his people. Big Hun says that all you need to do is pay enough and you will be left alone to enjoy yourselves and remain in your own homes. Later next year we will move you back to Assyria to some real good country there and put some other people here in Jerusalem in accordance with our transplanting policy, but you will get to live in a land rich with corn, and the biggest thing is that you will get to live.

You think God will deliver you? Where are the gods of the people of Samaria and some of the towns of Judah? Did the moon gods, or the sun gods, or any of the others save anybody from Big Hun? How do you figure that this small-time Lord of yours will save Jerusalem?"

The people on the wall did not say a word, however, as Hez had already instructed them not to answer the rabble-rouser.

Then the committee of Senator Fulbright, Wilbur Mills, and Harry Truman returned with their mouths down, their clothes dragging the ground, and they were shredding Kleenex in their misery.

Chap.
19

When Hez heard all this he was miserable and he went into the church to pray.

Before going, however, he told the committee to report to Isaiah, the prophet of the Lord. The committee said to Isaiah, "This is a sad day, one of difficulty, and one of blasphemy against God. It may be that the Lord heard the speech of Rickles and that the Lord is angry and will help what few of us are left in all this holy land."

"Well, you go tell Hez," said Isaiah, "not to be afraid of words. Also tell him that I will arrange to have a rumor spread in the camp among the soldiers of the Big Hun, and he will worry over the rumor, and return home, and get killed in the process."

Big Hun had already heard of a rumor of trouble from Ethiopia and so Rickles sent a written message to Hez repeating his speech and defying the Lord God of Hosts.

Hez took the letter and read it and then went again to the church and in the place of prayer he spread the letter in the presence of the Lord.

Then Hez prayed to the Lord saying "O Lord, Thou art the one true God, the God over all the kingdoms of the earth. You have made the heavens and the earth, listen now, and also Lord take a look at our predicament, and consider the big boasting of Big Hun. The Assyrians have demolished all the idols and defied all the gods they have faced, now, Lord, please save us from the Assyrian, in order that all the kingdoms of the earth may know that you are the one true God."

Shortly after this, Isaiah sent word to Hez saying that the Lord had indicated to him that the prayer of Hez had been received.

Isaiah then said that the Lord had authorized him to talk back to the Big Hun and say "You are despised and just a big laugh to the Lord. How dare you defy the holy one of Israel? You have even reproached God with your big lip messenger. Don't you know that God is above the tops of the mountains, that God blows down the tall cedars of Lebanon, and that God can dry up a river by stepping in it? Haven't you heard of these things? You have pushed around some small communities and taken advantage of weak people, but you are beginning to smell, and I've seen enough of your cruelty; so I will just put my hook in your nose and my bridle in your big mouth and turn you around and head you back to the north.

The Lord will save a remnant of the people of Jerusalem and their roots will grow deep in the land, but you ole Big Hun, shall not come into Jerusalem, nor even shoot an arrow over the wall, much less organize an attack. You will simply return by the way you came, for God affirms that he will defend this city for his own sake, and for the sake of his servant David, and in answer to the prayer of Hez."

And it so happened that night that an angel of the Lord passed through the camp of the Big Hun and a virus smote the soldiers so that they vomited most of the night and some died and many felt like they were going to die or wished to die by morning.

Big Hun then returned with his sick and straggling army. When he approached one of his home villages two of his relatives thinking that the straggling, weak army had been defeated, killed Big Hun and placed his son Little Hun[1] on the throne.

Chap.
20

Hez became old and sick and Isaiah made a sick call on him.

"You should make out a will, Hez," said Isaiah, "and get all your affairs in order for I don't think you have long to live."

Isaiah departed and Hez turned his face to the wall and prayed to the Lord and mentioned that he had been faithful in word and deed and asked the Lord to extend his time on earth.

Before Isaiah had time to leave the palace grounds the word of God came to him and as a result he returned to Hez and said "The

[1]Esarhaddon

244

Lord has heard your prayer, Hez, and he will heal you and in three days you'll be well enough to go to church.

The Lord also says that He will defend this city during your lifetime   for his own sake and for the sake of his servant David."

The trouble with Hez physically was primarily an infected boil and Isaiah took a ripe fig and placed it on the boil and the poison began to go into the fig and leave Hez.

Hez was greatly pleased with the word that Isaiah brought but he wanted a sign and proof that the word concerning the deliverance of the city was accurate.

Isaiah then asked the Lord to back up the shadow on the sun dial 10 degrees and this happened and Hez became happy and reassured.

The king of Babylon, Diamond Jim,[1] heard that Hez was sick and so he sent Hez a get-well card and several nice gifts. This pleased Hez and so he foolishly invited the messengers to see all his treasures, his antiques, and the jewelry in his vault.

A few days later Isaiah came to see Hez and asked "Who were the big shot visitors that you had the other day?"

"They were visitors from Babylon," said Hez.

"What all did they see here in Jerusalem?" asked Isaiah.

"Everything," said Hez. "I even let them look in my vault."

"You really blew it, Hez. They merely were here to case the joint and God says they'll come some day after you're dead and steal everything you showed them and probably take some of your sons as captives."

"I am sorry," said Hez, "but if this is the will of God then I am satisfied."

Hez, known widely for his conduit system of bringing water to Jerusalem, died fifteen years after the boil trouble and his son Lurch[2] reigned in his place.

Chap.
21

Lurch was 12 years old when he became king and he apparently responded to wicked advice for he began to do evil in the sight of the Lord. One of the things he did was to restore idols in the high places in the hills and he placed altars in the wooded areas to Baal and generally patterned his behavior after that of the wicked king Ahab.

As Lurch grew older he also grew worse and he sacrificed one of his sons and spent a great deal of time encouraging witchcraft and fortune telling industries. Lurch even erected a graven image in the house of David which had been built to the glory of God.

[1]Berodachbaladan   [2]Manasseh

Lurch led the people away from the one true God and the people forgot the promises of God and the faith of their forefathers.

The Lord spoke through his representatives that were left among the people and the Lord promised to bring trouble to Jerusalem and on the tribe of Judah and the Lord stated that the enemies of Judah would arise and capture the people and the people would become a prey and spoil to their enemies.

Lurch further aroused the anger of God by shedding innocent blood and creating a condition of violence in the city of Jerusalem.

Lurch died and his son Amon became king at the age of 22. Amon was also wicked and he served the false gods that his father worshipped.

Then one day the palace workers organized and killed Amon. This made the people of the city angry and they banded together posse style and hunted down all the palace workers and killed them and made Amon's son Jose[1] king.

Now Jose was eight years old when he became king and he was blessed with good influences and he began to do that which was right and proper in the eyes of the Lord.

One of the things that Jose did was to authorize the high priest to use the offering collected at the church to pay for the repair and remodeling of the temple of God.

The high priest did as he was told and he reported later to Jose that one of the workers had found the book of the law of Moses and the messenger brought the book to the king and read it to him.

Jose was tremendously impressed with the words of God as contained in the law of Moses and he expressed great concern that the people and the nation would be punished as God had promised for the sins of worshipping false gods and failing to follow the laws of God.

Jose requested that the high priest seek a true prophet of the Lord and that the prophet be told of the book that had been found and told of Jose's concern .

It developed that the best qualified prophet was a coed at Jerusalem University and she was told by the high priest of all that Jose had read and also for his request for clarification.

The prophetess at the university said, "Go tell the king that the Lord will bring evil and destruction on this place in accordance with the words that are in the book, because the people forgot God, and burned incense to false gods, and sought their own pleasures."

[1]Josiah

246

"Tell the king, however," continued the lady, "that the Lord is impressed with the spirit of Jose and pleased at his efforts to restore the worship of God, and that because of this, the Lord will delay the punishment of the people of Judah until after the death of the king; so that the eyes of the good king will not witness the scattering of his people."

Then Jose called an assembly of all the people at Jerusalem and he read to them the words of Moses, the commandments of God, and the words of the covenant which God had established between him and his people.

After reading this, Jose publicly proclaimed his intention of worshipping God and observing the laws of Moses. Jose told the people that the commandments of God would be the commandments of the kingdom of Judah. The people joined Jose in making this covenant.

As a result of this a mammoth cleanup campaign was initiated which took many years. All the idols, the symbols, the hill top shrines were all burned by fire. All the heathen priests were located and executed. The places for the sacrificing of children were completely destroyed.

The various statutes, such as the horses dedicated to the sun god, were all destroyed. As the various heathen shrines were destroyed, they were converted into burial plots and the bones of the dead were placed there, being all the bones of those who had worshipped false gods, as well as many bones of unidentified people.

The bones of the prophet of the Lord who had predicted that this would eventually occur were found and the bones of this prophet were not moved to the condemned area but left in their place as a memorial to the prophet who had been destroyed by a lion.

In the eighteenth year of the reign of Jose, after all the false gods had been denounced and the law of God was rather firmly established in the kingdom, Jose called for the greatest passover celebration of all time. This was used as a tremendous religious program and was the greatest passover feast ever staged or celebrated.

Following this, Jose began to remove the soothsayers, gamblers and deceivers of the people and to establish a solid reign of law and order under God.

Jose studied continuously the law of God and there had never been a more devout king in the history of Israel. Because of this, God delayed his punishment to Judah, but the Lord did not forget his anger with Judah and he merely postponed the punishment promised during the evil reign of Lurch.

After thirty-one years as king of Judah, Jose was killed in a battle against a raiding army from Egypt. After the death of Jose his son, Jed[1] became king of Judah and he lasted only 3 months, and he did evil during the 3 months of his rule. The Egyptian general didn't like the way Jed did things and so he captured him and sent him to Egypt, placing a half brother of Jed's by the name of Dru[2] on the throne. Dru agreed to pay the general the proper fee for protection, which money he raised by taxing the people. Dru reigned for eleven years and he did that which was evil in the sight of the Lord.

Chap. 24

There came into power in Babylon a king named Big Ned[3] and he caused the Egyptian army to return to Egypt and he forced Dru to begin to pay tribute to him instead of paying to Egypt. The Lord during this time was causing the people of Mississippi, and the gypsies, and Assyrians to rise against Judah and to desire to capture the whole of the promised land.

Following the death of Dru there came on the throne his son Sad Sack[4] who had a brief reign of 3 months. During that time Big Ned arrived on the scene with a large army and lay siege to the city of Jerusalem.

Sad Sack surrendered promptly and turned himself, his family, and all the treasury over to Big Ned. Big Ned then took all the strong men of Jerusalem, and all the skilled craftsmen, and blacksmiths and took them back to Babylon as captives. Big Ned then selected a young relative of his named Harpo[5] and left him in Jerusalem as king. Harpo, of course, followed heathen ways, and did evil in the sight of the Lord. With the taking of the captives into Babylon the Lord had finally destroyed the kingdom of Judah in punishment for their sins.

Some years after this, however, Harpo wearied of paying tribute to Big Ned and he revolted against him.

Chap. 25

As a result, Big Ned came back to Jerusalem during the ninth year of the reign of Harpo and he brought a big army with him and he lay siege to the city.

As a result, Harpo fled in terror and was captured on the plains near Jerusalem and what was left of his army left in the night through an opening in the wall, and remnants of the army were also

[1]Jehoahaz [2]Eliakim [3]Nebuchadnezzar [4]Jehoiachim [5]Zedekiah

captured.

Then MacArthur[1] who was a young captain in the Babylonian army led the storming of the walls and captured Jerusalem. The priests of the temple were captured and brought to trial before Big Ned, who had them all executed. Only the very poor and lowest grade workers in the vineyards were left to live in Jerusalem. This was the final carrying into captivity in Babylon of the people of Judah.

The small remnant that was left in Jerusalem were told by Big Ned that Gabby[2] was to be their king. Gabby told the people when they were assembled that all would be well with them if they would serve the king of Babylon faithfully and place themselves in subjection to the men of Babylon.

Seven months later a group of unhappy Jews got together and raided the palace and killed Gabby, but then they fled to Egypt for fear of reprisals from the Babylonians.

In the meantime, back in Babylon, Big Ned began to feel sorry for Sad Sack and he released him from prison and put him on a pension for the remainder of his life.

[1]Nebuzaradan   [2]Gedaliah